MAKING MUSIC WITH WHAT REMAINS

Rabbi Dovid Diamand

Praise for Making Music With What Remains

"A powerful true story about one man's pursuit of excellence despite terrible barriers. This is an extremely well-written book by a man who faced challenges in life that most of us only read about. I found it inspirational in the fact that despite these difficulties, the author persists to achieve more for himself and his family. He does this by recognizing (and ultimately accepting responsibility for) the mistakes made along the way. It is a sometimes humorous, sometimes sad, and frequently uplifting recitation of significant clips of the author's life."
- Max Carter, Author and CEO (Ret.) California Conservation Corps

"Fascinating. A beautiful and fascinating story. A worthwhile read!"
- Amazon Review

"Ability to self-analyze and improve. An honest account of a very unique life... Very inspirational."
- Amazon Review

"Making Music With What Remains - Well written! I am enjoying it."
- Amazon Review

Published and Copyrighted ©

Dovid Diamand

2018

All Rights Reserved

No part of this publication may be translated, reproduced, stored in a retrieval system or transmitted, in any form or by any means, electronic, mechanical, photocopying, digital, recording or otherwise, without prior permission in writing from the author/copyright holder. Permissions may be requested from rabbidoviddiamand@gmail.com.

Halachic Note: Jewish law normally prohibits sharing information that, while true, may be considered disparaging of another person (*loshon hara, rechillus*); of course, spreading false information (*motzi shem ra*) is always prohibited. Regarding a case of disclosing true information that may be disparaging, there are certain exceptions that permit or even require disclosure. For instance, if a person's *intent* in sharing the information is for a positive, constructive, and beneficial purpose (*to'elet*) and that may serve as a warning to prevent harm or injustice, the prohibition does not apply. It is important to note that even with positive intentions, there are important limitations regarding disclosure; and in some case names have been changed to protect privacy. Any disclosure herein that may unintentionally violate a rabbinical or biblical prohibition is my fault alone, for no one is completely innocent (*v'kulan b'avak loshon hora*). See Rambam Hilchot De'ot: 7; Chofetz Chaim Hilchot Lashan Hora: 10; Bava Basra 165a.

Dedicated to the memories of my dear grandparents:

Paul and Sonia Zeidel, A"H

Israel and Hannah Diamand, A"H

Table of Contents:

Preface   6

Prologue   10

Badlands   12

A Narrow Bridge   38

Black Hole   76

Where's David Diamond?   118

Coming Home   149

What Remains   250

Delusion of Consciousness   276

Appendices   287

Afterward   307

Preface

*"I went to the woods because I wished to live deliberately,
To front only the essential facts of life,
And see if I could not learn what it had to teach,
And not, when I came to die, discover that I had not lived."*
- Henry David Thoreau

"All that is gold does not glitter, not all those who wander are lost."
- J.R.R. Tolkien

"There is nothing to writing. All you do is sit down at a typewriter and bleed."
- Ernest Hemmingway

I was born in August of 1968. I will die, please G-d some day in the *very* distant future. It's customary for Jewish people to say, *"Ad me'ah v'esrim"*, (Hebrew for, "[May you live] until 120"); some who are generous simply say, "May you live forever."

No one who is healthy wants to die because life is so precious, and it also *feels* good. It feels right. It feels organically connected. That feeling of connection is each of our souls' lifeforce sensing and connecting with its Source; which translates into that viscerally good feeling of simply being alive. It resonates. There is a concept brought down in Chassidus (esoteric Judaism) that the Source, (G-d), is not just numerically *One*, but that He is the only truly existent reality. There is literally nothing else *but* G-d. He, alone, is creating everything out of nothing at every moment, intimately involved with every detail of creation. (*Tanya, shaar hayichud v'haemunah* & various other sources)

7 // Making Music With What Remains

So, the "reality" that you and I feel is simply G-d enlivening it. We are literally riding a wave of G-dly energy at every moment; each moment having a unique and G-dly purpose.

What happens in between those two dates of birth and death, no one can predict. The life I've lived thus far, (while I embrace all the details, some a little more and some a little less enthusiastically), is incredible, if not incredulous. It's like I was dropped into a world of perambulation and instead I was impelled toward avigation. If I could take (or make) another route to a destination other than the "normal" path, I usually took it. Sometimes I crashed and burned. Sometimes I soared. Most times people just stared, open mouthed.

There is a poem written by Jack Gilbert called, "Flying and Falling" and it takes a different leaning toward the mythical boy, Icarus, who thought he could fly by fastening wings to his back made out of wax. In the myth he starts to fly, but when he soars too close to the sun his wings melt and he falls, ostensibly, to his death. Most people understand this story as the *failure* of Icarus. I've always understood it as his sacred quest, not to any destination per se, but highlighting his achievement. This poem brings to the fore of what I always felt in my gut.

"Everyone forgets that Icarus also flew. It's the same when love comes to an end, or the marriage fails and people say they knew it was a mistake, that everybody said it would never work. That she was old enough to know better. But anything worth doing is worth doing badly. Like being there by that summer ocean on the other side of the island while love was fading out of her, the stars

burning so extravagantly those nights that anyone could tell you they would never last. Every morning she was asleep in my bed like a visitation, the gentleness in her like antelope standing in the dawn mist. Each afternoon I watched her coming back through the hot stony field after swimming, the sea light behind her and the huge sky on the other side of that. Listened to her while we ate lunch. How can they say the marriage failed? Like the people who came back from Provence (when it was Provence) and said it was pretty, but the food was greasy. I believe Icarus was not failing as he fell, but just coming to the end of his triumph."

I first read that poem when I was 37 sitting in a federal prison in McMinnville, Oregon contemplating the wreckage of my life and it gave me perspective and strength and hope.... *"Everyone forgets that Icarus also flew, not failing as he fell, but just coming to the end of his triumph."*

As I write this now at age 50 contemplating all I have experienced in life until present, I may have jettisoned into adulthood a bit on the extreme side. While I experienced early childhood trauma and aggressive toxicity leading up to (and continuing beyond) my parents' divorce and family separation... with all the fracture and heartache a young child experiences, Jewish law prevents me from providing a *full* public accounting. None of that stopped me from living a very full life, though. I've been married, done skydiving and class 4 level kayaking complete with Eskimo rolls, trained for two 300 mile eco challenges, run 2 LA marathons *and* a Sheriff's triathlon, learned Filipino martial arts, completed the LA County Sheriff's Department Reserve Police Academy, become an LA County Sheriff's Mountain Rescue Team Member, EMT,

9 // Making Music With What Remains

scuba diver, helicopter pilot, Jewish Big Brother, federal prisoner, presidential pardon applicant, father (of 4), Orthodox rabbi, living organ (kidney) donor and so much more. My life has had so many ups and seeming downs... and plenty of *sideways* that a story resonates with me describing Itzhak Perlman, and I retell it often:

Itzhak Perlman, a polio survivor and wheelchair bound violin virtuoso once gave a concert. When he was only a few notes into his performance, one of his violin strings snapped. The audience assumed that he would have to hobble offstage to procure another violin. Itzhak Perlman did no such thing. He closed his eyes and played. He played with passion and power unlike anything the audience had ever heard. Of course, it's impossible to play a symphonic work with just three strings, but that night Perlman refused to know that. The music he made was arguably more beautiful than any he had made before. After, he explained himself in one sentence. He said, "Our job is to make music with what remains."

There are moments, and then there are *defining* moments. I think if one thing captures the quintessential message that defines those moments of life between birth and death for me; it is to make music with what remains. Much lies broken, but you still need to play. And even if you only have three strings, play with three strings. Play with two strings. With such an imperfect instrument, you are capable of creating music that's more beautiful.

Dovid Diamand
October 25, 2018
Los Angeles, CA

Prologue

"Imagine you could open your eyes to see only the good in every person, the positive in every circumstance, and the opportunity in every challenge."
- Rabbi Menachem Mendel Schneerson

"The two most important days in your life are the day you are born and the day you find out why."
- Mark Twain

I'm led to believe that when the Creator of the universe created human souls that He had a special purpose for each individual one. And I think that everyone wants to believe that. Having purpose, feeling that there is meaning *fills* a gigantic hole; a hole that I believe G-d created in us whose purpose compels us to fill it with meaningful (good) endeavor. Sometimes human beings lose contact with their souls and therefore lose contact with their purpose, still the hole remains as does the resultant urge to fill that hole. Unfortunately, it can also be filled by other pursuits, some neutral, some dark; manufactured by us to artificially feel full. This urge to fill our hole, while less compelling than the urge to breathe, can be more compelling than most anything else we are confronted with. Therefore, we need to tread around each of our individual holes carefully, respecting and honoring each person's process and dignity in pursuit; for our purpose and meaning are tied inexorably to the G-d given *hole* He placed in every one of us, the unique hole that He wants each of us to fill.

There is a moving story about the previous Chabad Rebbe enjoining a certain chossid/devotee, Rabbi Zalman Posner:

11 // Making Music With What Remains

"The Rebbe began dramatically (in Yiddish) that when a neshomo (soul) has to come down to Earth, it doesn't want to go. Why? Because heaven is warm and comfortable, while life on Earth is cold and dark ('kalt un fintster'). What happens? In heaven the soul is ordered: 'You must descend below.' And to demonstrate the point the Rebbe took his index finger and repeatedly pointed downward in a deliberate motion, 'You must go down below into the dark and cold world, and there you must bring light (machen dort lichtig).' The Rebbe then continued and instructed his devotee to travel on a mission to a certain city, which may not be as comfortable as staying home, with the objective of bringing some spiritual light to the city. To this day he never forgot the Rebbe's finger pointing downward, 'You must go *down* and illuminate the dark and cold world.'"

The key to enduring happiness is to acknowledge this paradox and embrace it; that each of us was chosen for the journey and circumstances in which we find ourselves, in the living and breathing process of achieving the mission on Earth for which our souls *also* initially volunteered -- This book describes one journey, a mission, that I believe my soul was tasked with, that my soul was shown and *chose* to complete, knowing there would be lows and highs, trauma and heartbreak and joy; and most importantly of all, meaning. In the process I have had to recalibrate my compass a number of times; being bloodied and bruised and burnt but never regretting any of my collisions.

Victor Frankl writes, "What is to give light must endure burning." (*Man's Search For Meaning*, Beacon Press)

Chapter 1

Badlands

"All parents damage their children. It cannot be helped. Youth, like pristine glass, absorbs the prints of its handlers. Some parents smudge, others crack, a few shatter childhoods into jagged little pieces, beyond repair."
- Mitch Albom

"We are all broken. That's how the light gets in."
- Leonard Cohen

My great, great grandparents on my mother's side emigrated from Petersburg, Russia (what used to be the Soviet Union) to the United States in the early 1800s. It was still common for the Soviet Army to canvas Jewish neighborhoods and literally kidnap school age boys from their villages and conscript them into the army for decades. These children were called *cantonists*. If the children were religious, especially Jewish; they would be given non-kosher food, made to violate Jewish holidays and coerced to convert to the State religion of Christianity. These conscriptions could last 25 years and literally destroyed the child… and the parents frequently never saw their child again.

I am told that my great, great grandfather's brother was one such *cantonist*, and that his mother refused to have this happen again. So, she hobbled her other son by placing a log between his feet and breaking his ankles with a hammer, crippling him for life so that he would be able to obtain a medical waiver and be exempt from military service. My great, great grandfather had to hobble out of the Soviet Union, but I likely would not be here if he wasn't maimed. In any other eventuality it is certain he would have disappeared and been killed had he been drafted into the army. Their family settled on the East Coast in New England.

My grandparents on my mother's side, Paul and Sonia, had three children, my mother, a sister and a brother. They were denied a more robust Orthodox Jewish upbringing by their parents and grandparents because practicing Judaism in Russia could get you killed. Now free to practice in the United States, but unfamiliar with the Orthodox ways, my grandparents raised my mom and her siblings in the tradition of an East Coast Reform egalitarian-type of Judaism. They were pushed by my grandfather to excel in business and always increase financial success; and based on his formative experiences this makes perfect sense. A Yale University graduate, my grandfather yearned to realize the dream of American success denied to his grandparents. He carried the intergenerational PTSD of Soviet Communist cruelty, shame, poverty and lack of freedom experienced by his grandparents. This pushback towards material benchmarks of "success" may have manifested in an intrusive emotional construct; a feeling in the children that "conditionality of success" was placed on whether one felt loved or valued. I'm not sure my mother felt she was on the "right" side of that conditionality for much of her life, or if she ever felt she won the approval of her parents.

My mother went on to become a schoolteacher and then after her divorce from my father became a nurse. My aunt went on to create a multi-million-dollar speech pathology business, and my uncle went on to medicine and became perhaps the foremost kidney doctor in the world and is currently head of medicine at Harvard Medical School's Beth Deaconess Hospital.

My grandparents on my father's side, Israel and Hannah descended from the Sadigura Chassidic dynasty, a branch of the Ruzhiner dynasty. Hitler decimated them, murdering thousands of the Sadigura Chassidim and millions more Jews throughout Europe. Only a few escaped, my grandparents included, and they emigrated from Poland, by way of Italy (on the run from the Nazis), through Argentina and finally to New York. My father was born also on the run from the Nazis in Bari, Italy. My grandparents were forced to live in the attic of a train station in Italy for two years with another family before my grandfather was able to bribe a guard to allow him to sail to Argentina with his family. To get out of Nazi controlled Poland, my grandfather, who was a boot maker at the time, had to bribe a Polish guard to look the other way. He did this by making him a pair of "officer boots", the kind only worn by ranking Nazi officials.

I have no real idea what kind of living hell my grandparents went through, though I know that their families, brothers and sisters and parents were all murdered by the Nazis. My grandfather, though, had surviving cousins who settled in Williamsburg, New York continuing the line of Chassidic Jewish life. Today I

15 // Making Music With What Remains

literally have hundreds of cousins who live a very religious Chassidic Jewish life.

My grandfather Israel wanted nothing more to do with the Jewish life. After the Holocaust, and perhaps justifiably so, he was angry; angry with the Germans, angry with the Christians... and angry with G-d. Aside of the actual practice of Judaism, simply *being* a Jew for him meant that your family got slaughtered. So, he threw the whole thing off and moved to West End Avenue in Manhattan, NYC. There, he and my grandmother raised my father and my uncle largely secular. They spoke mostly Yiddish in the home – my father did go to some type of *yeshiva*/religious school early on but none of it stuck.

And while they were successful in running away from the Germans, they were not successful in running away from the anger that followed them out of Poland, and this weighed heavily on the household. My grandfather, like many who suffered from the firsthand horrors of watching the extermination of their entire families, found no healthy outlet for this anger. So, he went silent. Though I was told little about my father's growing up years in New York and even less about their tortuous escape from Poland, I was aware of a story about a years' long silent treatment inflicted upon my uncle who was 9 years younger than my father. Apparently, my uncle did or said something that upset my grandfather. So, my grandfather literally did not speak to him *for years* while he was living under my grandfather's roof. It is very hard to conceive of this sort of silence being inflicted on a child for years at a time... and today when I see my uncle, (and my father to a significant degree as well), I see how fragile they are and how silent anger must have fractured their childhoods.

So, my mother and father grew in their respective Reform/secular homes until my mother was 19 and my father was 20. They met at a social event and soon after they married.

After I was born, we lived in Massachusetts; then 5 years later in Rochester, NY, my brother was born. Shortly thereafter, citing bitter cold we moved to Los Angeles, CA and purchased a home in 1972 for about $49,000 in a city called Granada Hills. We lived on a cul-de-sac filled with other young families until I was 11 when my parents divorced.

What I recall in those six years in Granada Hills, California was how my reaction to my parents' relationship turmoil always ended up being with me acting out. I was very poorly behaved, always getting into trouble at school. Though never really being held to full account, and basically left without much direction; on my own I made poor moral choices. Perhaps because my parents were emotionally invested elsewhere or distracted by their own fractured relationship; simply unable or unwilling to establish, invest in or model proper deportment, I continuously rebelled against rules and norms, wanting to take back some sort of control into my life. As my parents' relationship continued to unspool, I felt more and more empty and I filled my life with mischief.

My parents enrolled me in private school called Carden Academy. I acted out there as well, from 3rd – 5th grade,

17 // Making Music With What Remains

and I'm not sure why I was not thrown out. But in the 5th grade, I decided to change my ways and apply myself... and behave. And the results were remarkable. Immediately I became a top student and earned the respect of my teachers and the principal.

So, I began to realize that I could also transcend myself and my upbringing and choose to take a different course than the one seemingly plotted out for me. I had also become adept at still being able to function even when I was placed in very dysfunctional situations. To this day, I notice how certain situations or types of people repel others by being "off" or caustic in some way. I find that having to enter into those orbits' caustic or dysfunctional debris fields does not always have the same pejorative effect on me as it does other people. And sometimes there may be some (hard fought) good to be found.

I had also been enrolled in a Reform Hebrew day school Tuesday and Thursday afternoons and on Sunday mornings. We met for Hebrew school and Shabbos prayer in a church, which was rented out to our congregation. Our classrooms were also on church property, which all seemed a bit odd to me. There was a picture of what I guess was the accepted Christian characterization of Jesus in the office, long blond hair, high cheek bones, a real Svengali look to it; and I even voiced my concern to the Reform rabbi about it; that this did not belong in a Jewish school. To my mind, its very presence gave a very bad appearance, communicated mixed messages and blurred the lines between what was acceptable within a Jewish environment and what was not.

He remained unfazed and said that we were guests in this place and had to respect the décor. I think the thing that bothered me, though I couldn't articulate it… was why was a Jewish congregation opting to be guests in a church in the first place?

My Jewish experience was largely watered down. I knew I was Jewish (and was proud of that fact); both my parents were born Jewish, and my mother wanted me to have a strong Jewish identity. She tried to accomplish that by enrolling us in Hebrew school and we (sort of) celebrated the major holidays, though in a fairly superficial manner. Most people simply do as they are taught by their parents; so, our underwhelming Jewish "observance" was simply part and parcel of what my parents experienced and felt comfortable with from their own upbringing.

Shabbos (Jewish Sabbath – weekly day of rest) was observed by lighting candles at home, then driving to our congregation for an *"Oneg Shabbos"* service, then off to McDonalds for dinner before returning home and waking up on Shabbos and going, not to pray, but to AYSO soccer games with my dad. Actual observance of Shabbos or kashrus (Jewish kosher/dietary laws) or other holidays was considered extreme. Passover was Seder and matzo the first day and then whatever we wanted the rest of the week. I had passing experience with more religious Jewish people, but only seeing them in theme parks and sometimes in Los Angeles; fathers with *yarmulkes* and kids with sidelocks called *peyes*. They fascinated me. They had this Jewish life I had no idea about. My mother told me that they were Jewish, but that they were Orthodox (extreme) Jews who could not eat at McDonalds. For my parents, Judaism was ingrained by their upbringing as an identity and feeling, but not by *authentic* observance.

Even though the emotional support and religious observance sides were severely lacking; to be fair, I did go to a very good secular school, which I credit for assisting me in being able to matriculate successfully to the next scholastic levels; and it taught me some measure of discipline and gave me some sense of normalcy. My parents sent me to camp in the summer, sometimes to Jewish camp at the JCC and sometimes to the YMCA. I had all the birthdays with friends and presents and had clothes and food and bikes and roller skates and even played 8 years of soccer, one season as goalie. I believe my parents tried to provide a childhood in some normal form, if not in the best function. My father took me to Indian Guides and Boy Scouts, and we went river kayaking and camping. My mother was very generous with her money and has assisted me in numerous ways throughout my life. My father, too, travelled great distances to see me and also took me skiing to the Matterhorn in Zermatt, Switzerland and Mammoth, California. So, despite the divorce and other onerous issues, I don't want the reader to think that they did nothing good for me. If this seems like a paradox of extremes, it's not.

There is something I learned from all of that, but it wasn't until I heard it articulated by a motivational speaker that I followed in my young adult life, that the paradox of dysfunction and growth could actually coexist in some sane place; that that paradox does empower growth beyond, while not shutting everything down into paralysis of victimhood. What I heard went like this, "...If you're going to blame people for all the *bad* you better blame them for all the good too. If you're going to give them credit for everything that's *messed up*, then you have to give them credit for everything that's great... If we can realize that life is always happening *for* us, not to us... pain and suffering disappear." – A. Robbins

Of course, this would take many years to internalize into my outlook. From each of my parents' specific life-challenges that contributed significant weight to my childhood outlook; now as an adult, I have learned to be highly introspective and a type of person who could care deeply and appropriately for others. I have become extremely persistent and sane, and someone deeply committed to faith and family and saving lives, specifically because I model the *opposite* of the intrusiveness and apathy that was shown to me.

I knew my parents' marriage was over upon arrival back from a visit to the East Coast. My mother had taken me and my brother to visit her parents, *without* my father. In those days anyone who wanted, could come right up to the gate and my father met us there as we deplaned. He tried to show some affection for my mom. He got a superficial and very cold hello but nothing more. I'm sure he was trying. But my mother was done. My father tried one last time to embrace her. Failing that, he walked with her down the concourse and tried to kiss her cheek. My mom kept walking and my father was only able to land a very weak kiss on her face. I felt badly for him. I felt badly for her; even as their relationship fractured into a million jagged pieces. It was a hard time to be a child in that home.

Trying to make sense of why they divorced, I know that my parents were experimenting in their social lives, having grown up in a very conservative geography, respectively. I'm sure their interactions with each other had been spiraling downhill for years; emotional intrusiveness cannot really tolerate emotional avoidance and silence. They were geared very poorly for each other.

I still recall the day my father left our family home. I felt as if my entire world had just ended. My dad had packed his bags and I was sobbing. I even wrote a letter to him about how much I would miss him and that I loved him and placed it in his bag. Feeling *so* vulnerable and in emotional pieces, I removed that letter. To this day I am still unsure if my father could have processed that pure letter of love and sadness from his son. My mother went into a morose state, started to spiral and became abusive. And she would not give me any healthy space.

My father moved to Marina Del Rey and my mother then graduated nursing school and announced that the only job she wanted was in Pennsylvania, 3,000 miles away from my father. My father did not contest the decision – meaning that he let us go and we would be forced not to see him very often, maybe every six months or longer, exacerbating the feelings of separation and loss.

That was a very lonely time for me. I taught myself to ride a unicycle on our cul-de-sac in California and ended up riding that unicycle all over our housing development in

Reading, Pennsylvania. People just stared at this odd 12-year-old riding on one wheel all over our community. Since you can't coast on a unicycle and you literally have to pedal up and down hills, I developed powerful leg muscles.

I began school in a bucolic town, not many Jews; and I was very much not a joiner, so I was mostly alone; however, on the East Coast, my mother found a Jewish Conservative congregation for us to join, and the education and observance went up a notch. I learned what I needed for my bar-mitzvah; I learned my Torah portion and the service and did a very nice job.

The secular day school I attended, Gov. Mifflin Junior High, was a bit different than anything I experienced before. It was a large rambling building with lots of kids. There were also lots of bullies and some fights, which were forced upon me. I recall getting my head bashed into a swinging door by a very fat older girl. I had a huge goose egg on my forehead and aside of it being very painful and embarrassing, I had no one to stand with me. I could not believe how vulnerable and how senseless getting picked on was. How hopeless. I felt extremely low at that time.

My mother, to her credit, also saw this low point in me and applied to Jewish Big Brothers on my behalf. So, when I was 12, she found a man about 14 years older than me who wanted to be my Big Brother. His name was Fred, and he was, and still is an ER doctor; though now semi-retired, he spends a lot of his time doing cosmetic Botox. Fred was like an oasis in this cold hell I was living in. He took me horseback riding, out to dinner and movies, included me in his family events and even sponsored me to a sleep away camp where he was employed as the camp doctor. Fred had one request of me; he told me that when I got older that he would be very proud of me if I, too, would become a Big Brother to someone who needed. I told him that I would. 15 years after his request, at age 27, I kept my promise and became a Jewish Big Brother, just like Fred.

And today, some 40 years later, we are still extremely close. We see each other every six months or so. He's been to my wedding and to my son's *bris* (circumcision). We've spent an entire Shabbos together in my home. I love Fred, as if he were a real brother.

Shortly after my bar-mitzvah my mother began to severely deteriorate emotionally and needed some time to find herself to stabilize. She made the decision to return *by herself* to California and place my brother and me with her parents in King of Prussia, PA. My father apparently felt leaving us with his ex-in-laws was an appropriate plan and did not contest this arrangement. He came once or twice from California to visit us in the year we lived there.

I attended Upper Merion High School and joined the football team. Still, I felt like an orphan; abandoned and off balanced. I felt some relief that my mother was getting the help she said she needed, but I missed my parents. My grandparents were already older; and this presented us with a major generational gap. There was not much more than a distant relationship coupled with grandparent pleasantries, and essentially no place to make a real or meaningful connection. So, here in King of Prussia, there was a kind of slog through superficial emotional isolation and malaise. And then suddenly, things got real *and* intense.

One evening as we were getting ready for bed, around 9 p.m., someone began pounding on our apartment door. My grandfather answered the door and in fell a woman who lived across the hall. She was face down inside our entry way and making a high-pitched whistling sound from her mouth. My younger biological brother witnessed this and ran away saying that he could not deal with what he was seeing. I was 13 at the time and recognized immediately what was happening from my previous CPR training and ran from my room toward the woman.

No time to get dressed, I had on only my underwear and some white tube socks. It's funny what sticks in your memory. I knew exactly what this was. She was choking. My grandparents were crowding her but not helping because they did not know what to do. I ordered my grandfather to lift her up; which he did. I positioned myself behind the woman as my grandfather tried to keep her up. By this time, I was supporting the bulk of this woman's weight as I started to deliver abdominal thrusts in the manner of the Heimlich Maneuver.

I recall grunting with the effort I exerted pulling my fist in hand back against her diaphragm over and over again. I think it took perhaps 7 or 8 thrusts, which seemed like a long time until finally a piece of apple flew out of her mouth, thank G-d.

25 // Making Music With What Remains

I stopped with the Maneuver and the woman regained her color and her composure and her breath. Now realizing I was not dressed very modestly I left the room quickly.

It was over so fast, and my grandparents never really spoke about it much. Perhaps they did not realize the severity of the situation or they were in shock. But I know what happened because I carried the pain of what I did for over a week in my hamstrings. I pulled every muscle in the back of my legs. That event had great impact on me, though I would not know how far it would influence me until many years later when I opted into extreme rescue work in law enforcement and then literally donated one of my kidneys.

Some people will never be able to help in an emergency, either because they are too jaded or immobilized by the horror unfolding, and/or incapable of action. Some people want to help but are simply not trained. And some people, people like me, not only want to help, but feel a deep visceral need to protect, save lives and they get trained. I think if any experience solidified or brought to the surface that need to be part of the solution instead of being part of the problem was that night in my grandparents' home saving the life of our neighbor.

It was around this time that my grandparents had had enough excitement in their retirement and found a boarding school for me to attend in Massachusetts called Worcestor Academy. I was about to embark on one of the most amazing and self-assured experiences of my life. Though it was only to be one semester of 9th grade, I grew tremendously during this time, living on my own, being responsible for money and grades and homework and new friends and working out and essentially came into my own as an independent young man for the first time in my life. And then that too would be taken from me. But I was so grateful every day for those next 6 months!

Nestled atop a hill located at 91 Providence Street in Worcestor, MA is Worcestor Academy, a boarding school situated on 71 acres. Its classic New England historic style architecture and old-world feel drew me in. I felt immediately at home. I moved into Dexter Hall and got my own private room. There was a dress code, jacket and tie, which I loved and no expectations except that I go to class, get good grades…. and nothing more. I got to set my own agenda, my own routine, my own workout schedule and my own friends.

And friends I made.

I was free from familial turmoil, worry and malaise of our post-divorce separation. I literally began to thrive. I enjoyed my classes. I enjoyed the ivy-league feel to the school and the environment I now called home. It felt vital. It felt real. It felt purposeful.

And then, after the semester finished, I guess my father got to thinking about how much time he never saw me and wanted me to come back to the State of California. I eventually came to understand his parental reasoning, but it still didn't make it any easier having to leave the only place I had felt whole in for such a long time. Upon this forced return to California, I lived in my mother's apartment in Van Nuys and began attending Grant High School.

I fell into a melancholy state; not quite depression, but something close to it, had trouble making friends and felt that my entire world had crumbled.

Now my mother was not done processing her own issues; (the ones that had originally forced her to take a leave from parenting us). Also, not expecting me to be returned to California so soon, she was not yet equipped to provide the parental support I needed, and she felt that perhaps I needed some time to decompress. So, at age 14, I went to live at an in-patient facility called, "The Westwood", which used to be horse stables. Though there was *zero* clinical reason I should have been there I used my time to grow emotionally. I learned a lot about human interaction and psychology and interpersonal introspection. I carry these skills with me to this day. I ended up earning the highest level in the program and leading the weekly patient group meetings.

I would come out emotionally stronger and self-assured and I realized my experience was largely of my own making. I got to see kids on every level of the socio-economic spectrum who struggled with trauma in their lives and became close friends with a few even on the outside. One previous patient, John, and I connected after he was discharged, and we spent a lot of time together. Eventually, our lives took different paths and for a year I did not speak to him. Then I found out that he intentionally drove to the Santa Monica Parking Structure and jumped to his death from the 5th story. I cried. His mother told me that John had always told her that there was something missing in his brain that he could never overcome and did not want to live that way anymore. I miss him.

I went to live again with my mother, in Chatsworth, CA. It was beautiful there, parks and rolling mountains with huge boulders for hiking and climbing. I started going to Chatsworth High School and earned my diploma.

While attending school, I also worked part time and was able to save enough to buy my first car at auction, a blue '67 Chevy Camaro with rear lifters and *mag* wheels. It was beautiful but not all of the electronics functioned; like for instance the fuel gauge did not work so I had to *gage the gauge* and sometimes I misestimated and ran out of gas. Also, the motor mount gasket was defective so if I pressed too heavily on the gas pedal it would get sucked down all the way to the floor and for a few seconds I would be unable to control the acceleration. Then the manifold cover over the radiator fan was held up and together literally with kite string. And the brakes were not so great.

Anyway, what it lacked in reliability it made up in giving me freedom; but with the car at age 16 came curfew which my mother set. I did my best to comply, but I was not always successful in meeting my curfew. One night I went out to visit a friend at 9 p.m. I was only meant to be out for an hour; home by 10. But I ran out of gas. With no cell phones in 1986, I had to walk to the gas station to get a can filled and when I finally rolled in at 12:30 a.m. reeking of gasoline, no excuse was acceptable. My mother decided

29 // Making Music With What Remains

that if I couldn't make the curfew work, I should go live with my father.

I gathered my things and put them in my car and drove to Marina Del Rey to ask my father if I could live with him. When my father saw me and heard that I had been told to live somewhere else, he did something I've never seen him do before or after. He cried.

I lived for the rest of the summer with my father in Marina Del Rey and drove every day to Chatsworth so that I could work in my capacity as camp lifeguard. When the summer ended, I got a job at Music Plus and moved in with a friend of mine from school in the Chatsworth area so I could continue to attend Chatsworth High School. My friend at the time was named Jef. He's since changed his name to Max, and we have remained close friends until this day. He bore a striking resemblance to Billy Idol and I looked a little like his guitarist, Steve Stevens. We ended up entering and winning our school's first lip sync contest with the song, "Rebel Yell."

Soon after, Jef got a motorcycle and I immediately wanted one too. So, I rented one. Jef and I would ride together, and it was very fun. I loved riding that bike. Helmets were not required by law, so I did not use one. But Jef did. One day we decided to ride out to Valencia together. I was on my Kawasaki GPZ 550. We stopped at a gas station at the bottom of a hill. I asked Jef if I could borrow his helmet; it had a face shield and the wind had been irritating my eyes and I needed some relief.

Thank G-d I put that helmet on. We began up the hill. I sped ahead of Jef super-fast because my eyes no longer hurt from the wind. As I crested the hill, I was in the lane closest to the right side, the side cut into a mountain. I was unaware that the road curved radically to the left at the top and I was going too fast to correct myself. I was unable to turn with the road due to my speed and I hit the mountain side at 60 mph. Instantly the handlebars twisted clockwise sending the bike crashing out from under my legs to the left of me. I was launched forward over the handlebars and then both rider and bike were rolling together on the dirt shoulder... and my world went black.

When I regained consciousness, I was face up with my head positioned downhill; my bike was a ramshackle wreck nearby. Jef's helmet was still on my head. I was in significant pain and not able to move. The wind had been knocked out of me and I could not yet breathe normally.

Just then Jef came running up to me and in his fear and excitement began to pound and push on my chest asking if I'm ok. He was (unintentionally) hurting me. Even in my delicate semi-conscious state I knew you are not supposed to be moved unnecessarily and I was at risk for spinal injuries, so I rasped at him, "Knock it off."

California Highway Patrol rolled up next, then a rescue ambulance. They put a cervical collar on me. I don't remember being loaded onto the ambulance, but I do remember that night in the hospital spending most of it on a gurney in the hallway. Since I had been in a very violent accident the doctors did not know how much if any internal bleeding I might have or broken bones, so for the next 6 hours I was placed in a sling and then hoisted up and down; repositioned every few minutes onto an x-ray machine so they could get a picture of every bone in my body.

Three days later, I was released with no broken bones and no internal bleeding. But I had a lot of road rash and small rocks embedded into my skin. My mother was an R.N. and enterostomal (wound care) therapist and to her credit, she bandaged and helped preserve my fragile skin.

I returned to Jef's house to recover and rejoined high school again a week later. Needless to say, I got rid of the motorcycle.

My mother helped save my skin, and things softened a bit between us, but I never officially lived with her again. For the last 6 months of high school, I was between being "homeless" and loosely staying sometimes by my mom. I lived with crew members from Music Plus while I waited for my acceptance to California State University Northridge to come through and when it did, I moved into an apartment with two friends also attending CSUN. I also joined a fraternity, Zeta Beta Tau (ZBT).

CSUN at the time was a commuter school of over 29,000 students. Today that number is closer to 39,000. It was very hard to meet people so I thought joining the Greek system would be a sure way to have a meaningful social life. Admittedly, I had some fun and it was nice having a group of people I could sit and socialize with. But after a very short period of time, the superficial fun grew stale. There are only so many parties to attend and only so much alcohol to drink until it gets old. I realized I was not a follower, nor was I cut out to be a "frat" brother; the relationships were artless and cliquey. I had little in common with most of the "brothers" besides the letters I wore on my chest; so, I quit.

In addition to all the academic core classes, I also enrolled in interesting and fun (non-academic) classes along the way like wrestling, modern dance and jazz and got NAUI and County of Los Angeles SCUBA certified. My instructor was an ex-Navy "Frogman", and training was military-like and intense. I came out with the equivalent of an Advanced Open Water certificate. I took a gymnastics class and did contortions and strength moves with my body then that I will never be able to duplicate. I also took and completed a mountain wilderness survival class. The one thing I learned that stayed with me was never to go anywhere outdoors without a condom. For those of you who are uninitiated, a condom is a fantastic water carrying device. It's very strong and can expand many times its size so that in an emergency you can carry a copious amount water from a lake or river to your camp site.

I was so enamored with SCUBA that I convinced my father to get certified so we could dive together. When he got his PADI certification, which in my opinion is a much weaker certification than NAUI; he and I took a boat from Oxnard, CA to the Channel Islands, which were a number of hours away. Diving off the boat was spectacular and pristine, though very dangerous. If you go down too far and ascend too quickly, you can have pressurized gas in your blood boiling out and develop an embolism in your lungs requiring emergency life-saving treatment. Drowning, hypothermia, ruptured eardrums and shark attacks were also other very real risks. There are depth challenge risks if you dive deeper than a few atmospheres of pressure, like 100 feet; the partial pressure of the nitrogen that naturally occurs in the oxygen we breathe on the surface and fill our tanks with increases such that the nitrogen can cause hallucinations. It's called *nitrogen narcosis* and it's caused divers to chase imaginary mermaids or simply take the air supply out and drown in a hallucinogenic haze. I took all of this to heart.

On our first dive together, my father and I made entry into the ocean from the boat and surfaced. We stayed on the surface to do a quick equipment check. Oxygen regulators worked, stage 1 and stage 2, BC (buoyancy compensator) worked, etc. Typically, a small amount of air is placed into the BC upon entry so that the diver can easily float to, and remain on, the surface during the pre-dive safety check. When the safety check is complete and the air is released, the weight of the gear allows you to submerge and dive.

I was clear. I took my snorkel out of my mouth, inserted my breathing regulator, and purged my BC as I began my descent under the water. I held my position about 20 feet from the surface watching for my father to follow suit. He purged his BC but did not have his stage 1 regulator in his hand or in his mouth and the snorkel was obstructing him. He started to descend and began to realize that he had forgotten a critical procedure and was now in way over his head. He had no way to breathe underwater because he had no oxygen source ready as he lost his bearings. And his PADI training did not help him. He tried to kick back to the surface to start over; to be able to take a breath. But the water was jarringly cold, and his kicking was ineffective now. He had previously depended on the BC to keep him on the surface and now his BC was empty, so he was starting to panic. He began to descend quicker now. Full panic.

I realized in those seconds exactly what was happening; and I kicked over to him, immediately taking my stage 1 regulator out of my mouth and reseating it firmly in his mouth. He began to breathe. I just blew bubbles watching him and I held him from descending further. We began to buddy breathe with the one regulator. Had we been further down in depth I would have used my stage 2 regulator as well, but at that depth, there was no need. I hit the automatic fill button on his BC, and it inflated and brought us both up those 20 or so feet very quickly.

I had just saved my father's life from literally drowning in front of me. I'm not sure if he realized it. He clearly would not have recovered from his involuntary descent had I not been there. That's probably the reason SCUBA diving requires that you dive with a buddy.

We spoke little of it after. It's possible he hadn't come to terms with how close to death he really was. We did dive together after that, but I stayed very close to my father during the next dives and never took my eyes off him for more than 3 seconds. After that, I think my father lost his zeal for diving, though I would continue for a number of years. SCUBA diving is a very time and energy intensive and high maintenance sport. I soon realized, like with most of the extreme activities I had in my life at that time, that the fun and challenge did not outweigh the time and energy it took to enjoy the sport; and just like skiing and kayaking, piloting a helicopter and skydiving, I found myself not the extreme thrill seeker I thought I wanted to be and very quickly, after mastering these sports, decided that they just weren't worth the time or effort required.

I took a summer day job as a city lifeguard while I worked as a bouncer and barback by night at a once popular, but now defunct, restaurant/bar in Westwood called, *Yesterdays*. One night I was out with my college roommate at a sushi bar, and I met a girl named Caryn. We started dating and soon that turned into a serious relationship. I ended up moving into her home located in West Hills.

A little more than a year before graduation, I began to intern at local hospitals as a physical therapist aide. This was required work experience if I was to meet my work experience requirements to get into the PT program at CSUN. I also had part time work as a dispatcher at the Auto Club to make ends meet. And I was still going to school full time. My girlfriend, Caryn, would later become my first ex-wife. She also happened to be a born Jew, secular, who was 5 years older than me and into Buddhism. Her father, Milton, had abandoned her mother and my girlfriend and her older sister when they were in their early teens. He had been cheating on her mother since almost the day they married. He married his mistress and settled just a few blocks from the family home, but never reached out to his kids. I recall walking with my then girlfriend in the mall one day and her father was approaching from the opposite direction; he passed us without a word until she turned and said, "Dad?"

He looked up, pretending that he hadn't seen us and came over to say hello, gave a quick hug to his daughter and then disappeared. My girlfriend broke down and wept right there in the middle of the mall. That was the first contact Caryn had had with her father in years and this casual apathy of her father was astounding to me. He didn't care that he was squandering a most precious gift, a daughter's love for her father.

While in university I had begun with a major in business, but a "D" in micro-economics and general disinterest in the subject led me to choose a different major. I then decided to go the liberal arts route as the quickest way out of school and changed my major to Radio TV and Film with an emphasis on media management. But then I lost interest in TV production. The fakeness and superficiality and ego all grated on me. So, I looked to do something else. In fact, I was preparing to enter the physical therapy program after a year and a summer of taking all the pre-med classes that would qualify me to attend. It all came down to my interview with the faculty of the program and I asked this fateful question, "I've worked very hard to get here, gotten good grades and good work experience... and I'm wondering why I would want to attend your program (and not another one)? What sets your program apart?"

After the shocked looks of disbelief that I dared to ask such a question, one of the faculty proffered just one thing; that their internship with practicing therapists in the field was a benefit of attending the CSUN PT program. It was a weak answer; they clearly had not been expecting me to ask and I was punished for asking the question by being denied entry after all that work! This was later confirmed to me by the Chair of the Department when I returned after being rejected seeking an explanation. The Chair could barely contain herself. She castigated me for having the temerity, the audacity to ask the faculty to convince me why I should attend their vaunted PT training school. And that ended my bid to become a physical therapist. Truth be told, physical therapy *is* hard, and working in a hospital environment is never easy; there are so many sick and dying people, so much trauma. And while rewarding, I could easily see that one could become burned out.

I flirted briefly with the idea of going into Chiropractic, but by then I was already making way too much money in investments as a Registered Representative. I realized after 4+ years of college that if I did not finish my original major I would never graduate; so, I opted back into the RTVF program, finished out all my units and graduated.

If there was any silver lining to matriculating through the pre-PT program, it was in befriending one of the hospital therapists. He told me about a specialized unit of the Sheriff's Emergency Services Detail (ESD/SWAT) known as the Sheriff's Mountain Rescue Team. He said they did cliff rescue, rappelling over mountain sides and out of helicopters, locating and rescuing lost hikers and recovering bodies. This was something special to me, the complexity and requirement for a specialized skill set meant I was immediately captivated by this. I decided soon after that I wanted to be on the Sheriff's Rescue Team.

Chapter 2

A Narrow Bridge

"The whole world entire is a very narrow bridge and the essence is not to fear at all."
- Rabbi Nachman of Breslov

My life seemed destined to its fateful turn; having missed an opportunity to attend physical therapy school, I was now looking for something else to do besides working in the field of my major, film and television production work. Closing in on graduation and having to finally get a post degree job, I was very dissatisfied with Radio TV and Film. As fortune would have it my girlfriend was having lunch at a sushi restaurant on Ventura Blvd., in Woodland Hills and saw two men sitting at the bar. She described how relaxed they seemed, and that they drove nice cars. She was curious about what they did for a living, so she asked them. At first, they were reticent to tell her, then told her they were trashmen; it seemed odd to me at the time that they were so reluctant to say… but after a few attempts they told her that they were brokers in investments. My girlfriend, thinking of my job situation, took one of their cards and gave it to me later that evening.

I followed up and spoke to a man named Joe, the sales manager at Consolidated Inter-Capital Corp., where the two men worked. He described the job but was not very accommodating about granting an interview, probably because I had never done phone sales, much less investment phone sales; but the money raise potential was intriguing, and I did not give up. I continued to call him until he agreed to grant me an interview. Apparently, I had a natural proclivity toward persistence.

If I had any illusions about the investment business being glamorous and sophisticated and computer generated before my interview, I lost those illusions quickly. The operation was in a professional building with a conference room, mail room and 6 offices, two for the principal, Ken, an old Oil and Gas investment guy and his executive assistant, one for the sales manager, Joe, one for compliance and two offices for the salesmen. There were essentially 12 cubicles in those two small rooms, each with desks, chairs, phones and scripts. Though I did not know the legal term for it at the time, it was a classic boiler room type operation; notwithstanding that it was legal and registered through the NASD. It wasn't exactly seedy, but it wasn't Goldman Sacks either.

The salesmen's rooms' decor looked more like junior high detention desks than what I imagined brokers' desks would look like. Every one of the salesmen had to be a broker in the legal sense, meaning they had to take and pass a securities exam and hold a license to sell the limited partnership investment being sold. In this case it was the series 22 (limited partnerships) and 63 (State securities regulations and rules).

The investment being sold was a sort of hospital accounts receivable factoring deal. CIC would purchase hospital receivables at significant discount with investor funds and when the entire amount was received from the insurance companies, the difference would then be paid to the investors in the form of a percentage of return on investment. It was touted as a win/win. The hospital got its money quickly and the investors received up to 21% return on their money.

Since *institutional* investors, those with $1 million net worth, were preferred, the unit price was set at $25,000 each. While CIC was required to validate each client's net worth, by making the initial buy-in such a large amount, the firm simply abdicated that requirement and played the odds. The firm assumed that if someone had $25k to invest in an LP, it was likely their net worth was in excess of $1M. I found that *not* to be the case with most of my customers, which is why I was only able to secure $25k most times from most people.

Commission was 8% to the broker plus a point bonus after $100,000 in production. That meant I could make $2,000 per unit sold right out of college. Problem was that I was terrified of phone sales. Asking someone to send me money on the phone who I've never met was completely outside my comfort zone. And yet, here were all these men calling people they had never met, pitching them and convincing them to send checks for tens to hundreds of thousands through the mail.

I was matched with one of the more talented men, "Michael Brooks" a/k/a "Michael Goodman", two of his chosen phone names. (To his credit, his real legal last name was long, foreign sounding, difficult to pronounce and impossible to spell; in a word: "cumbersome". A phone name solved that problem, but it also had the appearance of concealing one's identity.) And I watched him sell. It certainly wasn't rocket science, dialing phone numbers and reading from a script. But there was talent required to actually paint the investment picture in a compelling way to be able to sell to a total stranger. Yet incredibly when he read from the script, he sounded just like he was speaking "off the cuff". He was so smooth and so confident and so compelling. And persistent! At one point he dialed the next random number on his lead list and simply handed the phone to me, pointing to the script and indicating that I should do the selling on the next call. I froze. Nothing came out of my mouth. The person he called just stayed on the line saying, "Hello? Hello?" over and over but I could not bring myself to engage.

Michael took the phone back from me and then like nothing happened, pitched the man and tried to convince him to accept a brochure and his pitch. Whether he accepted his offer to send out a brochure and thereby become a "prospect" or not did not matter. It was just a numbers game. Out of 200 people called on any given day, the goal was to get 8 prospects and 5 pitches to be able to get one deal. At $2,000 per unit commission plus bonus, a broker's revenue could add up very quickly and this fact was not lost on me. The only small problem I had was my fear to actually sell.

I felt embarrassed about not being able to speak on the phone to the customer; still I knew I would have to eventually jump in if I wanted to work in this industry, so I stayed next to Michael listening to him for the rest of the day. But I made no attempt to sell that day. When it was time to leave, Michael walked out with me and we got onto the elevator together. When the doors closed, he turned to me and gave me his prediction of my future in investment sales. He told me a bit arrogantly that in his opinion this business of phone sales and investments was not for me and that I should try to find something else to do.

The doors opened. He exited, wished me luck and left.

As an academic exercise, looking back, had I listened to him I would have never gone to prison. As it turned out instead, I took his words as a challenge and decided that no matter how uncomfortable I was that I would push through the discomfort and do that job well. I wanted to prove to this guy, Michael Brooks a/k/a Goodman, that he was wrong about me. I wanted Michael to eat his words.

He indeed ate his words. I ended up becoming the number two salesman in the office during that same year, earning close to $100,000 in income from commissions in 8 months, having never sold anything before. I was the number one salesman the year after. And I did it right out of college, unbelievably, by reading a company approved script and by simply being persistent.

Aside of being persistent, there were relatively few other requirements to be successful, but they required practice and patience. The prospect needed to have 3 criteria to become a client. He had to have the money to invest. He had to be interested. He had to be controllable. If a prospect had those three criteria I relentlessly closed and kept asking for the money.

43 // Making Music With What Remains

To aid in my newly chosen career, I had become a devotee of motivational speaker Anthony Robbins and listened *religiously* to his tape program, "Unlimited Power." I used his techniques to motivate myself and move myself from where I was to where I wanted to go financially and materially, and I have to say the program helped me focus and achieve and be persistent. I actually became a helicopter pilot because of the inspiration I took from Robbins. It took me a year and $10,000 but today I am an FAA licensed private pilot – rotorcraft. I didn't just rappel out of helicopters. I also flew them.

I also went to a 3-day seminar of his and did the barefoot fire walk. There wasn't much substance beyond the feel-good moments, and I felt more and more that he was really about upselling his books and seminars, and he could have condensed his program into 1 day. Though he does have some very-good ideas and delivery, his style became a bit overbearing for me. After I inculcated techniques that I felt were most useful to acquire the wealth and materiality and peace of mind I was after, I quit following him. He does have powerful techniques and pithy motivational aphorisms; you just have to be able to put everything in perspective and take what is useful and leave the rest.

During my last year of college, I began and completed the application process and background check to join the Sheriff's Department and Rescue Team. After college graduation, I was accepted onto the Team and then into the Academy. I recall going to an Open House at the Lost Hills Sheriff's Station and met with members during their trainings. It was all very heady stuff. They were geared up in SWAT flight suits, sidearms, harnesses, helmets and had training modules and active operations consisting of lowering and raising systems, first aid, rappelling over cliffs and out of helicopters, rescuing lost and injured hikers, suspect searches and doing body recoveries. There was of course a law enforcement element to it as well; this was the Sheriff's Department after all, but that was significantly mitigated by the main job which was rescue. While most times people who feared law enforcement never wanted to see a Sheriff, in our case, people were *always* happy to see us.

It was against this backdrop that I entered the Los Angeles County Sheriff's Department Reserve Academy on the recommendation of my physical therapist friend. Located in Valencia, CA at the College of the Canyons, I was able to attend part-time, after normal work hours and on weekends, while still selling investments for CIC. After graduation I went on to get advanced certifications as a Search and Rescue (SAR) Sheriff Team Member and Emergency Medical Technician. I did this for no pay.

The LASD Reserve Academy was a full law enforcement training and certification program. We learned the law, powers of arrest and firearms, did p/t, practiced weapons retention and self-defense, baton training, small arms combat (at that time our sidearm was the Berretta 92FS) and shotgun target practice, plus patrol rides. We did roll play scenarios and lots of felony-stop training, handcuffing and officer safety.

45 // Making Music With What Remains

I enjoyed my time in the Academy immensely. We dressed in full "Class B" uniform and carried our batons, handcuffs and firearms throughout our training. We were told that our *primary directive* as officers was that we must survive our shifts; to be able to go home (alive) at the end of the day was the most important rule in law enforcement.

One thing that was constantly stressed by staff was to always "watch their hands" because its the hands of the suspect or subject being detained that can kill you. We were also not allowed to carry *anything* in our gun hands; for most of us our right hands had to be empty at all times. This practice, which became a habit of mine, has stayed with me ever since. The thought process is that if you have something in your gun hand like keys or a clipboard or your lunch, and you need to draw your weapon quickly to engage a bad guy, the time delay in dropping the item in your hand and then drawing your gun may cost you your life. That meant that all our police gear (and there was a lot of gear) had to be carried in our left hands or slung over our shoulders.

In fact, even today some 27 years after the Academy, keeping my "gun hand" free is so ingrained as a basic officer safety issue for me, that I have to fight the urge to go over to a cop who is holding something in his gun hand… and tell him to switch hands.

Sheriff's roll play days were intense. We were given every kind of scenario from car crashes with broken bones and brains splashed over the car to babies not breathing to burglary investigations to burglaries in progress and active shooters. It was one such burglary in progress my partner and I responded to and we came across a female being restrained by a male and the female was screaming for help. Upon rolling up to the scene, I completely sized up the situation incorrectly thinking the man needed to be cuffed and I did not bother to search the female. After I cuffed the man, I went to speak to my partner and turned my back for just a moment. Then shots rang out. The female had pulled a huge gun out of her bra and killed both my partner and me.

The gun was real, but the ammo fired were blanks. Still, they made realistic gun-shot sounds, and it really drove home what I was getting involved with. My mistake would have cost both of our lives on the street. It shook me to the core; this was real.

I took that experience very hard and almost quit the Academy. I had a heart to heart with my training sergeant, telling him what happened and stated that perhaps I should resign; but Sgt. Decker dissuaded me. He said that, "In every class a number of recruits get *killed* during roll play. That's the reason we have this as a training module, so that recruits can learn from it. If you learned from it, then it was worth it."

In the end, I didn't resign. But my demeanor and edge had hardened, and I never let any law enforcement situation ever get away from me again.

Part of the training required uniformed patrol rides, while still in the Academy, with Training Officers. Three times we went out with TOs and had to be positively evaluated to continue; on one such ride, my TO was a female deputy.

47 // Making Music With What Remains

She kept her back up weapon (a 5-round revolver) in the trauma plate pouch of her bulletproof vest. I was told that, "There is what they teach you in the Academy and how you do it on the street...."

Anyway, we're stopped under a tree in our marked black and white patrol vehicle as dusk was setting in. My partner was driving. She was giving instruction about use of force when some random guy just walked up on us from out of nowhere. He approached my partner's side, coming right up to the driver's side window. Without a moment's hesitation my partner un-holstered her Berretta and jammed it low across her hips, muzzle first, into her driver side door and just out of the guy's line of site. Her finger was pulling tension on the trigger, but not enough to engage the hammer yet. If she would have pulled the trigger the bullet would have exited the car door and gone right into his center lower abdomen.

That random guy just wanted directions; my partner gave them in a friendly manner and wished him well and off he went. He had no idea there were sixteen 9mm parabellum hollow point rounds aimed at his torso during that exchange. When the guy was 10 feet away walking in the opposite direction, she re-holstered her gun and continued on with her lesson.

What some people don't realize until they put on a uniform and carry a gun is how exposed and vulnerable you are; how much of a target you can be. What people also don't realize is that you never want to catch a cop unaware; a cop only has a micro-second to size you up to determine if you are a threat. Therefore, you want to give a cop as much time as possible to determine that you are not a threat before you close the distance too fast. It's always a good idea to self-identify what you need and/or what your intentions are well before you get close. That guy should have caught our attention a long time before he was actually at our door. It's called common sense. And I suppose we should have been more vigilant as well.

Also, I learned that when you are pulled over, the best thing for the driver to do is *show your hands*. When the deputy is approaching your vehicle, he has no idea what he is in for. There is no such thing as a routine traffic stop. More cops get killed in traffic stop related incidents than any other. So, the first thing is to make safe contact with the deputy. Stay seated. Turn off the car, unroll the window on the side the deputy is approaching from and *keep both your hands on the steering wheel*. Don't be rooting around for drivers' license or insurance and registration info just yet. There's plenty of time for that. Make contact. Find out what the matter is… and then when the deputy asks for them; give him those documents. Make sure that you tell the deputy exactly where you are going to reach, like your back pocket or purse or glove box. It's common decency, also known as common sense… and it may just save your life.

The greatest power law enforcement officers have is the authority to legally detain someone, depriving him of his freedom. On this, our instructors were clear: Taking someone's freedom is very serious; not to be taken lightly.

Training also included Code-3 driving (lights and siren), pursuits and felony stops. A felony stop is when you are pulling over a driver who you know is going to jail; usually someone with a warrant and charges that include weapons or violence, or someone who is suspected of committing any number of crimes or someone fleeing from a crime scene, etc.

The felony stop was coordinated with at least one other black and white. Using a secure radio channel authorized by the watch commander's desk, once both police vehicles were in position in a loose "V" shape behind the suspect vehicle (and assuming the felony suspect has complied with orders to stop); the lead deputy opened his door, stuck his gun out the car using the vehicle for cover, and then began to bark orders. By the way, if there are two black and whites, there will usually be 4 deputies all with guns drawn while using their patrol vehicles for cover.

I'm not sure if political correctness or polite verbiage has re-asserted itself in the many years since I was in the Academy, but when I went through this training, chivalry and all niceties were completely thrown out.

The deputy with operational command began: "Driver! Let me see your hands out the window! Driver, with your left hand remove your ignition keys and drop them on the ground. Driver, keeping your right hand out the window use your left hand to open your door. Driver, exit the vehicle with your hands up…!"

And so it went until the lead deputy had the driver backed up, visually checked and then ordered him on his face with his hands spread out away from his sides, left leg on top of the right.

50 // Making Music With What Remains

The tension was palpable as our training class was instructed to specifically order the driver *not* to move. Our instructors demonstrated with felony stop language that was a bit more aggressive than requesting of the driver, "*License and registration, please....*"

The deputy with operational command yelled, "Driver! Do not move! If you move, I will fucking kill you! Do you understand, Driver?! If you move, you are a dead man! Don't you *fucking* move!"

Then came an extremely high-risk moment. One of the deputies was required to emerge from cover and into the open, so as to secure and search the subject on the ground. Suspected of violence or weapons, the deputy still did not know for sure if the guy was unarmed or if there were other bad guys with guns in the vehicle up ahead.

Without giving away too much of the actual arrest procedure, the passenger deputy of the assist black and white would move in to handcuff the prone suspect, all the while with at least 3 other guns still trained on the suspect and his vehicle. After the suspect was secured in a patrol car, another deputy, sometimes with a canine, would have to clear the guy's car at gunpoint. Not for the faint of heart.

I also did one module in the jail working as a jailer; in the regular division, deputies have to work in the jails for 5 years or longer before being released to the streets. In the reserve division, there was no such requirement. Still, we all had our 1 night in jail. As it turned out, I would have to endure about 2,275 more nights in jail after I resigned from LASD. But for the time being, I was happy to learn the booking and fingerprinting and processing procedures as an Academy recruit.

After graduation, I had my POST (Police Officer Standards and Training) and Reserve Law Enforcement Officer Certifications and went to work, essentially volunteering my time for the Malibu Mountain Rescue Team (MMRT). This position was so dangerous that they called us *high risk* volunteers, and because regular deputies are not allowed to participate; only reserve deputies who are given $1 per year (as a ceremonial stipend) are allowed on the Team.

The training was rigorous and ongoing and very fulfilling. I spent 7 years on the Sheriff's Rescue Team. In that time, my Team and I were directly responsible for saving the lives of numerous civilians *and* law enforcement personnel. On most rescues I was assigned to the "Bash Team", which meant I was usually the first Team member onto a scene, be it rappelling out of the helicopter or over the side of the mountain or up the side of a mountain on a search. I was in incredibly good physical shape and I loved what I was doing. I also carried a Team pager, which meant I was literally on duty 24/7. Rescue pages could come at any time of the day or night.

Since I was making good money and did not have to be tied to a desk for 8 hours a day, this fit my lifestyle just fine. I would come to work for a few hours a day, pitch my customers and be available to respond to a rescue call if need be, or some other adventure.

I became very successful at CIC, but after a number of program iterations that we were fully funding, the principal, Ken, began to get greedy and jealous. I was actually making more with my commissions and bonus than he was in his entire capacity as CEO. He made 1 or 2 points on everyone's production, but with bonuses I was making 9 points on my production. So, he cut the commissions and I began to look for other opportunities, having since honed my phone and sales skills, earning myself a formidable reputation in the investment community.

After I left, the floor fell out at CIC. This "safe" NASD registered investment I had been selling had become noxious and then, "dead on arrival". Apparently, the factoring fiduciary Ken had hired who was responsible for purchasing the hospital receivables with the investors' money was actually using the money to buy methamphetamine, so the program shunted briefly to a Ponzi scheme and then completely collapsed.

As it turned out, that collapse was a harbinger of things to come in the high-pressure world of limited partnership boiler room type investment sales. With quick and easy money came greed and vice, debauchery and wolves in sheep's clothing. But still naïve to this new world of wealth and hoping to open a new horizon and with a new start, I had already hung my license at a broker/dealer called Portfolio Asset Management (PAM) and was working toward my series 7, so that I could also sell stocks.

The principal of the organization also turned out to be a fraudster, but I could not have known about it at the time. While I was working on my series 7, I was selling a video phone limited partnership called "Interlink" that

53 // Making Music With What Remains

purported to offer video teleconferencing services through the Wilshire, Los Angeles, California corridor via an ambitious fiber optic cable deployment. For each iteration we were supposed to be laying fiber for the project. We had one of the massive video routers in our office conference room as the prototype for the architecture being deployed along the Wilshire Corridor; and the technology it purported to house was the basis of many sales meetings.

But after the scientist who was hyped by the principals to have developed the switching technology for the Interlink router was interviewed on the Oprah Winfrey Show and it came out that he was a pedophile, I began to wonder. One day on an uneasy feeling, I went into the conference room to take a closer look at this massive monolithic looking router. I should have found complex circuitry and wiring and motherboards and a whole lot of technology, which I was looking to be impressed by. But when I opened one of the panels and peaked inside, I saw nothing but the back of the massive vacant frame. The entire 8-foot black steel monstrosity was empty!

After that I quit. The principal, Michael Gartner, went to prison and I was sort of free falling, not guilty of any intentional fraud, but with a very bad taste in my mouth from being associated with and selling what turned out to be a fraud. Unfortunately for me, I was now very adept and talented and committed to this life of investment phone sales and I was just looking for something safe and real to sell. But instead of pursuing a Morgan Stanley Dean Witter type position and getting my series 7, I took the path of least resistance and gravitated toward even higher risk but much higher commission investments that were in effect unregulated. I found that I could sell general partnerships without having to be registered (so I thought) for much higher commissions and of course the risk to the investor was just as grave; but based on my past "successes", none of my previous customers had realized any return. In my mind that did not mean actual success was unattainable and through naïveté and youthful hope… I set out looking for the next elephant. Realizing that even legitimate partnership investments are high risk and low return potential, I just decided to embrace the risk, find customers willing to take those risks and sell for a higher commission.

I found what I was looking for in the cellular lottery.

Every so often the Government would offer cell bandwidth that could be licensed for private parties to either buildout a cellular service or compete against established cellular carriers or sell it off to the highest bidder.

To sell the investment you needed a sales office that was participating in it…. I had lost contact with my old trainer, Mike Brooks; but when PAM fell apart, I called him and asked for some direction. He invited me into a new sales office selling the cellular lottery.

The sales office shenanigans I witnessed in this new wild-west unregulated investment world I had signed onto could best be described as a mixture of *"Glengarry Glen Ross"* meets *"Boiler Room"*. The manager was a guy named

55 // Making Music With What Remains

Tim, who was actually a doppelganger for the manager in the movie *"Boiler Room"*. The principal, known as "Lopo", (because his last name was also impossibly hard to say), had previously been involved in some shady dealings but now had embraced something that seemed above board, albeit risky, and potentially profitable as well. But it was an artificial bubble. Eventually deals like these and guys like Lopo always cross the line. Still, I felt at the time that if I could just do my job with the same work ethic and set of skills I had employed during my registered representative days as a licensed broker; that even though I would at some point literally witness the Titanic sinking underneath me, somehow, I could stay dry. I thought to myself, investments are investments. Limited partnerships, general partnerships, what's the difference? Sales are sales. All I was doing was reading a script and asking for the money.

I had the reading of the scripts down to a matter-of-fact science that could be duplicated over and over again; and like magic, customers invested their money. But what I failed to internalize was that while my role was "mechanical", my customers were investing actual money that they earned that could not be so easily replaced in the event of a program failure. Yes, every customer had to sign risk disclosures and you can't protect people from themselves if they want to invest in risky stuff; still, you don't have to help people do harm to themselves, either.

Setting potential regulation violations aside, the pressure I was applying, and the ferocity of my pitch also made it difficult, in my opinion, for my customers to process the risk factors in a way that would have been prudent for them. I guess that's why risk investments don't sell themselves. I justified it all in that the customers knew (or should have known) the risks and signed that they had read and understood them; (except that nearly no one actually does that; sort of like no one reads the electronic terms before they accept a new software download). And slowly, like the proverbial frog that gets incrementally boiled alive as the heat is turned up, I was cooked. It would just be a matter of time until I was flirting with illegality and within reach of actual fraud, perhaps too close for there to be a clear distinction. I allowed myself to be associated with shady characters and somehow rationalized that it would not affect me. So, I drank the Kool-Aid, (a reference to a cult leader at Jonestown who got his followers to drink Kool-Aid they knew had been laced with poison); and I sold.

Still busy purchasing gear not issued by Los Angeles County Sheriffs that I would need for my rescue work, I met a kayak instructor, named John, who was also working in the mountain climbing section at a Sport Chalet (like REI) in West Hills. This salesman got me interested in mountain biking and intrigued by river kayaking. Inboard kayaks are inherently unstable and in rough water, prone to capsizing. He agreed to teach me how to roll, so we met at a home with a pool in the backyard and we spent several hours doing Eskimo rolls. The whole process of being upside down in the water, "locked in" to a kayak and somehow righting yourself is so counter-intuitive that it took me a while to master the technique. But when I did, I was able to intentionally roll underwater, lean forward with the paddle parallel with the kayak, turn it perpendicular as it breached the surface of the water and then perform a very dynamic hip twist and paddle pull using my energy and the surface tension of the water to snap upright. It was the most amazing and empowering and scary terrifying thing I had ever done. After all, most of the time, the technique is being set up and performed in a very low-oxygen environment! Of course, there were times when I was unable to get the roll and would have to pull the skirt on the kayak and let myself up to the surface. But this proved very cumbersome and energy wasting and so I would go almost to the point of hypoxia, not to have to pull the skirt.

John and I became friends, and we went to the Kern River to kayak and try out my new skills. There had just been rainfall and now the river was swollen and raging. And cold! It was a whole different ballgame from the safe protection of a controlled backyard pool. This was real. And dangerous. The frigidity of the water caused me to seize and be unable to produce the dynamic force necessary to roll; and it was no time before I was pulling my skirt to surface after rolling.

I can recall growing up that I had always wanted to be in some sort of elite military unit, like the Navy SEALs, but being constantly tired and cold and wet was something my body would never adapt to. And here I was in the exact same environment I could never get comfortable in.

Slowly, slowly with sheer will and determination I began to get the roll and be able to paddle in the current, which was a Class I –II beginner part of the river. The next day, against my friend John's advice I agreed to try out the upper part of the river called, "Powerhouse Rapids". This part of the river was now a Class IV. Class IV rivers are defined as needing advanced skill, requiring "must make" moves to avoid hazards; and self-rescue is difficult, which means not for novices.

We dropped into the start of the Powerhouse and things soon got really hairy. Crazy waves and rocks and waterfalls; the sheer volume of the river was terrifying. I literally paddled to save my life. I was completely in the moment – I had to make moves I never contemplated making and exerted myself like never before; and then as I was trying to navigate between two rocks, the tip of my kayak caught one of the rocks and the force of the river took the back of my kayak and pinned it against the other rock, so there I was with the entire river pouring over me and against me as I'm pinned in my kayak against two rocks. Now this was a quandary because kayaks are known to collapse under such conditions, breaking and pinning the legs of the occupant inside and the kayaker sinks and is drowned. I struggled to free my kayak. There would indeed be no possibility of self-rescue here. The physics and dynamic pressure made it impossible.

My friend who had already paddled successfully past this obstruction saw my life and death situation and paddled back to me upstream. He made it look easy. He docked himself on the other side of the rock I was pinned to, reached over, and lifted the front of my kayak over the rock and into the cascade of water flowing through the

59 // Making Music With What Remains

two rocks. I was freed! But just then I hit a wave and rolled upside down.

Now I was underwater upside-down fighting against the violence of the current to lean forward and get my paddle out of the water and flip my kayak over. It was cold and dark, and my head was literally bouncing off rocks on the bottom of the river as I went. I did have a helmet on, thank G-d. I tried once. Couldn't do it. I tried again and was able to gasp some air for one last try. With all my strength, I muscled myself upright.

"*Whoo Hoo!*" I heard from my friend, "You just Eskimo rolled the Powerhouse!"

But by then I was a bit traumatized and realized that this kind of sport requires a type of skill that I did not really have yet, and I didn't really want to learn. White knuckling it and muscling through saved my life but there was no longevity to it. It just wasn't enjoyable to me after all.

I went back to flying my helicopter still as a student pilot, and after I was married for just a few months, my mother sent my wife and me on a 10-day trip to Israel. The day before the trip I took my final written FAA exam for my pilot's license. I wouldn't know the results until I returned.

Even as a secular Jew at the time, Israel truly had real impact. I especially enjoyed Jerusalem. And the Western Wall drew me in. I had a loose history of the place and was fascinated with everything I was seeing. I decided I wanted to see the Dome of the Rock atop the Jewish Temple Mount. I had no idea that I should not have gone up there for multiple reasons. First, as a Jew surrounded by Arabs it was simply unsafe for me. Additionally, I would come to learn later that it is actually forbidden for a Jew to tread up on the Temple Mount, without first becoming ritually clean and then significantly limiting where one goes. Certainly, one is not allowed to enter the inner Temple area itself, but as an American Jew, who was uneducated in the ways of Israel geo-politics and de facto Torah Judaism, I did not really appreciate the security situation, or the hostility leveled against Jewish Israelis from the Arabs who lived there; nor did I appreciate the spiritual gravity of the trip I would take; so, I made my way up the ramp.

Upon entry I turned to the right and entered the large mosque – It was huge with carpets covering the floor. There were lots of men in traditional white flowing garb. I was in jeans and a grey sweatshirt. I caught lots of hard stares in my direction, but no one directly threatened me or made any menacing gestures. Still, I was extremely uncomfortable in that place. I felt like I was in another world and that just under the surface was brewing extreme discontent and that my presence was adding to it. So, I exited.

I walked across the courtyard to the gold Dome of the Rock and climbed the steps. I entered the building. I walked to the center of the building, which housed a *huge* stone called the *foundation stone* that stood a few stories high, and I followed a random tour group. The reason the dome structure exists over the Jewish Temple Mount is because a main tenant of the religion of Islam is (military) conquest. By building on top of the Jewish Temple area, to the Muslims, this signified dominion and conquest which is part and parcel of Muslim divine service. The Muslim legend is that Mohammed, who journeyed to Jerusalem, stood on that stone, and then ascended to heaven. But Jerusalem is not mentioned one time in the Koran, not once. Jerusalem, however, *is* mentioned over 600 times in the Hebrew bible. So, any passing references to the actual place of a so-called Islamic ascension are so obscure as to forestall credible belief that the Koran is referring to the *foundation stone* in Jerusalem.

The real story, which preceded all others I would later learn, is that in the Jewish Tradition I was standing in the place where the world was created from, where Adam was formed, where Abraham offered his son, where Jacob slept and more recently, where the most holy place on Earth existed for the Jewish people called the Holy of Holies. Upon pain of spiritual/physical death, this place was to be entered once a year on Yom Kippur, *only* by the Kohein Gadol (Jewish High Priest). I did not know it at the time, but I was standing on the holiest ground in the universe.

I now know that G-d protects babies and the intensely naïve, because I was not a baby, and I did not die that day... or incredibly, the day after.

The next day was Shabbos. The day after, Sunday morning, I decided to go for a run. The Hyatt in Jerusalem was located on top of a hill and the staff provided me with a map with a running course. It looked pretty boring, the loop they laid out for me; so I decided to ditch the map and run *down* the hill. It was still early morning, but I was feeling pretty good. No shirt, earphones and running through the streets of Arab Jerusalem.

It seemed a bit odd, surreal even as people started coming out of the homes to watch me progress. I noticed someone looking a bit ragged with a machete standing outside his front door. I ran on and finally made my way out of the Arab section and back up the hill to the Hyatt.

Later that day we drove with our guide, Avraham, to Mt. Scopus. From that vantage point I could see the route I had run just a few hours earlier. I told our guide, "Look at that. I went down there. I ran that today."

He turned to me and became deadly serious. He lifted his shirt up, pulled out his gun and showed it to me. He said to me in his thick Israeli accent, "You know, I look like them. I dress like them. I speak the way they do, their language. And I carry this (gesturing with his gun) and *I* wouldn't go down there."

When we returned from Israel, I found that I had passed my helicopter test and now had my helicopter license. Training had been very intense. I started out with a 300 lb. instructor whose name was Jack. Now the helicopter I flew had a per passenger weight rating of 250 lbs., so I had to significantly compensate by pulling back with the cyclic (steering) control to keep the helicopter upright.

The two scariest parts of training were autorotation training and flying alone for the first time. Emergency training requires preparing for the loss of your engine. If you consider that the rotor tip speed for the helicopter that I was flying is 672 feet per second and then you consider that the speed of sound is 1,100 feet per second, you realize how dynamic flying a helicopter can be. It only takes 3 seconds of inattention, spatial-disorientation or vortex ring/settling with power to get your helicopter into a point-of-no-return crash configuration. If you also consider that for the rotors to spin that fast requires intense mechanism synergy and frictional wear, and that the helicopter is literally tearing itself apart with each blade rotation, you begin to appreciate the need for emergency procedures.

The instructor kills your engine for you without warning at about 1,000 feet alt. and 70 - 90 knots. You have less than 3 seconds to realize what's happening and embrace the situation in full; you are committed to an autorotation landing without power and there is no going back. Immediately, as I was trained, down goes the collective which changes the lift angle on the blades to be able to allow the rotor to spin free of the clutch and the cyclic is pulled back to keep the helicopter upright while at the same time grabbing as much wind as possible rushing up as the helicopter is falling. The wind that rushes up is what "autorotates" the rotors. The cyclic determines the angle of descent and the foot pedals keep the helicopter fuselage from spinning. And here you are falling out of the sky but if you do it right the air rushing up slows the helicopter's descent such that if you time it correctly, within 20 feet of hitting the ground you can lift up on the collective and roll the cyclic over and literally land as gently as if you were under power. In theory that's how it's supposed to work. In reality, it takes a lot of practice. The bottom line is while

I was trained for this eventuality, I prayed I would never have to use this skill set.

When I had the autorotation mastered, my instructor directed me to fly to Lake Piru, which is a deserted marshy wasteland close to Magic Mountain in Valencia, CA. There we could practice landings and takeoffs called, "*touch and gos*", and solo flying. Jack hopped out of the helicopter and off I went. His weight caused some adjustments on my part and I white knuckled my way through my first solo flight. But I was terrified. Once Jack felt comfortable with my solo flying, he approved me to take off and land from Group 3 Aviation at the Van Nuys airport and fly wherever I wanted. My first solo from the airport almost resulted in a crash. I was still so used to Jack's 300 lb. weight that when I first went to it pick up, I overcompensated with the cyclic and rolled the helicopter backwards. I almost bounced the tail rotor off the tarmac, which could have produced a dynamic rollover. My instructor and the owner were watching me from a safe distance. Their mouths were agape and I'm certain they would have liked me to land and walk away. But I did no such thing. I was already hovering about 3 feet above the tarmac and had no intention of setting it down.

I keyed the radio: "Helicopter *Zero Sierra Mike* leaving Group 3 Aviation requesting a Balboa north departure, with information *India*...."

The Van Nuys air traffic control tower responded: "Helicopter *Zero Sierra Mike*, you are cleared for a Balboa north departure leaving Group 3."

65 // Making Music With What Remains

India is a phonetic in pilot-talk for the letter "I". *Alpha* is for "A", *Bravo* is for "B" and so on. Each hour per FAA regulation, a new updated weather forecast is available for pilots regarding dew point, humidity, wind factors including strength and direction and temperature. This information is usually obtained pre-takeoff just before lift-off by the pilot using his radio. By informing the tower I was "with information *India*" (and next hour it would be "information *Juliet*"), the control tower was clear that I was clear on prevailing weather conditions and safe to fly.

And I was off. I had no other issues that day and the ride was exhilarating. I landed perfectly back at Group 3 Aviation and aside of a comment from the owner about how he almost shut down my first solo, I never received another negative comment. I think he realized I had been simply overcompensating for the weight of my instructor and let it go.

So many things need to be considered (and acted on) all at once in helicopter flight. Both feet are negotiating the foot pedals (to control yaw), the right hand is holding the cyclic (steering) and keying the mic, while the left hand is providing lift via the collective; also, the left hand is working the radios and electronic identifiers *and* controlling RPMs with a motorcycle-type hand throttle. Today the RPMS are controlled automatically mostly by a device called a "governor", a switch at the end of the collective. When I was a student pilot, I was never allowed to use the governor on takeoffs or landings because in case of a malfunction, the rotor speed could get away from you; so, in addition to the hyperdynamic of everything else, I had to ensure that I did not overspeed or over-spin the blades and destroy the engine and tail rotor of the helicopter I was flying... or spin the blades too slowly and fall out of the sky. Today, the governor is always in play and while it provides protections against pilot error, if it does fail, I don't believe pilots are adequately practiced on manual takeover, especially during critical takeoffs and landings. Flying a helicopter is like being in a living breathing unending knife fight. You need constant training, vigilance, skill and attention to detail to survive. And there is no autopilot.

In my time I've flown to Torrance Airport and Santa Monica and all the way up the coast to Santa Barbara International Airport and landed there. I've flown over LAX, downtown LA, and skimmed the coastline water 50 feet above the surface up PCH and through Malibu. It's been an incredibly rewarding experience; and while today I fly the larger and more advanced R44, rentals are about $600 an hour so I've had to greatly limit my flight time.

So, with my feet on the ground for the time being, just back from Israel; and while still working with Lopo, another salesman named John approached me and asked me if I would be interested in starting my own investment business by launching a competing cellular lottery program. I liked the idea because I could make more money as the broker *and* co-principal and I could offer my customers an additional opportunity to win a cellular license and sell it for a big profit. As I was negotiating for a higher percentage the promoter told me that if he could take his name off the program entirely and replace it with my name that he would give me what I wanted in terms of fees. Since I did not believe we were doing anything illegal and I did not understand the huge liability this placed on me, I agreed. I left Lopo's shop to begin my own one-man sales operation; and this upset Lopo and Tim very much, as you can imagine.

We structured the deal that if the program failed to produce the hoped-for results, that the majority of the proceeds would be deemed "fees" and non-refundable. We took a portion of the proceeds and placed them into a client trust fund which would be earmarked to purchase the lottery units and do the build out as required by the Government. In the entire money raise, only one of my customers asked for his money back. And I gave it to him.

As our new sales company was just getting traction, the 5-year relationship with my first wife was becoming very fractious. I can recall shortly before we married in Monterey, CA getting into a particularly bad argument amongst many arguments. She was extremely self-critical and suspicious and caustic, suffering from pernicious and pervasive toxic shame. I believe this was because of what she experienced from her overly critical mother and her emotionally and physically absent father. She was also in this cult of *chanting* Buddhism, materialist at its core, chanting foreign mantras for all of her heart's material desires under the aegis of "praying for world peace". But it could not have been more transparently opportunistic.

The scheme went something like this: By chanting, a practitioner allegedly synchronized his vocal cords in tune with the energy of the universe and in doing so, aligned the universe's energy thereby bringing about world peace. As an added benefit (that was certainly not lost on all my wife's starlet friends), the religious dogma asserted that all of their materialist desires would also come true conterminously. As a real-life example, my wife's friend said she wanted a new bejeweled bustier. All she had to do was chant for it because *really* the chanting was for the peace of the world, but as an added benefit the universe would also enable her to somehow acquire the bustier. The same procedure could help you acquire cash or a new job… and it's totally this "noble" endeavor, chanting for the lingerie or cash or a job promotion or whatever your heart desires, because *really* in this scheme, you're chanting for world peace. So, her thinking and her worldview were already unrealistically entitled and unhealthy in affect; in short, she was emotionally unbalanced. During that pre-wedding argument I came to an awful realization that I couldn't marry this woman. We were literally worlds apart. And yet like most of the awful situations in my life, I found (or manufactured) the good and swallowed the rest.

I drank the Kool-Aid and I married her.

Then 5 years later I threw up the Kool Aid I drank in order to marry Caryn, and I divorced her. In an ironic twist, I later needed to get a restraining order against her. Even as she continued to chant for "world peace", she had aggressed, accosted, and harassed me and my attorney outside the Van Nuys courthouse, had physically chased me in her car and sent me burnt up old love letters in the mail and mentioned a gun. She told me in her letter that she had truly lost her sanity.

69 // Making Music With What Remains

Coming off this difficult separation and divorce from my first wife I had moved from West Hills to south of Ventura Blvd., with my 4Runner rescue outfitted vehicle, a new motorcycle, a Honda Magna 750 and my black German Sheppard, Tonka. I purchased some showroom furniture to furnish my new rental home on a hill and settled into the single life and profitable high-risk sales.

A tattoo parlor on the corner of Baza and Ventura opened and one day I got a really massive tattoo on my right shoulder of a sun and a Filipino martial arts design of the style I had been affiliated with. It was totally an impulsive ego move, indicative of the state of mind I was floating in.

Biblical law (Leviticus 19:28) forbids Jews from getting tattoos. And though there is absolutely no requirement to have a tattoo removed once its already in your skin; years later when I returned to Jewish observance, I became palpably repulsed by the image on my flesh and I had no rest from that revulsion. So, it needed to go. I tried to have it removed non-invasively; but when every type of laser available could not get all of it; I had it surgically cut out at great pain and expense. I paid a plastic surgeon to excise four 8-inch x 2-inch strips of tattooed flesh on my right shoulder in 6-month intervals. After each removal, he would tightly stitch the skin together and wait for the skin to stretch enough to remove the next strip. This would go on for almost 2 years. And then it was completely gone! All-in-all, 64 square inches of tattooed shoulder skin was cut out using only lidocaine injections to numb locally. Today I am most grateful for that 8-inch-long scar.

I spent a lot of time riding my motorcycle along Mulholland Hwy to the Rock Store and other places, mountain biking and running with my dog. And I was looking for other things to fill my time. I became good friends with a full-time federal DEA agent, who was volunteering his time like me on the Sheriff's Rescue Team. He was a Tang Soo Do master (like Chuck Norris) and also a certified sky diver. He convinced me I should give skydiving a try.

I traveled to Brown's airfield in San Diego's Otay Mesa and learned how to jump. We spent 8 hours in class on the ground and then it was time to go up in the airplane and jump out. I have to tell you that the airplane we used was very rickety and it crammed in about 10 divers and some instructors. The pilots also wore parachutes if that tells you anything about the airworthiness of the plane. We took off and ascended to 14,000 feet. Now most people will opt to have an instructor attached so the training time is less, because the instructor does all the work. I wasn't interested in having some guy *mounted* to me; I wanted to jump and pull my own rip cord.

So, when it was my time to exit the plane, with the door open at 14,000 feet, my brain literally balked. It was *screaming* at me not to jump. SCREAMING. I was beyond terrified. Then I jumped and my two instructors jumped after me along with a cameraman I hired to videotape my first jump. I immediately got into a neutral position and stabilized. The two instructors were simply falling with me to ensure I did not freak out and that I pulled my parachute in time. At 5,000 feet according to my altimeter,

I waved them off and pulled my cord. I went from about 200 mph to 35 mph in just a few seconds. Then I toggled my way to the ground and landed fairly gently. Wow!

I did it again and again and again. After the 5th or 6th jump, I was allowed to exit the airplane by myself with no in air supervision. I ended up jumping 13 times, but I never lost the discomfort of jumping out of an airplane at 14,000 feet. On one of my jumps, something convinced me that I probably should give up skydiving. I exited the plane with jump goggles on. Under the goggles I was wearing expensive prescription frames and lenses. As I was falling, the wind whipped up the plastic goggles and blew them off my face. Along with them went my prescription glasses. I was so upset that for the next 5,000 feet I lost track of where I was or what I was doing. When I finally realized that I should check my altimeter, it was 5,000 feet and time to pull. I deployed my chute without incident. As I was toggling to the ground, I found my glasses flipped up, but firmly, on the top of my head.

But I realized at that point, besides the absolute discomfort every single time jumping out of the plane that if I had lost my bearings over a pair of glasses, I had no real business jumping out of airplanes any longer. I ended my skydiving pastime shortly thereafter.

All was going well in my cellular investment and we were getting ready to open another investment round when suddenly the Federal Government announced that they had changed the rules, and that no longer would the awarding of licenses be left to chance. They reasoned that perhaps the winner would squander the opportunity.

Instead, the Government would award to those who could demonstrate a technical ability to build out the licenses. This effectively ended our program. Only the small percentage that was set aside for the clients' licenses was returned. On this *force majeure,* the unforeseen circumstance of the Government changing the rules midstream prevented us from fulfilling our contract. Since this was one of the risks our clients signed to, with very few exceptions, most accepted this eventuality with grace and walked away with their losses. The State of California, Department of Corporations, however, did not walk away gracefully. They issued me a *"Cease and Desist"* order requiring me to stop offering securities for sale without a license or registration. Even though the lottery was long over, I was still issued a *Cease and Desist*, which specifically precluded me from again offering these types of investments. It seemed that the Government oversight community was beginning to gain some traction and focus; and this concerned me because the order precluded me from doing my job. Perhaps my days were now numbered offering these types of investments. Suddenly once again, with zero history of making any money for any client, I was in free fall, looking for my next deal to sell, while not sure how to avoid being in violation of the DOC.

As it turned out I did not fall for long. I met in passing, Lopo's ex sales manager, Tim. He, too, had left Lopo's operation after the Government effectively ended the cellular lottery. He had some hard feelings because I had been competing against Lopo, but now with that in the past, Tim was interested in recruiting me to his new deal, of which he was the principal.

I really had a bad feeling about Tim and was not interested in working with him. He had a shyster's demeanor and what turned out to be a serious cocaine habit, though at the time I did not know it. But my German Sheppard knew. One day he came to my home and my dog went after Tim like I've never seen him do before or after. He bared his teeth, and he was scary ferocious. Tim departed very quickly. He had a nervous *sweatiness* about him, and I believe he was also off gassing the smell of whatever mind-altering chemical he had been ingesting, probably cocaine or meth... and my dog was able to smell it. My dog knew he was a bad guy and wanted Tim far away from me. But I didn't listen to my gut or my dog or internalize any of the writing on the wall.

So, during our impromptu discussion, Tim told me we would be affiliated with two other known shady guys, Marc and Ira, who had spent their entire professional lives running risky type deals. These guys really turned my stomach. They just exuded greed, copious consumption and arrogance. It was unreal to me that after so many years of running programs like this they were still unindicted; so in my head, despite what appeared to be a certain fiduciary disaster, I thought that perhaps they had found a legitimate way to stay in legal territory. That did not mean I wanted to work for them, though! I do recall seeing the junior partner, Marc at a sales meeting promoting his newest investment and I gazed at him. I could not believe he was still walking free in the world based on previous and current conduct. My body language must have had its effect because he approached me after the meeting and asked me half joking, "Why do you look at me like I'm guilty of something, like I'm a criminal….?"

We both laughed uncomfortably and went our separate ways. Today I place a lot more stock into people's body language and the vibes they give off, but back then I wrote off so many clear signs and gut feelings as random when all the alarms were going off. I mean the entire corporate head office, Marc and Ira included, wore pirate costumes to a costume themed event that they had organized.

Pirate costumes… every single one of them.

So, when Tim caught up with me after that meeting, I was making 20+ points on my previous deal. He offered me 25 points if I would work for him. I demurred. He offered me 30 points.

I said, "No."

He upped it to 35 points. I laughed.

He raised it to 40 points, and I stopped laughing.

"You are going to pay me 40% on every deal I bring in?" I asked incredulously.

He said, "Yes."

"But I'm not working for Marc and Ira," I said. "So, no deal."

He said that I would not be working for Marc and Ira directly; they were only the promoters. I would be working directly for Tim. Tim said that as an Independent

75 // Making Music With What Remains

Sales Organization, he could sell any program he wanted and was not beholden to sell Marc's and Ira's investments.

But that did not ring so true because it was Ira who had approved and set up Tim in the ISO. Yet, Tim assured me he could dissociate himself anytime he wanted from Marc and Ira, even though I don't believe he ever had that intention.

Still, I pushed him, "And I would have no management responsibilities or promoter or principal liabilities?"

He said that while I would not be a manager or promoter that he would appreciate it if sometimes I could give advice and sales tips to newer "brokers".

At the end of the day his offer was 40 points, with no fiduciary or promoter liability. It wasn't such a difficult decision.

I drank the Kool-Aid.

Chapter 3

Black Hole

"Your faith was strong, but you needed proof. You saw her bathing on the roof. Her beauty and the moonlight overthrew you. She tied you to a kitchen chair. She broke your throne and she cut your hair. And from your lips she drew the Hallelujah."
    - Leonard Cohen

In my 2nd to last year at CSUN, three years before I joined the Sheriff's Department, I was traveling along in my car one day and almost become a victim of road rage. A short muscular Latino fellow and his girlfriend had been tailgating and honking at me; driving in a very belligerent manner. I was the lead vehicle. They pulled in right behind me as I was stopped in a left turn lane. I decided that I did not want them following me any longer so at the left turn signal, I intentionally waited until the light turned red to make my left, thinking that the guy would have to wait until the next light cycle. I wanted to lose this guy. No such luck. The guy saw what I was trying to do and became enraged even further. He ran the light from behind the crosswalk, taking the left turn against oncoming traffic, almost getting into an accident in the process.

I saw what was happening in my rear view and I got scared. He skidded through the intersection, accelerated, and then actually passed me going southbound on a three-lane street. He raised a fist as he passed me. Then he got in front of me in the center lane and slammed on his brakes. He was fully stopped in the number 2 lane. I had to stop as well. He exited the car and ran over to my passenger side and slammed his fist into my window. I'm surprised that it did not shatter. He was screaming at me that he was going to do serious harm to me, so I put my car in gear and sped around his car to the left and made my escape, down one street and then down another. I lost him.

That incident shook me. I realized in that moment that I was literally defenseless. I had no means of protection other than the car that surrounded me. I didn't really know how to fight, and aside of school hallways had never had a real fight. I thought that if he had been able to get me out of my car, that he would have killed me with his fists. I actually became angry that I had allowed myself to be so vulnerable up to this point. So, I decided to change the equation. My first experience with fight instruction was upon enrollment in a local West Hills Taekwondo karate school; and while I learned how to kick and do *katas*, street fighting was not real high on the agenda. It was more about competition and belts, not practical self-defense.

MMA was not yet in existence and proven street fighting credentials besides the hype were hard to come by. I did know that I needed to learn how to use my hands better, so I found what I was looking for in the middle of Reseda, California. The owner/head instructor was a devotee and student of Dan Inosanto, one of Bruce Lee's former teachers and training partners.

Thus, began a very intense 7-year Filipino martial arts education that fused many styles together: Wing Chun, Gung Fu, Jeet Kun Do, Kali, Escrima, Silat, Muay Thai and Kickboxing. There was a loose standing grappling, stick and knife fighting, punching, kicking, knees and elbows. It was a very violent way to spend 60 minutes. After a few years, I advanced to the upper level, which was a closed full-contact class. We would don full body armor, hockey pads, helmet and gloves and literally beat the tar out of each other. I still have scars from stick fighting; and one from a knife fight. We used very large steel training knifes, which were still sharp and pointed and heavy. I got one of those scars in a dynamic live training of disarming my opponent by fanning his arm, flipping, and grabbing his wrist and then forcing the flat of his blade up against my triceps and pulling hard against his wrist. This forcefully dislodged the knife from his hand. It flipped up fast and its point gouged into my left eyebrow. I was fortunate not to have lost my eye.

Being trained was a blessing; not that I would ever look for trouble, but now, I felt I could hold my own in any situation. Even today, when I think back to that potentially explosive car situation, the healthy fear is still there; but now I know I could handle myself just fine.

I had moved to the advanced fight training level when I first met Tim again. Despite his offer and my acceptance of 40% commission; before I agreed to sell again for him though, I needed assurances that my efforts would not subject me to any legal jeopardy moving forward. Tim referred me to the lead counsel for the organization, Jim, who incidentally was indicted in the very deal I would be selling; but when he went to trial, he would be acquitted.

I told Jim who I was, that I had a DOC *Cease and Desist*, and that I wanted to sell for Tim but that I could not offer sales of investments without being registered; so first off he told me that he was going to give me the "family rate" and then he wrote up a legal agreement for me that basically informed Tim that I would not be interested in selling anything for him, nor would I be conducting any investment sales for him per se. I would simply be acting in the capacity of an "introductory consultant", whereby my legal working relationship would simply be that I would be introducing prospective clients to him for a fee. It would then be up to Tim to technically offer for sale the units to the customer. In reality nothing changed; but on paper I felt safer using this arrangement. Tim agreed to be bound by this document.

Now Jim served as the corporate and General Partner counsel for each of the 7 programs Marc and Ira ran. He knew exactly what was going on. But he was able to claim privilege with no knowledge of the internal workings, and skate on his indictment. My working letter, defining the legal nature of my relationship with Tim that Jim drew up for me, would come up in my discovery, but the prosecutors dismissed it outright because they were also indicting the (dirty) lawyer who penned it; so to them it was "fruit from the poisonous tree."

Then there was the issue of registering with the State Attorney General anyone who was conducting telephone sales in your office. The requirement was on the boss; in this case Tim, who was required to contact the State Attorney General and simply provide a list of names of people who would be telemarketing from his office. Tim swore that he fulfilled this requirement and that he registered all of us. I felt that I could "sell" legally now.

The problem was that Tim lied. He never registered any of us. The registration requirement was incumbent on the principal, so even if I had wanted to, I was not allowed to register myself. I had to trust Tim. This requirement was also a strict liability law, which meant that even if I had no intent to remain unregistered and even though I was lied to; the penalty of not being registered was on the person selling, no matter what the reason. If I had known, I would have called Sacramento to see if Tim had met his requirements before I started. But like so many other things up to that point, I just trusted. A criminal misdemeanor violation would be the first prosecutorial volley. Many more felony charges would follow.

Then there was another problem, which I never really thought through until I began to close significant sums. A number of clients thoroughly read the small print and detailed risk factors and highlighted something that seemed glaringly inappropriate in the deal: 85% of the clients' money would be coming out of the deal and going into "administration" and "fees"; which seemed obscene, even predatory. I then realized that Tim's office got 50% of the deal for commissions and the promoters, Marc and Ira, et al., got 35%. Only 15% went into the actual deal as I and most of my customers now understood it.

Tim couched it this way: "Firstly, each deal raise was approximately $750,000 - $1M for the investment itself." Tim then asked me rhetorically, "If I gave you a million dollars for a business do you think you could make money? Mark and Ira are giving the investors a ready-made business; it's essentially *turnkey*, so all they have to do is have their partnership meeting and then start making money."

Tim led me to believe that in addition to the investor's $750k, that significant promoter expertise with additional funds were also being invested outside the investors' money by the promoters preparing the business, getting things ready to roll.

But 85% as an up-front load?!

I still wasn't exactly convinced. Tim tried another tact; telling me that there was plenty of money to make the customers' money back plus a huge return with what was being invested. One of the examples he touted was an internet mall that was in the pattern of our program. That one sold, according to Tim, for a billion dollars, with significantly less capital than we were putting in our internet program.

My retort: "But doesn't 85% seem to you a bit excessive; with appearances of impropriety?"

Tim just turned the conversation back on me with a clever non-sequitur: "How much do you think it costs to make a can of Coke? One penny. How much do they mark that can up? Like 70 times its original cost, which is 7,000% and nobody is complaining. Coke doesn't break out the ingredients' cost; they just charge you. We don't have to break out the cost of providing a working investment. Coke does it. We can do it."

"But with Coke, you're getting a product," I countered.

"So are the investors," he shot back, "They're getting a running, turnkey business with a million dollars. This structure is industry standard for these types of programs and every investor knows it. They read the risks and they signed to the risks...." And so, it went.

I could either accept the rationalization and trust that Tim and Marc and Ira and Jim, their corporate lawyer, knew what was flying and were prepared for all contingencies; could make a lot of money with a bulk sum for the investors... or I could choose to quit. I lulled myself into a negligent trust once again. Somehow, I forced all the clanging alarms bells to go silent; I convinced myself that all I could go on was what I was shown and what I was told. But I would come to realize that in the process I did damage to myself, my customers and my moral compass by continuously ignoring my gut, my better judgment and by breathing in the ether that Tim spewed.

I was now working very hard, trying to make the most out of my custom arrangement. I was making approximately $25,000 per month in commissions by then. My individual production was what supported the office and it blew everyone else out of the water. There were several other ISO's in the southern California area and my personal production alone was more than the other ISOs' entire production combined. My boss, Tim, understood what motivated most salesmen: Vice - Drugs, money and women, but mostly greed.

But I was an enigma. I was not really motivated by these things. And Tim knew I was working with LA County Sheriff's and was not into *vice*. Still, he was very persistent, even manipulative. He told me I should get a Harley and a Porsche and that I should buy a big house on a hill, because of course I "deserved" it and could now afford it.

"Why not?" he intoned, "That's what you do when you make the kind of money that you now make. You buy a Porsche and a huge house. That's what successful people do."

What he didn't tell me is that the reason he wanted me to buy those things was because I would then always need more money to service those items and that would keep me beholden to working for Tim and beholden to needing a large income stream; essentially, I would always need to sell high income investments (for Tim) to make the money necessary to live this new rich lifestyle. At first, I just ignored him. I was happy in my home rental driving my truck and my stock motorcycle; but after a while of Tim nagging me, my ego turned baser. It wasn't an emotional swoon that Tim tapped into. It was a cold intellectual coming to terms in a rational sounding way. And how did I rationalize feeding into my animal desires in such a prolific and ostentatious way? I simply thought to myself, *Why not? I'll still be the same person. Even with a Porsche and a Harley… and a big house on the hill.*

I commissioned a custom build "Harley" *Fatboy style*, out of a Pro One Fat chassis raked and lowered with a 180 rear tire and 6-gallon gas tank with a true dual cross over fishtail exhaust. 1340 cc. Beautiful. I think the only actual

Harley part on the entire bike was the brakes. All-in, it was $28,000. I paid cash.

Motorcycles are notoriously hard to see in traffic so based on a pithy aphorism that, "loud (motorcycle exhaust) pipes save lives", my pipes were completely un-baffled and literally deafening. I think they were among some of the loudest pipes in Los Angeles.

Then I decided to get the Porsche, because of course Tim had a Porsche and he decided I needed one too. So, I went over to Ogner Porsche in Woodland Hills and special ordered a 1996 Carrera 4 Cabriolet black and tan with carbon fiber *everything*. It was still 1995 and the base price on that car was $72,000. I put $20,000 into upgrades and at the end of the day, with transportation and taxes and DMV fees (of $2,000!) the all-in price was something like $120,000. I put $76,000 down on it and got a $44,000 car loan, which I extinguished in about 10 months. I opted for the Euro Delivery package whereby I would be able to travel to Germany, tour the Porsche factory and drive my new car on the Autobahn, and then have it shipped back to the States. I even memorized the 17-digit VIN. Let's just say that it would be very hard to remain humble driving that Porsche.

And then I bought a huge custom build home in Woodland Hills, a stone's throw from Calabasas. The neighborhood was multi-million-dollar castle homes and then, only just a few "normal" homes on my street. There were a few lots still available, and I closed on a corner lot with 88,000 sq. ft. of property, a 12,000 sq. ft. pad and 4,300 sq. ft. of actual living space, which was small for my neighborhood. The price on the house was $620,000. Today that home is worth over $2M. But at that time, I could not get a normal loan because the mortgage companies wanted proof of income and all I had was deposit slips since I was working as an independent consultant. I also needed a jumbo loan because of the dollar amount, and I wanted to avoid the PMI (private mortgage insurance). The only way I could get a jumbo loan with the terms I wanted and be able to avoid the income reporting and PMI requirements was to put 20% of the appraised value of the house down in escrow. In other words, I had to come up with $124,000.00 cash, which I did. In the industry, they called my loan, "a drug dealer loan"; because of the amount of cash required and the lack of reporting requirements.

So, I was working for a bunch of dress up "pirates" in a "boiler room", having just gotten "a drug dealer loan". You can't make this stuff up. Then, who moved into the house literally across the street; a house that I looked at (and turned down) before deciding on my house....? Tupac Shakur, who had just signed with Death Row Records' Suge Knight. So, there was ol' Tupac rolling in and out at all hours in his custom Humvee and then he bought these two Pit Bulls and built a gigantic, enclosed chain link fence on all sides, top included, to keep them in. One day he didn't come home. He had been shot and killed in Las Vegas presumably over East Coast West Coast rivalry. His home went up for sale very soon after.

Now most of the neighborhood was fascinated with our rapper neighbor and so when the house went back on the market and the realtor decided to do a walk through to assess for an open house, most of the neighbors, myself included, followed her inside. Aside of the makeshift memorial gathering traction on his front doorstep (flasks of liquor, some cards, flowers, candles, etc.,) there wasn't much to see but two things stuck out in my head. First off there was this huge living room with the most beautiful white plush carpet, and there were literally grease and oil stains and skid marks all over it, as if he actually parked his Humvee in the living room. The garage's juxtaposition and its open construction actually afforded access between the two, so it's not implausible.

Also, there was an unused baby's diaper in the middle of the skid marked white carpet. And inside the diaper was an unused (live) shotgun shell.

While I was waiting for my car to complete production and my new home to finish construction so I could actually move in; and when I wasn't working or training or flying my helicopter, I used to frequent a Sports Bar called Yankee Doodles. I did not go for the food or the alcohol. I didn't drink. I went to play pool. One night I met a girl I liked. Her name was Shannon. I asked her out. We met a second time and then a 3rd time and soon started dating. I liked her very much. After the insanity of my first marriage, Shannon seemed simple and uncomplicated and with very little drama; low maintenance. And we got along well. I saw potential in this relationship. I felt she understood me.

I told her about my challenging family dynamic, my difficult growing up years… and her reactions were impressive. She was unflappable, seemed immune to manipulation and was very protective of me. This also elevated my esteem of Shannon significantly. I was hopeful for the continuation of our romantic relationship.

There was one problem at the time. She professed to be a "fallen" born-again Christian. And I was an irreligious secular Jew, who had no interest in religion, except that I seemed to tolerate whatever spiritual journey the women in my life were into. I had tolerated Caryn's Buddhism, even went to a few meetings with her... I didn't have any major issues tolerating Shannon's religion, either. It had nothing to do with me. The problem was that fundamentalist Christianity is not so spirituality divorced from real life; it is a way of life to its adherents, and this is where things got really interesting in my life....

As we began to get closer, Shannon would spend the night until soon she was staying with me often. Most Sundays she would go to her church and she asked me if I wanted to join her. Shannon had enough foresight to know that even in her "fallen" state that the relationship could not last. I was an irreligious Jew and everything in her upbringing and background frowned on her current choice as a long-term relationship. Knowing that a breakup eventuality over this was brewing, and since I really liked this girl, I agreed to push some of my own boundaries and perhaps appease her by going to church with her one Sunday.

When I arrived, it was nothing I was used to; it was actually foreign and not at all comfortable. To make matters worse, I was only there as a friendly gesture being supportive of my girlfriend. When I opened the service bulletin I cringed. Inside, after the announcements were various names of people who ostensibly asked for prayers to be said for them. Midway down I saw my name typed in this church program I had never known about until that very day. It read, "Pray for David Diamand who is a Jew and needs to be saved."

Now this shocked and upset me. I felt ambushed. Here I was simply joining my girlfriend as a show of support to her. It actually jarred me that I had become an unwitting intervention charity case/appeal by a group of people in a foreign religion I had never met before. By "saved" I rightly assumed that they were praying their level best that I convert to Christianity… and I certainly wasn't about to do that!

There is a joke that has a lot of truth to it: A Jewish atheist sends his son to a Catholic school because the secular education in the parochial school is top notch. One day the Jewish boy comes home and tells his father that he learned that G-d is actually a trinity. The father very assertively tells his son, "Listen to me, son, there is no trinity. There is only ONE G-d, and we don't believe in Him!"

Even though I put no stock into my birth religion, I still wasn't about to abandon who I was. I was a Jew. Christians and Jews don't mix religions. Period. I left the church with Shannon, who was also very uncomfortable with what had happened. She told me that she had only asked that my name be mentioned in prayer; she had no idea it would be printed up in the weekly church bulletin. We did not speak further of that event. But my reaction to the event told her all she needed to know about my

89 // Making Music With What Remains

receptivity to her religion, and it was not long after that we stopped seeing each other.

About two weeks before we officially ended our relationship, my car in Germany was ready to be picked up. On a lark I asked Shannon if she would like to accompany me. She, having never been to Europe before, agreed. We took a limo to LAX and boarded Lufthansa business class. When we landed in Germany, we went to the hotel to rest. I could tell that Shannon was happy to be in Europe but not so happy to be there with me. Still, I tried to be accommodating and rekindle something from our previous relationship.

We got a tour of the Porsche factory the next day, were shuttled around the Porsche race test track at speed and then finally picked up the Porsche I had specially built. We drove it back to the hotel and then the next morning drove on the Autobahn at ridiculous speeds into Amsterdam. We spent a night there, and then we drove to Paris, France the next day.

Nobody stopped me for ID or to check our passports. It was still 1995 and we were driving a brand new 1996 generation 993 Porsche no one had ever seen before, and we were just waived through all border check points. Even when I got it back to Los Angeles, I couldn't get a speeding or parking ticket to save my life. Every single time I got pulled over by LAPD/CHP (except for once) I was let go with a warning.

I had heard that the French were extremely rude to Americans, especially those who could not speak French, but all I spoke was English and I stopped to ask directions frequently and no one was ever anything but friendly and accommodating. Maybe it was my Porsche ambassador "talking". We climbed the Eiffel Tower and did some additional sight-seeing and then left the next day.

On our way back to Germany I decided to take the car to speed. The Porsche had a 6-speed manual gear shift and I decided to go for it. I was able to find a relatively quiet part of the Autobahn and got the RPMs up passed 5,500 in 6th gear.

We ended up passing Euro Disney on a downhill at 165 mph (265 kph). And I still had room to go faster, but I backed off. I was actually *passing* cars on the road that were doing 60 mph at 165 mph, which meant, however you measure speed I was passing other moving cars at over 100 mph. At that speed there was no room for error, and I had witnessed some horrendous Autobahn wrecks earlier and decided that speed time was over.

We made it back to Germany later that night, turned the car in for shipment back to the States and caught a plane back to the US the next morning.

The relationship had significantly deteriorated between Shannon and me and I realized that bringing her had been a mistake. We were already over before we left and the trip to Germany just extended the painful break-up process. She and I walked off the plane. I dropped her at her apartment, and she was now sadly, out of my life.

I needed diversion, and still on my Euro Delivery high, I decided that I didn't want to wait the 3 weeks for my car to arrive via ocean transport, so I purchased a $3,600 first class ticket on Lufthansa for my car to be placed on a pallet and delivered to me the next day. I had dropped off my car at the German factory in Stuttgart, and two days later I was driving it again on the 101 freeway in Los Angeles.

For a couple of months, I had fun with my new toy, but then thoughts of Shannon's faith being so profound for her, that she would let it come between us, perplexed me. The imperative of her faith; the fact that she felt that she had a real connection to something she believed in pressed upon me, besides the fact that I missed her. So informally I thought I would investigate a little deeper what it was she felt so passionate about.

And that is what I did. Beyond the need for some religious meaning in my life that Reform Judaism had not provided me with, was my emotional need for human relationship. Shannon and I had broken up because I could not blindly accept the tenants of her religion and I was unhappy about that; and unwilling to accept that that decision could be the end of our relationship.

So, I was also motivated to learn more about it if only I could find some way to accept enough of the tenants and still keep my sensibilities, so as to maybe win Shannon back.

Let's just say I had a lot of emotional motivation to find a way.

Author's Note: The following section until the end of Chapter 3 contains information that may be extremely offensive to some people; Gentile Christians, in particular, are advised to skip this section.

What I am about to reveal, writing this memoir today as an Orthodox rabbi, disturbs me tremendously; but we all have our journeys, and this just happened to be mine. Today, of course I have repudiated Christianity entirely and returned to the faith of my fathers. But at the time I knew little about Jewish Mesorah (Tradition) and even less about the Hebrew bible.

I started with the (false) premise that there were intelligent people on both sides of the issue and the sheer number of intelligent people on the side of Christianity dwarfed those on the Jewish side. The problem with my reasoning was that my definition of "intelligence" had more to do with (secular) college or graduate degrees rather than Talmudic, Hebraic or biblical erudition. I just figured that anyone could read and interpret a translation. I also didn't know that the Christian translation I was reading from was mistranslated; and that the out of context non-Jewish explanations given took into account none of the millennia-accepted rabbinical commentary or biblical Hebrew context. Most of the time, in the mistranslated, non-contextual Christian world, the literal text on the page was simply taken as "gospel", as is.

I would come to find out much later that apparently there is a special mission to convert non-believers to Christianity and if that non-believer happens to be Jewish, then the imperative is even greater. I have heard that missionaries would rather convert one Jew than 50,000 non-Jews. And the reason is clear: Who else but the Jewish people should have accepted the Christian deity and messiah candidate, but the Jews? The man whom Christianity worships was a Jew, who claimed that he came for "the lost sheep of the house of Israel." (Matthew 15:24)

That the Jewish people, as a whole century after century, until today have rejected this message is really a thorn in the side of Christianity. Jewish rejection degrades the Christian message's credibility and standing, especially when the very people for whom the message was supposedly meant; the people who actually speak the language of the bible and who are the Chosen of G-d reject this message almost without exception.

Why do Jews reject the message? This book is not meant to be a polemic or exhaustive resource on the matter. Suffice to say, that after exhaustive research, I came to the irrefutable conclusion that forestalls any chance of Christianity being kosher for a Jew... or for a non-Jew, for that matter.

If the reader wants to learn more on the matter, there are excellent books and resources available:

- *"The Mythmaker: Paul and the Invention of Christianity"* – Maccoby
- *"You take Jesus. I'll take G-d"* – Segal
- *"The Disputation of Barcelona"* - Nachmonides
- *"Faith Strengthened"* – Troki
- Outreachjudaism.org
- Jewsforjudaism.org

For me it came down to a painful but honest accounting of biblical texts and proper application. It came down to proper translation and in-context exegesis. I learned what G-d was not and what the messiah was not, and I came to the inescapable conclusion that Jesus was not the messiah anyone should have been waiting for.

The *Tanach* (Jewish Bible) clearly states that, "G-d is *not* a man... nor the son of man...." (Numbers 23:19)

Hosea 11:9 states this categorically, "... For I am G-d and *not* a man, the Holy One in your midst...."

See also 1 Samuel 15:29: "G-d is *not* a man." This is clear.

Israel, corporate Israel, is in-fact G-d's son. "When Israel was a child, then I loved him, and out of Egypt I called my son." (Hosea 11:1)

G-d Himself adjures His people that He does not have a physical form and does not take forms and therefore we are not to become corrupt to worship an image or anything that takes the form of any created being in Heaven or on Earth, *including a man or a woman*. (Deut. 4: 15-19 and 5:1-7)

The Jewish prophets state clearly what the candidate must do to be considered messiah. He must be a human man. He is not divine. He is not to be worshipped. He must observe all the commandments G-d laid down in the Torah, not set them aside. He must usher in an age of *world peace*, not watch as his adherents kill Jews in his name. (It is quite ironic that Christianity has killed more people in the name of the man that they worship than virtually any other causation.) 100 million people murdered by

Christianity is hardly the face or candidate of (a religion of) world peace.

In-point-of-fact, during the Disputation of Barcelona, Nachmonides (also known as "Ramban", a leading medieval Jewish scholar), looked out in the killing fields of Christian Europe and bemoaned, "Woe to the world if messiah has come"; meaning if this is how the world looks *after* messiah has already come, the world has no hope. Even today, at this book's publication, the world has not yet come to peace. So, then, it is clear that the Jewish messiah definitively has not yet been revealed.

Further, the Jewish messiah must *also* re-gather the Jewish people to the land of Israel, not see them scattered throughout the world. He must compel the Jewish people to similarly observe the 613 commandments and the non-Jewish people of the world to observe the 7 laws of Noach. (These Noachide laws include not denying G-d, not blaspheming G-d, not murdering, not engaging in immoral relations, not stealing, not eating of a live animal, and establishing courts of law to ensure law and order.) The Jewish messiah must also see that the 3rd Temple is rebuilt and sacrifices resume. And finally, there must be a *complete* resurrection of the dead. (See Ezekiel 37.) If *any* of these things have not been accomplished the messiah is not here.

Alleged, unverifiable events like walking on water, changing water into wine or multiplying loaves of bread, etc., while "very nice", all fall into the same class of so-called "miracles" claimed by many religions. Yet, *none of them are biblical signs of the messiah*. We see that the Jewish prophet Elisha multiplied oil, and also resurrected a dead child; but nobody ever thought he was G-d or attributed messiah-status to him for those deeds. (See 2 Kings 4.)

Certainly, by being killed (or dying) *before* the biblical job is complete definitively means you are no longer the presumptive messiah or even a candidate. In the Jewish Scriptures (Ezekiel 18), everyone is responsible for his own sins; so, no man can die in my place, even if he claims to be G-d. In addition to G-d clearly stating that He hates human sacrifice is the fact that the messiah dying for others' sins is not one of the biblical messianic signs or requirements.

There is no "coming" a second time; as creative and desperate as that is, the so-called "Second Coming" is made up. The messiah is *the* messiah his first and only coming. What is so glaringly offensive about the Christian message is that not only did none of the biblical requirements G-d set fulfill, but after Jesus' death, the Temple was destroyed, the Jewish people were dispersed and evil and darkness engulfed the Earth; in short, the very opposite of what G-d requires the Jewish messiah to do. It is so clear that the birth of Christianity heralded the advent of an *anti-messiah*, certainly *not* the Jewish messiah.

However, if the Jewish people were right to reject Christianity, then the Christian message should have largely disappeared. Relegated to history's junk pile, like so many other failed Jewish offshoots and messianic cults, it should have only gained adherence by a small but obscure cult-following, like the Karites and Sadducees, who have essentially all but disappeared. And for most of the legitimate Jewish world, that was the case – Jews rejected the Jesus message as irrelevant because he met none of the biblical messianic requirements and taught us nothing new; instead, he died a rebel's death. That antinomial non-Jews misunderstood, co-opted and then perverted this message; literally starting a brand-new religion, had nothing to do with authentic Judaism.

Still, this fledgling religion of Christianity was able to spread like wildfire amongst the largely ignorant masses of the Gentile nations because they found something therein (however mistakenly) that "spoke" to them; giving them the false promise of a relationship with the G-d of Israel on *their* terms, all without having to give up their idols or go through the difficult process of converting to Judaism. Once the NT (New Testament) myths took root, no matter that those tenants and theology could be *factually* disproven, the Gentile world had at its core what it *felt* it needed… a wholly emotive message that resonated with its greatest hopes and fears, a message of a professed connection with what they believed was the G-d of Israel rooted in a fear-based faith of "salvation from damnation".

Is it any wonder that the Christian world remains unable (or unwilling) to acknowledge the truth of Hebrew biblical context? Since its inception, Christianity at its core is a religion obsessed with death, with what will be in the afterlife; so, the single-minded focus is on the need to be "saved" in this life from some eternal punishment. Christians are terrified of going to hell. They shake from this fear and this motivates *everything* that comes after.

Nowadays, Christians also place inordinate emphasis on their "born-again" experiences, (self-manufactured or imagined *feelings* of euphoria, wholeness, love, or dreams in which Jesus comes to them). It is important to note that in Hindu countries, Hindu gods also come in dreams to people and in Muslim countries Mohammed comes. In Catholic countries, Mary comes. *Everyone* claims "miracles", euphoric experiences, and visitations/dreams of their particular savior. Now, no one has a corner on the market when it comes to so-called "born-again" experiences, yet those very *experiences* make up the Christian's foundation, currency and primary focal point; rather than the contextual meaning of actual biblical texts.

Since Christian salvation is predicated solely on fear-based *belief*, there is a kind of dread at entertaining a contrary perspective that might cause one to question this tenuous salvation. Fear of seeming ungrateful for this "gift" of unearned salvation becomes pervasive and cloying… and shuts down an exchange that might lead to countenancing a Jewish view. As any perspective that contradicts their current salvation belief-set could send them to Christian hell, honest discussions are generally too scary for most Christians. This explains how a Jewish scholar can bring biblical proof of Christian fraud and a Christian will still incredibly reject that proof in favor of his fear-based emotional attachments. Intellect has absolutely zero sway.

How is it that what was so clear to the Jewish people throughout history was also not *initially* understood by their non-Jewish neighbors? One firstly must understand the context of the times. In the days of early Christianity, I would come to find out later, paganism and idolatry were rampant. Gentiles worshipped rocks and stones and bugs and trees and their own grandparents, the moon, the stars and even deified humans with all the dysfunction of their mortal counterparts. (See Greco-Roman mythology.)

By taking a Jewish character who may have aspired to be a Jewish leader or teacher and then deifying him, Christianity was born and fit in with the profile of all the other false religions of the time. In their culture of god-men, it wasn't a giant stretch to worship a man and then call him the One G-d of Israel, even as they attributed a non-historical, non-biblical and oxymoronic triune status to G-d in His Unity. Despite the resultant cognitive dissonance, the Gentiles were able to keep the paganism they were already steeped in and then got to (fatuously) claim salvation vis-à-vis this idolatrous belief-set coupled with a sophomoric, facile belief ascribed to as "G-d"; and further, without any effort of having to keep the commandments. In this new salvation blood cult amongst many others, all one's sins easily being forgiven by a belief in a dying Jewish god, while the Jewish people were replaced as G-d's Chosen by the non-Jews, was heady stuff. Who wouldn't want that? Everyone knew the G-d of Israel was enduring, eternal. So, Christianity "gave" it to them by holding that the way was through acceptance of the New Testament's definitional twist on messiah. Ironically even then, in the NT, there was no deification of their messianic candidate.

It's only because of a *vote* at the Council of Nicaea (325 C.E.) that made G-d into a trinity based on the man-god worship tradition that sprung from institutionalized Gentile idolatry and human deification of the time. Coupled with a gross misreading of the New Testament texts (and later by mistranslating the Hebrew texts); this contributed to solidifying the myth that turned a so-called "nice Jewish boy" into another Gentile god.

In our days when we know that worship of the moon or stars is already not real, because we know the moon is a "dumb" rock, stars are masses of gas, and Zeus is an accepted myth; how did Jesus-worship then survive? Simple: The Christian always started with belief in the "New" Testament first and once he accepted *that* message, he was then forced to believe in the Jewish Scriptures, (called, "The Old Testament" by Christians), after the fact. "'Old' Testament" denotes for the Christian something no longer binding. So, a Christian may give lip-service to belief in the Jewish Scriptures, but then only as his support to "foreshadow" what he already believes from the NT.

Now there are serious problems; the New Testament diverges with the Jewish Scriptures (Old Testament) so much that in order to keep one's Christian faith, the "Old" must be forced fit, changed, or simply determined that it no longer applies. And once you have an emotional connection to an ideology, it's not easy to overcome that with logic, especially when you have what you believe is "salvation". It becomes expedient, even opportunistic, to ignore or manipulate the Old Testament in favor of the New. And Christianity has been doing that for millennia.

To the faithful Jew who always started and ended with the Jewish Scriptures, the Jew judged anything that came *after* in light of what the Jewish Scriptures said. If, as Jewish people have done since Moses transmitted the Torah, a Gentile also would have done the same and simply read and applied the Jewish Scriptures *first* in its original language and *then* judged everything in light of that, s/he could never have accepted the New Testament!

Indeed, by the time a non-Jew finally gets his bible, the authentic Hebrew portion has been grossly manipulated, mistranslated and re-translated numerous times from Hebrew or Greek to Latin to Old English to Modern English… and then another extra biblical pamphlet called, the "New Testament", is attached. And this misnomer is *also* called a "bible". How would a non-Jew even know that his bible has been mistranslated or that the authentic bible is really the Jewish books alone; which do not include the New Testament (or the Book of Mormon)? The point is if someone would have picked up a real Jewish bible in its original Hebrew or in an authoritatively translated English and read it from Genesis to Chronicles, there would be no room for Christianity in the conversation.

To impress the point, the *bon mot* goes: Why did G-d create Mormons? So that evangelical Christians would know how Jews feel. When you ask a Jew to show you his bible, there is no New Testament attached to it. The New Testament has nothing to do with a Jew and nothing to tell a Jew. It simply underscores another false and idolatrous foreign religion, which is forbidden to the Jew. If evangelicals have difficulty countenancing that, then hand them the Mormon "bible" which also contains the Book of Mormon *next* to their New Testament and then they will balk. Which proves the point and the punch line: "Now you know how we (Jews) feel."

The point is not to disparage Mormons... or even evangelicals. *Anyone* is entitled to believe whatever one wants to believe; but when it comes to tenets of what is authentically Jewish and what is not, there are boundaries that cannot be crossed (no pun). Evangelicals (Protestants), Catholics and Mormons follow entirely different religions using the imprimatur of a mistranslated bible along with other non-Jewish texts as a basis for their new beliefs.

To that end, practically speaking, it is considered idolatry for a Jew to accept or embrace Christianity under any banner, (Baptist, Evangelical, Catholic, Mormon, etc.). 100% idolatry. Christianity has taken a Jewish man and elevated him into a god, calling him G-d and has taken G-d, Who is One and Indivisible; and turned Him into a godhead of 3 parts in partnership with one another. This belief set is contrary to our bible and is forbidden for a Jew.

However, when it comes to a non-Jew, whether Christianity is outright idolatry is a difference of opinion among Jewish Sages. Some authoritative codifiers of Jewish law say that Christianity is absolute idol worship even for the non-Jew. Others say that it is not outright idol worship *for a non-Jew only*. Now it has always struck me as odd that non-Jews should be held to a different standard when it comes to idol worship. But this has more to do with how one comes to parse out the Christian ideology and how our codifiers understood Christian theology in different parts of the world.

For the Jewish people, there is no other consideration; it's either an idol or it's not; but non-Jews are generally given a bit of leeway if they erroneously view G-d as working within His creation in a sort of "partnership" called *shituf*, whereby G-d designates certain powers to certain created beings. There may be room to be flexible. Still others say that since from the beginning, the Gentiles did not hear about the idolatrous nature of a trinitarian concept of G-d before it developed into a worldwide phenomenon, that they are not guilty after the fact; that they want to follow the One true G-d and are held harmless by their attribution of a falseness to G-d in their well-intentioned error.

Still, it seemed simple enough through a logical geometric progression of reason and logic: The Jewish people were entrusted by G-d to disseminate the Jewish Scriptures to the world and apply its laws. *For over a thousand years*, the Jewish people were entrusted to transmit and interpret their Scriptures; (the entire religion of Christianity falls apart without that trust), but suddenly after they rejected Christianity, they could no longer be trusted to interpret their own bible. Jewish intellect would be no match for the emotional hysteria and brute force that impelled the non-Jewish Pauline/Jesus myth.

Notwithstanding, the unambiguous clarity of the Hebrew Scriptures made Jewish rejection of Christianity an imperative, while at the same time making it equally impossible to legitimize Christianity. An intellectually honest person recognizes that the Jewish people, since the beginning and without interruption, are the originating, quintessential experts, and sole, enduring custodians of transmission of authentic Hebrew bible, Jewish religion, theoretical and practical biblical law, proper translation and application. Judaism's wholesale repudiation of the

Christian message, therefore, was crushing. It made the Church look like it was on a fool's errand, and Christianity, a practical joke. Jewish rejection profoundly off balanced and hurt the Church deeply.

The way the Church responded to Jewish rejection and tried to counteract the ensuing cognitive dissonance was by promulgating incongruent, noncognitive NT narratives plagued by mistranslation, misinterpretation and misrepresentation of the Hebrew bible; and then for "good" measure, it dismissed the Jewish people outright as "spiritually blinded" or "spiritually veiled" to the truth.

The Christian a priori is that Christianity is already "true" and therefore the Jew from the beginning is spiritually corrupt; without first feeling the need to investigate the arguments as to why these "spiritually blinded Jews" rejected the message in the first place. Therefore, the focus is on conversion of the Jewish people as a top priority in many evangelical Christian circles. Conversion of the "blind" Jew heals the mortal wound of Jewish rejection and thus solves the entire Christian conundrum.

In reality, Jewish rejection of Christianity does not signify any "spiritual blindness" of the Jew, but millennia of Jewish Scriptural, contextual and translational expert erudition. However, the Gentile nations were denied that primary intimacy and were then ripe for misdirection. Even though many non-Jews may be intellectually advanced, once they believed the message and an emotional bond set in, it became very hard to displace emotion with (Jewish) logic. And since the Hebrew language and Jewish Scriptures were largely closed to

105 // Making Music With What Remains

Gentiles... with the intentionally mistranslated versions having to come from the Catholic Church and other later bad actors, a "perfect storm" of misdirection was created.

There's a pithy aphorism piqued in Jewish circles that when something is so off it screams, "What's a Kohein doing in a cemetery?" (Kohanim/Priests are not normally permitted to enter a cemetery for fear of becoming ritually impure and this is the accepted Jewish practice.) In other words, having written all the foregoing, how could a Jew end up embracing this religion in any form?

Clearly stated, most who fall for this are simply uneducated Jews misled by non-Jews who convince them with a mistranslated English version of a Christian bible; showing them out-of-context, mistranslated "proofs" they had apparently missed in their anemic Jewish upbringing.

For me, this was true as well. And it was compounded by the fact that I was suffering without any healthy love or companionship from my own biological family; I also wanted to belong to something meaningful. And, perhaps in fulfillment of some need that I had not yet realized was *already* available in my own birth faith, my need for a personal and uplifting intimacy with the Divine had been denied to me by a lack of understanding and a proper religious Jewish education.

Just as in sales, to varying degrees, you paint a picture, hammering on hot button needs/wants/desires of your intended customer/victim and then you give an intellectual solution with an emotional close. With my ridiculously inane and subpar Jewish education/practice and at the time, only a perfunctory, rudimentary knowledge of the Hebrew language I was literally inveigled by the translations placed in front of me by many Christians who I believe were mostly well-meaning but equally beguiled like me.

It didn't dawn on me until much later that *none* of these non-Jews could speak or read Hebrew and here they were, Gentiles, teaching me about my own bible from a mistranslation of a mistranslation. Now it is virtually unknown within the Orthodox Jewish world for a knowledgeable, *yeshiva* educated practicing Jew to convert away. A religious Jew has an intimacy with his bible that is imperious to mistranslations and misapplications and made-up stories of the missionaries. If a Jew, G-d forbid, embraces the Christian message, it is almost always the Jew who is ignorant; one who does not grow up learning about his faith is at risk for conversion.

And while it's no great achievement to deceive an ignoramus, the Church exults in counting these poor deceived Jews as "saved"; while Judaism counts them as ignorant victims and worse, *shmad* or *meshumadim*, (Yiddish/post-biblical Hebrew for "destroyed ones").

None of this is to say that I am anything but supportive of non-Jews praying to G-d and having a true personal and real intimate relationship with the One true G-d. But I believe because Christianity is based on fallacy, also having been the source of so much evil in the world, that there is no reason that a non-Jew needs to seek a relationship with G-d through a religion whose designs were formed vis-à-vis such an odious foundation of idolatrous tenants.

It is true after Christianity went through its major reformation, that today many people who identify as "Christian" do significant good in the world. Notwithstanding their motivations or beliefs, the point is that as a whole, self-identifying Christians *are* interested in having a connection with the Jewish G-d; (although they miss His essential nature entirely), while still walking the "golden rule", (a very Jewish concept), conducting themselves with honor and honesty, and wanting to protect Israel and the Jewish people.

But they do so in a subtle egotistical fashion, ironically holding up a manufactured tradition of the so-called "humility of Jesus" as a duplicitous self-standard bearer. It's an ego I recognized, mine being fomented in Tim's office – the ego telling me that I knew best, that I alone had the truth and correct perspective and reasoning, that I deserved it, that I didn't need to seek out or listen to expert rabbinical council (or legal counsel) outside of the influence that was stoking my ego, and that I got to make G-d in my image and impute what I wanted as what G-d wanted, instead of the other way around. Then I got to interpret bible in a manner and fashion that matched my base drive, all under the guise of being "humble"; because let's be honest… as an evangelical Christian, the whole non-believing world, even if it does tremendous good like build hospitals, adopt at risk babies, etc., will *still* go to hell, but the humble Christian is saved. Christian *belief* (faith) is superior to any good deeds because belief gets you into evangelical heaven. Yet, Jesus' "humility" does not allow for anyone to be "saved" outside of belief in him. But this is not humility. Its stunning arrogance.

Now most Gentile Christians who (against the author's advice) will read this debrief, would demur. But when put on the spot, they will all agree (in theory) that no matter how much good you do, unless you believe in the Christian man/god, you will be rejected and sent to hell. Conversely, (and mind numbingly) no matter how much evil you previously did; if you have even one moment of belief before you die, you go to heaven.

What I have described is not how people stuck in evangelical ether will want to see themselves or their religion. That's fine. Ignorance and self-interest can prevent an honest accounting sometimes; but the *only* way to becoming a Christian (besides being born into it) is simple self-interest and ego as described above; and for those who require a textual basis, a first run reading of the New Testament and then out of context mistranslation and misapplication of the Old Testament as its "support".

I recently watched an interview with Ben Shapiro, a Modern Orthodox Jew of the conservative Daily Wire column and John MacCarthur, an evangelical Christian leader, which captures the smug evangelical Christian presumptive ignorance and psychology perfectly. First off, most assuredly, like most non-Jews, MacCarthur does not read or write a word of biblical Hebrew. So, he's lecturing Ben Shapiro from his understanding of a non-Jewish mistranslated, reinterpreted bible. Then he imagines Jesus as some kind of "super Jew who saw to the heart of the

Jewish law clearer than any other; that it's not only about the practical application of the law, but also the heart of the law", as if no other Jew ever thought in those terms... as if the Jewish people have been thumping and bumping along for 3,330 years, clueless.

And then suddenly, thirteen hundred years *after* Mt. Sinai, Jesus came to witness to his own people, and failing that, then non-Jews (who were previously worshipping rocks and trees reductio ad absurdum) were able, all at once, to understand / internalize this Jewish (Hebrew) message of reproof; now themselves witnessing to the Jewish people, as if the nation of Israel never had a concept of their own religion. It was complete subjective egotistical arrogance. Evangelicals don't realize how offensive their message delivery is, or how presumptuous their *strawman* or how circular their "reasoning" is, all wrapped up in one hot mess of: "I-alone-have-the-truth-and-I-will-mechanically-stand-my-patronizing-testimonial-emotive-faith."

The result is that Jesus gets elevated by the ill-informed above all the other Jews who ever lived simply because the non-Jew, who never researched anything before the Christian message, suddenly heard a Jewish sounding message coming from a Christian book. When a non-Jew hears, "You shall love the L-rd your G-d with all your heart, with all your soul and with all your might"; it gets falsely attributed to NT Christianity, when in fact it was lifted from Deuteronomy 6:4. You see there is nothing true in the NT that is new; and in the reverse, nothing new in the NT is true. Christianity is in-fact a new religion, even as it falsely purports to be a continuation (and fulfillment) of Judaism and the Jewish Scriptures; while at the same time mistranslating Jewish Scriptures, denigrating and demonizing the Jewish people and believing the rabbis to be lost and ineffectual.

Debate with Christians is mostly useless. As Thomas Sowell wrote, "It is usually futile to try to talk facts and analysis to people who are enjoying a sense of moral superiority in their ignorance."

The Christian stands on artifice and his own deluded understanding of his moral superiority simply because he accepted Christological "salvation"; and then insulates himself from any discussion on the matter by making sweeping and gratuitous and ignorant statements like, "Jesus was the purist Jew, the most righteous Jew, etc., etc., who ever lived. He went above the rabbis."

Having now inculcated this mindset, some Christians "dare" their listeners by pushing them to choose: "Jesus was either the messiah and G-d, or he was lunatic or a liar. Those are your only choices."

There are, of course, *other* choices. Perhaps Jesus never said those things and the New Testament writers simply placed the offensive comments Jesus *supposedly* made onto his lips. Or they misinterpreted or misapplied what he actually said. Or he indeed was a lunatic and/or a liar. Either way anything he may have said that was in line with accepted Jewish sources prima facie is true. Anything he said or was purported to have said that is not found in the Jewish sources is false. That a heretic or non-Jew then took some words that on their face may have been true and then twisted them into a non-contextual meaning explains how Christianity became a non-Jewish religion.

Christianity is neither a continuation of Judaism any more than Islam is a continuation of Judaism, just because the Koran mentioned Moses and Abraham. Christianity (like Islam) is a brand-new distinct religion; it's not Judaism and not for the Jewish people. Its fatal flaw was in trying to draw legitimacy for its existence by attempting to attach itself to Judaism. In trying to attract the Jewish people, Christianity actually shot itself in the foot by appropriating the very Scriptures that G-d gave to the Jews, that make Christian worship idolatry and forbidden to Jews. The Jewish bible makes it very clear that *G-d is One* (a Unity) and not three (a trinity). It also makes it very clear that G-d is not a man and that His Law is eternal. Even the man who Christianity worships told his followers in Matthew 5:17 that (as a Jew), "I did not come to put away the Law or prophets but to fulfill (keep) the law (Torah)."

And so, our Jewish G-d-given eternal Law had already illegitimatized Christianity from the very beginning. If Christianity would have simply been honest and claimed that theirs was a brand-new religion that placed faith in a man-god to save you, well and fine. Everyone is entitled to believe in whatever faith they want. The world is full of these types of religions from Hinduism to Buddhism to Islam and thousands of others. But Christians in their headlong egotism took Jewish Scriptures that they did not understand and tried to prove their new religion thereby, and this carries over today. When I hear a Christian "standing his testimony" or repeating a slogan, trying to push his belief in Christianity by inanely quoting a Jewish Scripture, (invariably out of context and mistranslated); if I show the error by translating his "proof text" or "foreshadowing" or "typology" in context and properly translated there is usually an unwillingness to accept, a cognitive dissonance, a burying of the head. And there is only one word that could account for it: *Ego*. Ego brings you squarely to: "My people are destroyed for lack of knowledge." (Hosea 4:6)

Christianity presents a biblical lie and then hides it in plain sight. It hopes its adherents will not possess the education or be able to investigate its claims before that adherent forms an emotional bond with its myth. Once the emotional bond is formed, it's virtually impossible for the intellect to have any sway. Christian apologists simply mount a non-sequitur bluff, confidently spouting meaningless, nonsensical and misleading phrases like "intellectual faith" or "evidence that demands a verdict" or "biblically based" or "harmony of the Gospels". They essentially stand their faith on old slogans and the same out of context, mistranslated texts. New Testament Christianity is like an emperor who has no clothes, standing naked in plain sight while being lauded by generation after generation of sycophants… when in reality, it is only a cacophony of noise and fraud.

And further, because of the intense anti-Semitism fomented (along with the idolatry that resulted) from within the New Testament and the subsequent writings of the Church fathers (Luther, Calvin, et al.), that today if a Christian loves the Jewish people as a distinct religious entity and accepts Jewish worship of G-d in a non-Christological way, it is always in spite of the New Testament and not because of it.

In 1543 Luther published, "*On the Jews and Their Lies*" in which he writes, "The Jews are a base, whoring people; that is, no people of God, and their boast of lineage, circumcision, and law must be accounted as filth. They are full of the devil's feces... which they wallow in like swine. In sum, they are the devil's children, damned to Hell..."

And John Calvin wrote, "*A Response to Questions and Objections of a Certain Jew*" in which he says, "Their [the Jews] rotten and unbending *stiffneckedness* deserves that they be oppressed unendingly and without measure or end and that they die in their misery without the pity of anyone.... I have had much conversation with many Jews: I have never seen either a drop of piety or a grain of truth or ingenuousness – nay, I have never found common sense in any Jew."

Let that sink in for a moment. Luther and Calvin were rabid anti-Semite Church Fathers; yet even in death, they continue to be *the* definitive progenitors of modern-day Protestant Christianity with approximately 1 billion adherents, second only in number to Catholicism.

While today, despite the horrific things that the Catholic Church also did to the Jewish people throughout the Church's despotic, barbaric and creepy history, its reformation specifically allows that even without acceptance of their savior, a Jew (and by extension, any person of good moral conduct) can be "saved". Now a Jew is not looking to be "saved" in the way a Christian understands that word. A Jew is more uniquely concerned about his conduct here on Earth than with any rewards in the World to Come; but it's nice to know that Catholics now view the Jewish people in a more egalitarian manner, and that the Jewish people are still considered by them to be G-d's Chosen in a special relationship with Him. They respect our relationship and our path and do not attempt to actively convert Jews. Evangelicals on the other hand maintain that everyone who does not hold by their savior goes to hell, so active missionizing is part of their calling.

These evangelical beliefs and tactics dishonestly delegitimize the Jewish people, as my mentor and teacher, Rabbi Dr. J. Immanuel Schochet, OBM, wrote for his final book, "For the Love of Truth", page 157 on the subject of Judaism and Christian missionaries:

"I say to you [Christians], by all means be a good Christian; but never forget that nothing, absolutely nothing, can or may ever supersede truth and honesty. Remember a very profound statement attributed to Coleridge (English Poet and Philosopher, 1772-1834): 'He who begins by loving Christianity better than truth, will proceed by loving his own sect, or church better than Christianity, and end in loving himself better than all.'

"The ultimate meaning and practice of religion is love of truth, pursuit of truth and commitment to truth. Anything less than that is not religion, is not worship of G-d, but worship of self, worship of your personal feelings, worship of your private opinions and prejudices. It is, in effect, the worst and lowest form of all idolatries. For truth is synonymous with G-d, and G-d is synonymous with truth." (Mosaic)

As it turned out, many years later after I returned to Orthodox Judaism, I had the merit to learn from all three of the Schochet brothers. I learned in a *yeshiva* headed by Rabbi Erza Schochet, dean of school, and I received my rabbinical ordination from Rabbi Dovid Schochet, head of the Orthodox Rabbinical Counsel of Toronto, Canada. All three Schochet brothers had profound and far-reaching impact on my life.

Now I am very much in favor of *any* religion that contributes to the good in the world even if the origination or core theology does not. It's the paradox of living in a world that has so much good and evil intermixed. It's our job as human beings to unwind the good from the evil in any permitted way possible. And good Christians and Catholics today are also capable of this; still any good that a Christian does while identifying that their faith inspired the good deed, is always tinged to a lesser or greater degree with the ego of replacement theology and somehow seeing in their hero and religion what no religious Jew was ever able to see... and not thinking that to be strange, odd or untenable somehow; that the Gentile alone could see truth, but not the Pharisaic Jew.

And so, it was, without being inoculated or properly educated, that this Jew who had no real understanding of, or intimacy with, his own birth religion first, went ahead and embraced another religion. It was the beginning of an odyssey that almost ended in the tragedy of ending my line of any future Jewish descendants in an all too familiar story repeated time and again, within the assimilated ranks of the Jewish people. Once I believed I could countenance it, I called Shannon and told her that I had had a change of heart about her religion; I asked her if we could try again.

She eventually agreed, but I have to say that even though I had all this new understanding in my head, all these "proof texts", etc., there was still a significant dissonance in me. But I had already invested myself and made certain commitments to this. It was still one of the most difficult things I have ever had to do, to embrace the Christian message… and when it came time for me to actually accept, my mind and my heart both screamed at me, that this was wrong. I could feel my entire body shudder and I almost passed out from psychic trauma and mental anguish. I could not breathe. I could not speak. I felt as though I would fracture inside by having to accept what was so foreign and so unnatural for me. I literally felt a palpable tearing of my moorings. I believe this was my Jewish soul being torn, crying out, fighting for spiritual oxygen, fighting for its life. In the end I almost listened to the voice screaming, *No*! I almost got up and walked away. But for the girl…. Almost.

Instead, and being so conditioned to imbibing emotional toxins growing up, that I must have felt a kindred connection to this kind of internal dysfunction, a kind of normalcy to embracing that which is venomous; I drank the Kool Aid, and in the process, drowned my Jewish soul.

Having now eliminated the religious barrier, Shannon felt she could move forward in a committed relationship with me. She moved into my new home in Woodland Hills, and we began our lives; soon we were civilly married and expecting our first child. Shannon initially did not want to become pregnant. I literally had to beg her to have a baby and she agreed. Our daughter was born on February 13, 1997 and I was so happy to be her father. My daughter was the light of my life.

Our lives were idyllic, and yet there was always something nagging at me; something pulling on me that did not seem to fit with my new life. I still had not come to terms with the fact that I had been given this "true" understanding of the bible and not one of the rabbis in any of the streams of mainstream Judaism accepted this. How was this possible? I continued to have unsettling dissonance. And so, as a pet project I engaged with rabbis and read books on the matter from so-called anti-missionary groups if only to understand what they knew, that I did not.

Shannon had no such misgivings or dissonance. Born into this world, she was simple, unassuming, and congruent with herself and her faith. And since I had married her on her terms, I was the one who had to maintain my side of things. She expected me to toe the line even as I had begun struggling to maintain those terms; yet it would become increasingly difficult as the foundation I thought was so secure began to wash away under my feet as I learned more and more about the reasons why Jews don't accept the Christian message. Still, because frankly I had way too much to lose, I maintained my distance for the time being and lived my nice life in a big house on a hill with my wife and baby and my German Sheppard.

And Tupac across the street.

Chapter 4

Where's David Diamand?

"I can bear, and ignore one's idiocy, however, not the lies since that break, damage and destroy innocent lives."
- Ehsan Sehgal

Each weekday I arrived for work at Tim's office. One Monday morning I opened the front lobby door of the main sales office on my way to my desk and I froze. Inside the office was a bunch of State law enforcement agents from the Department of Corporations, Enforcement Division. There was a swarm of them in blue raid jackets. Up against the wall were all the salespeople having their pictures taken and lots of records were being piled into boxes ostensibly for removal. I had just walking into a DOC raid. Their investigators had law enforcement authority... and this looked serious.

I decided in that moment, that while my worst fears may have been confirmed, I also did not want to be there when whatever hammer came down. I thought, let the DOC do what it needed to do, and I could come back later. But just then as I was about to close the door, an agent turned and demanded, "Hey, stop, what's your name?!"

Since I was not yet inside the office and I had no intention of coming in, I told the agent that I was simply visiting a friend and it didn't look like it was a good time; so, I shut the door and left. Incredibly the agent did not follow me. Perhaps he had too many other fires to put out where he was or perhaps his jurisdiction only extended to the confines of the office delineated on his search warrant.

In any event, the sirens in my head were screaming off the hook. I was now actually very concerned. A DOC raid, I thought. I guess we're done now. I was almost relieved, but still scared. I called Tim. But once again, he soothed me to the point that I felt silly for even hinting at concern. He actually made me feel sophomoric for questioning, that I must have had no faith in my own sales history and that I was missing the essentials. He said, "DOC raids happen all the time and there is nothing to be concerned with. As soon as they complete their *audit*, we can go back to work."

Sure.

Tim was a master at hiding the most dysfunctional things in plain sight and then making those dysfunctional things into positives. 85% load was a *good* thing! DOC raids were a *good* thing! It was all a *normal* part of the industry.

So, the next day we were back to work. Whatever the DOC did or did not do I have no idea. They were there to collect records of investments and scripts and sales materials as part of a larger investigation into the ISOs and Marc and Ira I would postulate. What they alleged or what evidence was sustained, I was never told except that, "This is all standard procedure."

I do know that a few weeks later Tim was actively looking for another office space and he had changed the name of his business from Brookside Consulting to Granite Consulting. We vacated that building and set up shop a few miles east on Ventura Blvd.

Tim explained that sometimes customers complain... and the DOC has to investigate. To be able to do a complete investigation there has to be an allegation of securities violations. But allegations are only sustained if you don't fight them, or you lose in court. And the worst thing that happens is that they issue you a *Cease and Desist* order. Happens all the time. So instead of fighting them and wasting a whole lot of money on a DOC judge, who likely rubber stamps the DOC recommendations anyway; most people, according to Tim, simply accept the *Cease and Desist* and then open up under a new company and continue on.

Tim would then intone, "Just because the DOC conducted an administrative action doesn't mean that there is anything to be afraid of or that there is any fraud. It's always possible that some *'i'* wasn't dotted or an infraction of administrative policy or the DOC interpretation of what constitutes a security violation might cause a notice to *Cease and Desist*. Standard stuff. Plus, we still have full support of our in-house legal department and our promotions team is sailing full steam ahead. If there was anything wrong Marc and Ira would have shut everything down. They know what they're doing. At worst, it's only a fine. Oil companies do it all the time; they dump illegally and then pay a fine."

According to Tim, because the current landlord was giving Tim problems growing his office and Tim said he needed a bigger space, the office now had to change its location.

I had to hand it to Tim. He knew what I had to hear to get me to stay. He gave me just enough of the truth stuffed with a lie that I was unable to unwind, and I remained in Tim's ether. I was also clearly motivated financially, though I knew in my heart that aside of the moral implications of pressuring people into such high load investment there might also be legal consequences and that unnerved me; just not enough to get me to call it quits. Besides, what if I was wrong? What if Tim was right and I threw away my fortunes on my fears? So, I had a daily tennis match with myself.

I continued to bury my head in Tim's explanations and the fantasy that so long as I kept selling and the investments were running, then they must be legitimate; and my clients had not lost their money. I was betting everything, my future, my family and all of my clients' money now and into the future on my hope and need that everything was legitimate and legal. It was a fool's bet, but by now I was in over my head; so much of my clients' money was sunk in and I was completely committed to what I had been pitching people that I needed to believe it. I kept excavating for proof because I wanted to believe that I was operating on moral fiber; and Tim exploited it. Giving up and getting out would mean that I would have to admit to myself that it had been a fraud all along, that my customers' money was a complete loss, and that was simply too painful for me.

Sometimes other salesmen would bring me potential customers who they had opened but just couldn't close. If I was able to close that customer, we would split the commissions. One of the salesmen, Steve, brought me a number of prospects he could not close, and we teamed up. As we worked together, I used to confide in Steve my core concerns about what Tim was telling us in sales meetings and what the reality on the ground was. By this time a few of our programs had busted; one or two of them were in bankruptcy (which Tim also spun as a "good thing") and I told him I was concerned despite the promises that Tim was making. I even tried to soothe myself by touting Tim's explanations in a way to be able to move forward despite my doubts.

But Steve wasn't having any of it. He was clear. He believed, and stated as such to me, that at the core, Tim's programs were scams, and the customers had no chance to make any money. He believed he was lying to them. I was shocked. How could he sell something he *believed* was a fraud?! Steve said that this was his job; and this was how he made money and whether it was viable or not, was not his responsibility.

So, I admonished him (taking a moral high ground), "If you believe you are selling a fraud, then you are lying and intentionally defrauding the customer; you believe the customer will definitely lose his money."

He smiled sardonically, nodded, chuckled and lifted his shoulders sheepishly in a *what can I do?* shrug and said, "Yup."

He tried to say that I was no better than him, because I was doing the same thing. I took extreme exception to that assessment. I wasn't selling what I believed to be fraud and I wasn't intentionally lying and further, I didn't need to lie to sell. I pointed to all of the "proofs" Tim gave as my support. I would never have knowingly sold something I knew was a fraud or had zero chance of working, but Steve dismissed Tim's proofs. It was hard working with Steve after that knowing that he felt he was definitively conning people and thought I was doing the same, even as I doggedly clung to my fantasy that it *could* be real. The irony was that Steve, the salesman who admitted to me that he believed he was knowingly selling people into scams, and who was also indicted for wire fraud and mail fraud went to trial but was acquitted, while I did not end up so fortunate.

Anyway, the woman Steve had been pitching for a while, for some reason had never closed with him. I engaged with her. Over the course of the next year plus, I spoke to her regularly, but she would not invest. I would always seem to be just on the cusp of closing her, but her investment money was somehow always locked away or she wasn't quite ready. Still, she gave me buying signals that told me she was interested. I must have spent over 20 hours pitching her, reading and re-reading the scripts. I could never figure out what the problem was.

The problem was that she was not really a (potential) customer at all. She was a CI (confidential informant) for the FBI, and she was recording every single one of our phone calls. The FBI was listening in as I was reading my scripts, most always in a very forceful manner. When it later came out that Tim's sales meetings and scripts were all misrepresentations, and therefore most of what I had been pitching to the CI were misrepresentations; even though I always maintained I did not know, it was my ambitious, sometimes aggressive sales style that did not play well for prosecutors. And it would not have played well for a federal jury, either. I don't think a jury could have made the necessary distinction between *what* I believed and *how* aggressively I sold. Steve on the other hand plodded along and sounded like he was reading; in short, he was not a good salesman; so even though he was also recorded, his pitching was not compelling. So, he got away with saying he did not know anything other than what he was told to say.

Fast forward one year. We were still selling, but by now something like 7 programs had gone by and not one had made anyone any money, and now finally Steve's assessment started to ring true for me. I began to really doubt the veracity of what I was selling, though I had no absolute proof of it. Still the writing seemed to be very clear on the wall. I began to ask Tim very pointed questions and I would not stand for his non-sequitur arguments or explanations any longer. I kept his feet to the fire demanding answers to my questions about why none of these programs were working or an admission that what we were selling was a fraud. Tim did neither. Instead, he called me into his office one Friday and said, "Here's your last check. You're fired."

Wow. Just wow. This was unexpected. I was his top salesman. He said that he could not have me in the office causing negativity to the other salespeople and that my lack of trust in him was too much and he was letting me go.

125 // Making Music With What Remains

I went home in shock and very conflicted. I thought to myself that if indeed it was a fraud, why would he fire me; why not just continue to placate and scam me and get me to continue selling for him until the bitter end? And if it wasn't a fraud, then I could understand perhaps why he fired me. Maybe I wasn't seeing things correctly? In the end, I realized that Tim was playing me. He had just foisted a huge take away close on me and would end up reeling me back in. The "hook" came in the form of a phone call later that weekend.

Me: "I'm sorry about what happened. It's just that I had so many doubts and none of the other programs were making any money…."

Tim: "You didn't trust me, and you were making it hard for the other salesmen to do their job… but I wanted to let you know that Mark and Ira were able to take our programs public! Stock certificates have been issued and we are now a publicly traded company. It was real the whole time. If it wasn't, we could not have gone public and the customers are going to make money. You can have your job back if you want it."

At the time I was so glad that things were "good" again between me and my clients and Tim that I accepted everything he said without taking the time to truly investigate what was happening

It was executed masterfully. Tim had wrecked me with my own concerns, and then in one call put all of my objections on a shelf, forever. If it wasn't legitimate, how could he have fired me? If it wasn't legitimate, how could it have gone public?

Of course, I would later find out that it was a reverse merger into a shell, whereby the promoters simply took the customers' remaining 15% and paid a nominee corporation controlled by the promoters to acquire a shell corporation and issue stock on it. But these type of transactions and shell corporations are a dime a dozen and the prosecutor told me in a debrief meeting that, "The stock was not worth the paper it's printed on."

To add insult to injury I would later learn that doing a reverse merger, while sounding great, was just a way for the promoters to get their hands on the remaining 15% and put it into their pockets as well.

So, this "great" stock investment I was now unwittingly selling as "legitimate" was effectively taking 100% of the investors' money.

Sigh.

Now perhaps, even more misled to the true nature of the investment but still conflicted for non-specific gut feelings, I continued to pitch to the CI with this new public stock offering... until the *very* bitter end culminating in an alphabetical soup of law enforcement agencies descending upon the main office and every ISO office.

One Monday morning in early 1997, the FBI, LAPD, DOC, USPS (Postal Inspector), IRS and FTC raided Tim's new offices.

They screamed, "Federal agents! Don't move! Hands! Let me see your hands! Stay at your desks! No one leaves! No one moves!"

Salespeople were in shock. There was silence in the office until the lead agent yelled, *"Where's David Diamand?!"*

I still get queasy in my gut when I recall this - I was not actually present for the raid to unfold or to hear the agent asking about my whereabouts. I usually came to work around 11 a.m. and the raid was around 8 or 9. I was told the details after by others who had been present for what unfolded.

Indeed, as I was rolling up into the office parking lot, in my convertible Porsche, top down, I noticed two things out of the ordinary. Firstly, there was a tall man with a fanny pack (holstering a gun) unknown to me standing outside the building entrance and secondly, one of my co-workers, Sylvan was walking away from the entrance toward my car in the parking lot. As he walked past, he whispered emphatically, "DOC raid!"

I put my car in gear and drove past the man standing in the front and out of the lot. As usual, I felt no need to present myself to any agents. I would just have to wait and see how Tim was going to spin this one. The man in front yelled, "Stop."

Then, knowing that Sylvan had tipped me off, he turned accusatorily toward Sylvan and snarled, "What did you tell him?!"

Apparently, he was one of the investigatory agents supervising the exit. I ignored him and drove off.

Another salesman, Ed, caught up to me in my car and seemed to be extremely concerned. He said, "All they were asking for was you, David."

My stomach fell. I drove home and found a Federal Trade Commission box of evidence waiting for me on my front yard. Inside was voluminous amounts of transcribed recordings and evidence of all the programs we had sold with Tim, plus a demand that I be present at an FTC deposition later that month. I also found that all of my bank accounts had been frozen, and I was adjured by court order not to remove any money from them. At that time, I had been expecting a paycheck for tens of thousands that would now not be coming, and the FTC had frozen over $120,000 of my cash.

I called Tim in a panic. "Tim, the office was just raided by the FTC. Everything's frozen. Agents were specifically looking for me." Then haltingly I asked, "Were we lying to our customers…?"

"We were not lying," Tim responded. "Everything you told them was true and if the clients lose their money, it's because the FTC froze the funds and didn't let the investment work."

Either what Tim was saying was true or he was simply a pathological liar until the very end. In any event, I was in extreme distress; this was nothing like the DOC raid. This was a federal matter now and I was literally terrified that the FBI was going to show up and arrest me. As it turned out the FTC only conducts civil cases so for the time being, arrest and jail were the least of my concerns. But still, there was the sum of all my fears now on full display -- gut-wrenching realization and despair. *Oh my G-d, my customers really have lost all of their money. Oh my G-d....*

I normally kept $5,000 in cash in a home safe and was just getting ready to pull more money out of the bank to replenish that, but it was not to be. I had almost no cash, living on a hill and driving a car that I could not afford to put gas into. We actually had to sell jewelry to buy baby food and diapers. It was a very scary time. I carried a lump in my throat through much of it.

I suppose this was G-d's way of making me feel how my actions had probably made lots of others feel over the years; pounding away at investors until they invested, without a look back when the money was lost, without a hard thought about how my investors might make ends meet or pay their bills or even buy food. In Hebrew we call it *midda-knegged-midda* (measure-for-measure); what you *measure* out to others gets *measured* back to you. In that moment I felt sick, and I realized that as much as this situation was terrible and how badly l felt for my clients because I was now living it, that I would never be able to sell another investment again. I made that determination right there and right then.

Yet, still under an illusion that I couldn't have done anything illegal, I contacted the criminal lawyer assigned to our case being paid for by the promoters. His name was Irv and I adjured him in the strongest terms that he had to somehow get my money back. He was astonished I would have even asked. He said, "I heard the tapes! I can't believe the things you said."

Then he admonished me, "You're not getting your money back...."

I tried to explain to him that everything was Tim; Tim gave me the scripts and I just read the scripts. He said that it was my compelling voice on tape making misrepresentations and that I would be lucky if this did not go criminal.

The day of the FTC depositions arrived, and Irv advised all of us as the group's counsel that everyone would be taking the 5th. I felt this was preposterous. In this way I would be protecting those who deserved to be prosecuted. And I would look just as guilty, which I felt I was not. I truly felt that while the risk was high, that the investments theoretically could have made money. Further, I had merely been the voice for Tim, (who continued to tell me it was real) and the promoters; and that I believed that I would literally be held harmless if I could only tell my side of the story. It was unimaginable to me that I could not explain everything I knew. Surely, the FTC must be incorrect in their assessment. The tapes just had me reading a script, the script that Tim gave me. How was I culpable for that, especially if Tim kept telling me it was all good and I believed him? And even *if* I had maintained some healthy skepticism or doubt, ultimately, I believed the evidence of the investment's viability given to me. Period.

I ended up taking the 5th but felt horrible about it. So, I fired Irv and took another attorney who I felt would better represent my interests. We asked that the FTC re-conduct the deposition so that I could fully cooperate and answer their questions. They agreed and a new date was scheduled for me to fully depose with them.

In the meantime, we had already moved out of our Woodland Hills house and into a smaller home in Westlake Village. Thank G-d I had placed all my assets like my house and cars into a Family Limited Partnership controlled by a general partnership. Neither my wife, nor my FLP were named in the restraining orders. By allowing my wife who was a 1% partner at the time to become general partner, (because my GP was unable to oppose her due to the restraining order), she was able to sell the Porsche and our home to get us some legal fees paid and some breathing room on the other side. When the FBI finally showed up at our door, we had long since moved to Westlake Village having already sold the home for exactly what I bought it for. I paid off a $540,000 jumbo mortgage loan and still had some cash for living expenses. The FTC and the FBI were incredulous and furious that they could not seize those assets, but there was nothing legally that they could do.

Still, I had major State and Federal tax liabilities that needed to be paid and I had no idea how I was going to swing that. The account that the FTC froze contained all the money due the FTB (Franchise Tax Board) and the IRS.

Every so often I went into the bank to conduct business and in one such branch I was able to scan the teller's monitor over the counter. I was able to see that the freeze put into place by the FTC had to be renewed every 90 days. I kept that fact in the back of my head.

One day, about 100 days after the initial raid freezing my account, I went into another bank branch and asked if the account in question still had a freeze on it. The teller said, "No."

"You mean I could liquidate every dime out of this account in cash, right now?" I asked incredulously.

The teller smiled and said, "Every dime. There are no restrictions on this account; however, if you want the $120,000.00 in cash, it may take about 30 minutes."

The feds had dropped the ball. Apparently, the FTC had not remembered to renew the freeze; so, as I was flirting in my head with liquidating the entire account holding my cash, I immediately *arrested* that thought and did something far more elegant. I asked the teller to liquidate only a portion of the account into bank checks to the following entities in the following amounts:

State of California Franchise Tax Board - FTB: $11,000

Federal Department of US Treasury - IRS: $29,000

I did not touch another dime in that account because while the actual bank freeze was not in force technically, there was still a federal restraining order in effect forbidding my personal use of those funds. I knew that the FTC attorneys expected that those funds were to be disgorged to the FTC should their complaint be upheld, and I also knew that I was walking a very fine line here, and I did not want to be in *overt* contempt of court.

My attorney freaked out after I told him what the bank allowed me to do. He told me that I could be in serious trouble; but I had already caused the funds to be moved and was not about to put them back, exacerbating a potential violation of court order. In the end, my own legal rationale was that I had not violated the letter of the law because I had not taken the funds for "personal use". There was a tax debt that was obligated to be paid and I was simply allowing the transfer of the money out from under control of one Government agency (FTC) to two others (FTB/IRS), having never had that money in my personal control. I held my breath and mailed the checks.

Risky business, indeed.

The FTC deposition began soon after. I spent 3 days at the FTC offices in Los Angeles answering every question truthfully; I was hoping that I would not be asked about the accounts, since I knew they had not checked on the efficacy of the R/O they had previously placed. I think it was at the end of day 3, when we were wrapping everything up that the lead FTC attorney, Monica, asked me, almost as an afterthought, a bunch of final boilerplate questions. She was already certain that all my answers would be, "No."

One of her last questions was, "Have you removed any of the money from any accounts subject to the FTC freeze?"

I simply answered, "Yes."

Monica had already moved on to the next of the final boilerplate questions she had wanted to ask when she stopped, midstream, now uncertain of how to continue.

Since she had been expecting a *"No"*, she seemed to have a bit of trouble processing my affirmative answer to her last question. She slowly walked back her focus, trying to process what I had said and the implications therefrom.

"What did you say?" She asked me.

"I said 'Yes.'"

"What, how…?" She stammered.

I explained the whole thing to her, from the moment of my entering the bank, to noting that the freeze had expired, to asking the teller to generate bank checks payable to the IRS and FTB, to my mailing them, to me not touching another dime in the account… and my lay-person legal rationale for having done such a thing.

She shrieked, "What?!"

Then Monica was suddenly speechless. She was literally white as a ghost and then she stormed out of the room. Her junior counsel followed obsequiously. My attorney followed them. I could hear his low calming voice and I could hear her screaming at him. She was clearly very upset that I had the temerity to move out of her reach what she considered FTC money. At the end she came in flustered and threatened to have me held in contempt of court, but it was a hollow threat. She knew she was beaten, already. She would never see that money back from the

IRS because it had never left the technical custody and control of the Federal Government. It was a one in a million lock.

And the judge, to the continuing dismay of the FTC and Monica, also did not see it their way. Once the FTC freeze expired, the court found no harm and no foul. In the court's opinion, I was always in compliance with the letter of the court's restraining order. The money in question was never in my personal possession and was simply transferred between federal agencies; despite the fact that the FTC argued that I would benefit personally from having my taxes paid.

In the end, without admitting to any violation of any law, and further, with an affirmative agreement from the FTC that my agreement to settle with them did *not* constitute any admission of law violation, I agreed to have all my income from all 7 programs "disgorged" and paid a fine to settle the FTC civil lawsuit. When the federal judge signed off on the income "disgorgement" I filed an amended tax return with the IRS on advice from my tax accountant that my income was now considered legally "disgorged", and therefore *all* of the taxes I had recently paid through those bank checks were now null and void. The IRS then sent me back *all* that money I had just paid in taxes, which had just been transferred legally out from under the FTC freeze, *nunc pro tunc*; a Latin term I used on my amended form that means, "retroactively to correct a previous filing."

Three years later at my criminal sentencing the federal prosecutor would bring up this *nunc pro tunc* filing to the court with the intent to bolster his crushing sentencing recommendations, even though it was legal. So, for the first time in a long time after the FTC fiasco settled, I began to breathe easier and perhaps it was all behind me now. Part of the FTC agreement called for me to liquidate certain assets to them. I had to part with diamond earrings I had gifted Shannon, an Omega watch, a Ruger Mini-14 .223 rifle, an FM High Power 9mm handgun and my "Harley" motorcycle. But after the motorcycle rolled out, I was done with the FTC.

We had been living in our Westlake rental for about a year after and I was now working at a computer systems design firm, a business partner with IBM, as legitimate as you could get. I had turned over a new leaf, having kept my resolution to never offer another investment again. But the Government could have cared less. Two FBI agents showed up at my home one day while I was at work. Shannon let them in. They had a *Target Letter* from the United States Attorney's Office that they wanted to hand deliver to me. My wife tried to defend her husband, telling them that, "He's a good man."

The FBI, however, was only interested in my cooperation in a criminal case in which I was about to be charged. How much prison time I got would depend on my cooperation and then of course pleading guilty early on; two things which I refused to do. First off, I did not feel that my actions constituted a crime. Second, I could not fathom being taken away from my young daughter and wife or having to do a day in jail; and third, I did not want to lose my position with the Sheriff's Department or be burdened with a federal felony and the lifetime discomfiture that would convey.

In life, there is the shorter long way and there is the longer short way. In other words, there is the easy way (that looks difficult) and there is the hard way (that looks easier). Had I chosen the easy way, I would have done maybe 18 months in prison (reduced to 9 months), been charged with perhaps 1 count of fraud (rather than 66 counts) and never lost my two daughters to attrition of our relationship and the ensuing parental alienation of affection inflicted on them by their caretakers in my absence. My recalcitrance in acceptance of responsibility would become a dark 6 ½ years of my life and loss of my children; tragic, with traumatic reverberations to this very day.

The *Target Letter* let me know that it was likely I would be charged with multiple felonies to include wire and mail fraud and conspiracy to commit fraud and that I would have to appear. I was not requested or ordered or required.... but *commanded* to appear to give testimony to a federal grand jury convened with the express intent of the prosecutor to indict me (and all my "co-conspirators"). In addition, I was required by court order to show up at the Boiler Room Task Force in San Diego to give handwriting and voice samples and to make myself available for possible criminal questioning in the Mark and Ira deals I had sold.

Now I had heard of the Boiler Room Task Force while working at Tim's office; and that they had made inquiries into Tim's and Mark's and Ira's operations, but I just assumed they were a bunch of senior citizens on a PTA or

AARP-type board who wrote reports about various investments targeting their age group. I foolishly thought they had the enforcement or oversight power of a school crossing guard carrying a stop sign. In actuality, the Boiler Room Task Force is an arm of the US Attorney's Office made up of full time FBI agents specializing in phone room and investment scams.

And the hits would just keep coming.

I went to San Diego with my new criminal attorney and gave my voice and handwriting samples. The agents all looked like they wanted to kick my teeth in. I was still in denial about how serious this was or how I was being perceived as the bane of everything good in the world because of the pervasiveness of my sales of those investments the Government felt were already illegal.

Then I went over to the federal courthouse to be questioned in front of the grand jury. The grand jury is a prosecutorial tool that votes whether or not to indict a defendant. All the grand jury hears is the prosecutor's theory as to an alleged crime. No defensive arguments may be mounted in a grand jury proceeding and it's so blatantly one-sided that they usually indict. It's said that a federal prosecutor can get a grand jury to indict a ham and cheese sandwich; so, I knew what would be coming down the line.

There was just one caveat: San Diego previously had no jurisdiction... until I began to pitch a certain confidential informant, who happened to be located in San Diego. The entire case hinged on the tapes I made unwittingly with the CI I had been pitching for over a year. That's it. As it turned out this entire case was over the tapes and it was my voice using Tim's scripts that essentially brought down an entire criminal enterprise.

After my testimony, the prosecutor asked my attorney if we would like to discuss the case. On the elevator up to his office, he was all smiles and jovial with me. He probably expected that I was going to make his life so much easier and simply plead out pre-trial taking my felony and a year or less in prison. But I had no intention of doing so. If there was ever a failure to see the other's perspective, it was our first meeting. The prosecutor lost all of his smiles and joviality about 30 seconds into our meeting. He told me that he would be charging me with a crime when the grand jury indicted me and I told him that I was innocent of fraud, intentional or otherwise, and that there was no way I would be able to stand in front of a judge and plead guilty to something that I had not done and/or had no intention to do. It should be mentioned that although San Diego became the charging venue, no other US prosecutor would have touched this case with a ten-foot pole. The San Diego prosecutor was hell bent on charging this case, notwithstanding.

This case was originally out of Los Angeles, but after the US Attorney's office there reviewed the case, they declined to prosecute. In their opinion there was nothing illegal to charge, however bawdy the terms of the investor's agreement or coarsely obscene the sales pitches may have been. There was no crime. I am also told that 20 years ago nobody anywhere would have thought to indict. Investors were presented with a risky program and signed to it. However, an overeager prosecutor in San Diego was making his career in telemarketing fraud and wanted this as his show case, even though the basis of charging a crime was weak to non-existent. However, where there is necessity, a crime can be created, easily.

Just look at the Mueller-Trump probe that reached far beyond its original mandate and then created new criminal offenses where none previously existed. Allegations that don't fit statute and legal theory could make a criminal out of anyone. In fact, Michael Cohen, Trump's lawyer pleaded guilty to, among other crimes, federal election finance violations *that don't exist*. If Cohen had gone to trial on those charged campaign finance "violations", he would have surely been acquitted.

So-called "hush money" payments during a presidential campaign made with personal money are not illegal, so long as there are other legitimate reasons for those payments, *in addition* to influencing a campaign. It could have been easily argued successfully that Trump had a legitimate interest in simply protecting his family and other business entities from embarrassment *in addition* to protecting his campaign from tawdry allegations of improper conduct. Hence, there was no campaign-finance violation.

But, for whatever political motives the AUSA wanted Cohen to admit to a violation that would somehow "touch" and embarrass President Trump. And in my humble opinion, Cohen admitted to it simply because if he didn't the prosecutor would have hammered him with numerous other tax fraud counts that he *did* commit and would have turned his 36-month skate in the park into a 20 year to life prison sentence.

Prosecutors literally have a federal defendant over a barrel because they have a tremendous amount of leverage at their disposal. Statute allows them to threaten a defendant with onerous amounts of prison time, decades in prison if you lose at trial... or if you simply plead guilty, mere months to a few years in prison. Most people, when facing those prospects simply plead out by taking a deal, which is one of the reasons the federal conviction rate is 98%. Less than 2% of those who get charged beat their charges in front of a federal jury.

And there is no more parole, or any meaningful good time offered in the federal system. Currently the feds only give you 15% time off your sentence for good behavior. And after 1987 if you are convicted and sentenced to life in the feds; it's actual life. Your "out date" on your confinement and committal documents is "upon death." Or you can be sentenced to effective "life" if the judge gives you a significant enough sentence. There are people, like Bernie Madoff, who do have "out dates"; but the amount of time until the release date is so long that Bernie will have long been deceased by then. Bernie Madoff was given 1,800 months or 150 years. His out date is Nov 11, 2139. Either way, if you decide to fight the prosecutor, your chances are slim that you will be acquitted. Any recalcitrance to admit guilt thereby forces the Government to prove up their case against you using time and money; in this process to do so virtually guarantees a much harsher sentence from the judge. In my case it went from 18 months to 88 months; and *could* have gone to 168 months. That's 1 ½ years to 7 ½ years to 14 years. No joke.

I wanted to give my account again before things moved any further. Clearly the AUSA did not understand the frame of mind and perspective I had while I was selling; my *mens rea* specifically was *not* to commit a crime and I had gone to a lot of trouble both emotionally and intellectually to be clear that I was not committing crimes while I sold… and if I could only convince him of this, he would see the error of his charging ways and dismiss me from further prosecution. The meeting I was after to accomplish this is called, "Queen for the Day." The defendant gets an opportunity to debrief with the prosecutor and attempts to explain evidence, convincing him not to indict or prosecute; and the prosecutor typically agrees that none of what the defendant says will be used against him at trial.

On the day I met with the federal prosecutor again, he was ready for me. He had his assistant counsels in the room, along with the two FBI agents who had shown up at my house, the Postal Inspector, and an IRS agent from the CID (criminal investigative division) who was conspicuously reviewing my last year ending tax returns.

I asked my attorney, "Is this a tax audit?"

"It's much worse," he replied sardonically. It was almost funny how he responded. Almost.

The meeting went on for over 2 hours. And there would be zero forward movement. I doggedly held onto my defensive position, which the prosecutor's team kept trying to shred. The prosecutor held onto his theory of the crime and had each of the agents there to try to help him bolster his case, which I kept trying to shred. In the end, they did not buy that I was an innocent salesperson who did not know that the investments could not work... and I did not buy their theory that the investments could not work or that what I had been saying to customers qualified as fraud. Further complicating things, is that while State courts allow defendants to plead out *nolo contendre*, Latin for: *a plea by which a defendant in a criminal prosecution accepts conviction as though a guilty plea had been entered but does not specifically admit guilt*; federal criminal court does not recognize such a plea. Federal court requires that a defendant specifically admit actual guilt to each of the charges and there was no way I could bring myself to do that. I did not intentionally or wantonly commit a crime. Therefore, I could not accept an agreement that specifically required I admit as such. Stalemate.

I returned to my life treasuring every minute with my family but carrying a terrible burden. I couldn't bear to think about being separated from my child, so I buried my head as to how the feds viewed my culpability and the punishment on the other end of the inevitability of a criminal indictment. Still, I knew enough to know that I would have to end my tenure with the Sheriff's Department soon, for a federal indictment was certain. I needed to resign my position before I would have to be arrested. It would have been very embarrassing to have been working and have the FBI or my own department handcuff me on duty or in uniform. So, after one last rescue, I resigned.

In fact, as fortune would have it, my very last affiliated rescue with the Team was off Pacific Coast Highway on a canyon road, where an elderly lawyer afflicted with early onset dementia had been horseback riding. His horse had returned to the stables, but he had not. So, after dark, our Team was activated, and we staged at the bottom of the hill. We got our assignments.

My Bash Team made it to the top of the dirt hill in about an hour and began our hike down. As we descended 1/3 the way down the hill, I noticed that nobody was searching over the side well. If this man had been thrown by his horse, then likely he would have gone over the side.

Sure enough, as I shone my light down about 60 feet away and under a large Manzanita tree, pinned under its roots, lay the elderly lawyer. His position suggested he was indeed thrown from the horse and slid down the steep embankment under the roots. The steep grade of the hill from which he was pinned prevented him from freeing himself. It was a life and death find! I called it in on my radio:

"Robert 22, I got him." (My Team designation was 100R22.)

"Are you sure?" came the reply.

"I have him," I radioed back.

By that time, I was over the side and next to him taking vitals. Another Team member quickly slid next to me and started cutting him out of the root system he was lodged into. We got him out and he was transported to the hospital.

Despite the approbation, "Nice job Dave..." by my sergeant at the end of the rescue or the numerous commendations I had earned in my 7 years on the Team, that lawyer rescue would be my last "caper" with the Sheriff's Department.

And with that last rescue in the bag, I simply retired and waited for the hammer to drop. It took more than a year for the FBI to finally show up at my door at 6 a.m., demand entry with guns drawn and take me into custody.

In my time with the Sheriff's Department, I've risked my own life in profound ways to save the lives of civilians *and* other law enforcement personnel. I've assisted in reuniting families, recovering loved ones and contributing to overall community peace and safety. I've had to tackle fleeing suspects and bagged more dead bodies than I care to count; but I have to say working LA County Sheriff's was one of the most rewarding endeavors I have ever taken on. And I miss it.

We moved from Westlake Village to the San Fernando Valley seeking to downsize our expenses, to Chatsworth, finding a 3-bedroom home with a huge backyard for $1,200 per month rent. I was at work one day when my previous Westlake landlord called me. She said someone from the Federal Trade Commission had called her, telling her some crazy story that, "'An arrest team was currently outside of your previous rental and they were looking to serve a criminal complaint and take you into custody… and where's David Diamand?'"

The house stood vacant, and they did not have a forwarding address to be able to serve their arrest warrant. She said that she did not know where I was and then she told me that the call seemed fishy because she knew I was in law enforcement and had always paid rent on time; and while she would not share any information with the caller, she also wanted to let me know. I thanked her and hung up.

I called my attorney and he said that there was indeed a warrant issued for my arrest. Apparently, the FTC was still very upset with me for clearing a significant portion of my account and paying my taxes out from under their expired freeze; so, they decided to lodge a misdemeanor criminal complaint with the City Attorney for telemarketing without being registered with the State Attorney General. Remember that Tim had sworn to me that he had registered us? Well, he lied. And I was now the one to be held criminally liable. The FTC filed their complaint on the last day before the statute of limitations would expire.

I contacted the arresting agency, LAPD and spoke to the lead detective. He told me I could turn myself in and bail out the same day, for $15,000. Now if that seems a bit excessive for an unintentional white-collar infraction, it is. When you consider domestic-violence defendants bail out for $5,000, you get the idea. The FTC was really upset with me.

I borrowed $15,000 from my boss and showed up at the LAPD Van Nuys location. I met the detective. Instead of causing me embarrassment by handcuffing me, he asked me to place my hands in my front pockets and then he escorted me into a dungeon of a jail. He knew I was bailing out, so he decided to sit with me in the jail while they processed my paperwork.

He turned to me in all sincerity and said that his team was also part of the FTC/FBI task force investigating this case and he'd seen all the evidence that they had against me and told me that it was going to go criminal federally. He advised me charges would be coming and that it would be best if I pleaded out rather than fight the criminal case. I was in denial as to the awfulness or seriousness of what he was telling me, so I smiled and thanked him; smugly thinking that perspective and context was everything and somehow, I would be able to convince a federal prosecutor or federal jury that I was simply a tool in the hand of the real criminals and just doing my job without malice. He nodded and left me alone... until I bailed out. All in all, I was in jail for an hour.

On the misdemeanor "crime" of selling without being registered, I pleaded guilty to a business and professions code 17511.8 unregistered telephone sales violation; paid a fine and served 2-years-probation. I applied for and received a subsequent dismissal of the charge under 1203.4 PC, which allows a defendant to ask a judge to remove the misdemeanor conviction from one's record as if you never committed the crime in the first place. Case dismissed (after the fact). While largely a formality, it did feel good to have it off my record.

My daughter turned 3 and now that I wasn't so focused on the FTC (because that was finally over) or the AUSA because there was nothing I could do about it, my attention turned toward my family and specifically what I wanted to start infusing my daughter with in terms of life values. I hadn't thought of it much until then, but I thought I might like to return a bit to my Jewish roots and give her some of the original Jewish value system with which I was familiar; and not knowing any better, I started taking her to a Conservative Jewish synagogue.

In Jewish thought, it's not the parents who save their children, but the children who save their parents (Midrash Tanchuma), and my three-year-old was about to save her father.

I was about to get the wakeup call of my life, simply because I took my daughter to a Jewish synagogue.

Chapter 5

Coming Home

"Your destiny is tied to the destiny of those shattered things that await your repair."
- Anonymous

Sitting in synagogue on Shabbos morning with my 3-year-old, still not understanding what the point was, I opened a siddur (prayer book) and leafed through some of the Sabbath day prayer service. I kept hearing my friend, Rabbi Tovia Singer's voice, in my head. He used to say, "Everyone has an opinion. But who cares what Tovia has to say?! What does G-d have to say....?"

I noticed that most of the siddur was comprised of psalms and one psalm in particular (chapter 18) caught my attention, much for what it said and what it didn't say: King David is speaking to G-d, about how G-d, *alone*, saves; He rescues from hell without help, without intermediary, without needing any redefinition as to the very nature of One G-d. In the same psalm, David extols his being rewarded for his righteousness based on the cleanliness of his own hands; that he kept himself from sin, that he could be righteous, and that G-d "delighted" in David. David being a type of every Jew, describes how he kept all of G-d's ways, His statutes (*mishpotov*–rational laws) and ordinances (*chuksav*–supra-rational laws). "You, G-d lighten my darkness... As for G-d, His way is perfect...."

Then in Psalm 19 David writes: ".... The law of the L-rd is perfect, *restoring the soul...* the precepts of the L-rd are right, *rejoicing the heart*, the commandment of the L-rd is pure, *enlightening the eyes*... More to be desired are they than much fine gold, sweeter than honey and the honeycomb... Who can discern his errors? You (G-d) will clear me of hidden faults... presumptuous sins; then I will be faultless... clear from transgression...."

This did not comport with the Christian concept at all. I began to feel that the Jewish faith, my birth faith, was already "perfect", and I needed nothing more for spiritual fulfillment or perfection than simply to return to my Jewish Source.

Then in Ezekiel 18: "The soul [alone] that sins will die, *the son shall not bear the iniquity of the father*. But if the wicked turn from all his sins that he has committed, and keep all My statutes, and do that which is lawful and right, he shall surely live, he shall not die. None of his transgressions that he has committed shall be remembered against him; for his righteousness that he has done he shall live."

No blood and no Christian savior required here.

But I was told that keeping the Torah was too difficult, except that that wasn't true either:

Deuteronomy 30: "If you will listen to the voice of the L-rd your G-d, to keep His commandments and His statutes which are written in this book of the law; if you turn unto the L-rd your G-d with all your heart, and with all your soul. *For this commandment which I command you this day, it is not too hard for you...* But the word is very close to you, in your mouth, and in your heart, that you may do it."

This is what G-d says. It's basic Hebrew bible 101 in context and it makes all the difference. Here the Torah of G-d is perfect; it restores a person; it's doable and desirable *and salvational*. Not only am I required to keep it, but G-d says that I can easily keep it. (It's not in the heavens i.e., beyond my ability.) And that in keeping it lies my intimate relationship with G-d; that it's sweeter than any material thing; that it's perfect and restores my soul; and that I can save myself from my own sins. And further that any wicked person can save himself simply by turning from his sin; and by keeping G-d's commandments he is restored, and his sins are forgotten. Clear.

But what about the idea of blood atonement? Nowhere does it say you need blood to return to G-d to make full atonement. Kosher animal and bird blood (*not human*) sacrifices were *tentative...* and even when available, were *not an exclusive means* of divine service; by no means the only way to make atonement and generally *not for intentional sin*. In the narrow channel when a blood sacrifice might apply for *unintentional sins*, so then G-d gave a very detailed description of how to bring it in Leviticus. But even when a blood sacrifice was still an option; when the sin qualified and the Temple was in existence, *even then*, blood was not literally required to qualify for the efficacy of a blood sacrifice. Flour also worked just fine. See Leviticus 5:14. If someone was so poor that he couldn't afford a lamb or a goat... or birds, he could bring flour. No blood. Same sin atonement!

Note that Ezekiel's formula above clearly does not refer to blood in order to be fully restored to G-d and forgiven of all sin. Even without blood *there is full forgiveness*!

Moses on Mount Sinai achieved forgiveness for the Jewish people without blood, simply with words: "Pardon, I pray of You, the sin of this people... And the L-rd said, 'I have pardoned *according to your word.*'" (Numbers 14:19-20)

Further, Daniel continued as a prophet, even in Persian exile, when the Temple was destroyed. Daniel was not offering any sacrifices. A clear sign that you cannot be a prophet is if you have sins that have not been forgiven. But with no blood atonement sacrificial system what could he do? He did what Solomon and Ezekiel adjured. He returned to G-d like Jews have always returned to G-d without the need of blood: "And when Daniel... went into his house -- now his windows were open in his upper chamber toward Jerusalem -- and he kneeled upon his knees three times a day, and prayed, and gave thanks before his God, as he did aforetime." (Daniel 6:10)

King Solomon knew there would come a time when the Temple would no longer offer efficacy for atonement and to forestall any thought that atonement or forgiveness of sins was in any way contingent on the animal or bird sacrificial system, he said this:

"If they sin against You -- for there is no man that does not sin -- and You be angry with them... and they turn back, and make supplication unto You... saying: 'We have sinned, and have done iniquitously, we have dealt wickedly'; if they return unto You with all their heart and with all their soul... and pray unto You... then hear You their prayer and their supplication in heaven Your dwelling-place, and maintain their cause; and forgive Your people who have sinned against You, and all their transgressions wherein they have transgressed against You." (1 Kings 8: 46-50)

Forgiveness is bloodless. Clear.

And Hosea makes it clear beyond any doubt that we are now to take our words (our prayers) and return to G-d, for our prayers take the place of blood:

"Return, O Israel, unto the L-rd your G-d; for you have stumbled in your iniquity. Take with you, *words*, and return unto the L-rd; say unto Him: 'Forgive all iniquity, and accept that which is good; so, will we render for bullocks the offering of our lips.'" (Hosea 14: 2 -3)

Even the term, "New Testament" misunderstands the Hebrew text from which it was lifted. Jeremiah 31 speaks of "a *bris chadasha*", literally, "a new covenant/promise", which Christianity retranslates / mistranslates into, "The New Testament". But if one reads in context, G-d's new promise does not negate His older promises or His Laws. The new promise describes Israel *keeping* all the laws G-d gave at Sinai and knowing G-d *through* His laws!

Of course, after I learned the foregoing, the next two prophets describing messianic times needed no further explanation:

"Thus, saith the L-rd of hosts: In those days it shall come to pass, that ten men [non-Jews] shall take hold, out of all the languages of the nations, shall even take hold of the skirt of him that is a Jew, saying: We will go with you, for we have heard that G-d is with you (Torah observant Jews)." (Zechariah 8:23)

"O L-rd, my strength, and my stronghold, and my refuge, in the day of affliction, unto You shall the [non-Jewish] nations come from the ends of the earth and shall say: 'Our fathers have inherited naught but lies, vanity and things wherein there is no profit. Shall a man make unto himself gods, and they are no gods?" (Jeremiah 16:19 - 20)

When I read all of that and thought about it, I realized l'havdil (though there is a major distinction) like Eisav, (Esau) I had sold my birthright for a bowl of bean soup. I felt physically ill and repulsed, like I had spiders crawling all over me and I had to get out of the non-Jewish life I had been living.

I read Maccoby's book referenced above, *The Mythmaker*, and everything fell away and into place at the same time. I could no longer be married to a non-Jew, could no longer tolerate a non-Jewish household and told my wife simply that, "I'm out. I don't subscribe to your belief set and I can't embrace your religion any longer. I want to return to my people and the faith of my fathers. I want to live as a Jew."

In the lead up to this epiphany, I still felt unfulfilled going to a Conservative Synagogue. It was still the same type of watered-down unauthentic practice I was used to that made me not want to practice my faith from my youth. I asked someone if there was anything else besides this kind of practice. I was told that I should try Chabad. Chabad is an Orthodox Jewish line of Chassidic Judaism, considered "Ultra-Orthodox" in practice but very welcoming to those who aren't (yet) observant. I walked into a Chabad shul (synagogue) in Northridge, CA and that was it. I knew exactly who I was and felt something real and vital and warm. I felt my soul rise as authentic Judaism began to open up within me profoundly. It is no exaggeration to say that I became fully observant within 90 days of walking into that Chabad shul.

From morning services, I befriended an elderly Jew who had lost the function of his kidneys and three times a week he had to go to a dialysis center to have his blood cleaned. This process took about 3 hours per treatment, *3 times a week*! I used to sit with him, and his pain had great impact on me. I wished I had a way to alleviate his suffering. Dialysis, I would later learn, is a last-ditch stopgap. It takes only some of the toxin out of the blood, and eventually after 5, at most 10, years the patient dies from toxicity. As soon as you leave dialysis you are exhausted, and your day is already ruined. The next day you are already building up toxins again and so by the next day you have to go back to dialysis. It's no way to live. But all I knew to do was to sit with my friend.

Shannon tolerated all of this for a while. She loved me and did not want to lose our marriage. She actually purchased my first kosher mezuzah for me. She even went searching for me on Shabbos in her car when I would walk the 6 miles to shul and 6 miles back to bring me water. She was sweet about it. But I was impatient and still feeling icky from the realization of having spent years being subject to a foreign religion. I was not the easiest to tolerate at the time.

The closest thing I can point to is the visceral feeling of disgust after wading into a lake full of leeches and realizing that some of them are still attached to you as you emerge. You act like a crazy person making all kinds of wild gestures trying to get them off you and if people are nearby, they might get hit or think you're insane; but all in an effort to remove the filth you have been steeped in. Anyway, as a metaphor for what I was feeling spiritually, my disgust was coming out in actuality. I was not always kind in this process of divesting myself from what I previously embraced. And I feel remorse for that.

I asked Shannon to come *with* me, to convert to Judaism; I shared all that I had learned and even brought her to Jewish events and Shabbos meals and services at a local Chabad. As a last ditch I asked her to attend an anti-missionary 3-day conference to learn in-depth why Jews never accepted the Christian message. Of course, I was motivated not to have to divorce her. I loved her. I had a daughter with her, and we had a life. If only she could embrace me on my terms. If only. But that would require a complete repudiation of her birth religion, her whole life and her friends and her family's belief set, all of her holidays and every warm emotion connected with her faith, in addition to every bit of bible she understood (wrongly, but sincerely) from a Christological perspective. In short, it would short-circuit her world, her being, her very existence. The Jewish faith does not go out looking for converts, but I was emotionally compelled and felt that in this case I would try to prevail upon Shannon to convert – maybe there was a reason she married me; maybe there was a Jewish spark inside of her. Maybe.

In the end she could not, and I could not really expect her to. Even though I had unwittingly and ignorantly betrayed who I was, she would not betray who she was. I had embraced her on her terms and here I was flipping the script on her; and what I was asking her to do was very unfair. Still, I persisted in asking her to leave her way of life and join mine, if only that we could stay married, until one day she finally had had enough. She came apart and all niceties were gone. She said (exact quote), "I don't even like Jews. Why would I want to be one?"

We divorced shortly thereafter. She took our daughter and left. I went and enrolled myself in a *yeshiva* for men who have returned to their faith in Morristown, NJ called Tiferes Borchorim and got down to learning and living as a *frum* (religious) Orthodox Jew.

When I returned from New Jersey, Shannon was not intent on sharing our daughter with me; and she forced me to court and into a child custody evaluation that came out very favorably in my favor until even her own attorney told her that the judge was going to award 50/50 custody and visitation. Being denied access to my daughter was very painful and financially costly, but for the time being that was over and parenting her, and everything that went along with parenting, was the highlight in my life. I loved my daughter then. And I will always love her.

With our legal separation and upcoming civil-divorce a matter of weeks away, I began to reach out on Jewish websites looking to re-marry. I found what I thought I was looking for in an Orthodox Convert to Judaism, a medical doctor named Miriam, just graduating from medical school in Louisiana. We met and we liked each other, though she always seems to have one ailment or another or knee pain, requiring prescription pain killers. It needs to be noted that I had zero intimacy with addiction or the signs of addiction so what came next ended up being a huge shock for me.

Before one of her visits, Shannon was made aware that Miriam was to be my wife and our daughter's future stepmother; Shannon had a meltdown. She asked me to come over to her home and when I arrived alone, she started to cry. She asked me not to marry Miriam and that I should come back to her, that she would do anything for me, even live as a Jew. I told her that it was too late and that I was sorry and already committed to another woman. I did not show Shannon the kind of compassion I wished I would have. But that relationship was over.

Miriam agreed to move out to California so we could be married and start a family. We had a baby girl together and she decided to do her residency at UCLA, but for one reason or another that residency never materialized. What did materialize was lots of prescription pill usage to the point that Miriam was non-functional and completely stoned. She was using her medical doctor's credentials to self-prescribe and self-medicate and when that wasn't enough, she would doctor shop (I once counted over 50 separate doctors she was getting narcotics from) and forge prescriptions.

Miriam was also getting erratic. One day she and I had an argument. In a gesture of "displeasure" she shattered a drinking glass in the sink and large shards flew everywhere. Unfortunately, I picked one of them up and showed her in my open hand that that could have cut my daughter's foot had she walked on it. Miriam grabbed the large shard out of my palm and violently began to cut at her neck by the carotid artery with the piece of glass.

I was in shock but had the presence to launch myself at her and grab her hand with all my force to prevent her from cutting a second time. After a brief struggle, she collapsed on the floor and I called 911. Miriam had just tried to kill herself in front of me, my 4-year-old daughter and our infant daughter. Police and Fire came. Miriam was handcuffed to the gurney and taken to a local emergency room locked ward where, after they stitched up her neck, they placed an involuntary 5150 psych-hold on her. I kept a copy of the admit form, which stated that she was a danger to herself. On that form she also signed a written statement to the nurse, which read, "*You (Miriam) made a suicide attempt after you had an argument with your husband. You (Miriam) took a sharp piece of glass and cut your neck by the carotid artery.*"

Aside of the drug use and suicidal ideation there were hoarding issues and she did not seem that sincere about her Jewish conversion. Miriam and I both agreed that she should take some time in Louisiana with her family to try to heal. So, after she stabilized, I placed her on a plane with my daughter, hoping that her mother would be able to help supervise and monitor Miriam with our baby.

In this same period of time, roughly a year had gone by with no word from federal prosecutors. I reached out through my attorney to let them know that if an indictment came down that I would like to be able to turn myself in, rather than be arrested needlessly.

The prosecutor responded that I would not need to turn myself in. He said to my attorney, "Oh, he'll know when he's been indicted…."

I can almost imagine hearing the prosecutor chuckle as he said it. So, I would just have to prepare for the knock I knew would be coming sometime soon.

That knock came a few days after Miriam went back to her parents' home to continue her recovery. I was in the bathroom at 6 a.m. and my cell phone rang. On the line was Special Agent Goldman. He told me that he was currently outside my front door and that I should open it up immediately.

I went to my front door and opened it. Some standing and some crouching on my porch, there were 5 special agents in street clothes wearing bulletproof vests and FBI raid jackets, and all of them were aiming weapons, 3 handguns and 2 shotguns at my head. I had obviously been indicted and the FBI was there to serve the warrant and take me into custody. I spread my arms and backed away from the front door slowly. Perhaps they were more aggressive because they knew I had weapons, (which they didn't know were in a locked gun vault at the time). They rushed me and had me handcuffed in about 5 seconds. They did a "perp" walk with me in front of my neighbors and then off to the Los Angeles FBI substation in the literal shadow of the FTC federal building, for additional processing. I was shackled to a bench and offered a Pepsi.

Then the agents took me downtown to the federal courthouse for my initial arraignment in front of a magistrate. Before the arraignment I was locked up in what's called Marshals' pre-trial unit where I would be evaluated by a Pre-Sentencing Officer as to my suitability in the Government's estimation for bail. The officer said that he would be recommending no bail for me. I was now sincerely worried. Plus, I was sitting with a kid no older than 17 who was in for bank robbery. He told me he was expecting to get 17 years for robbing that bank. The kid would be 34 when he left prison. The incarceration numbers being thrown around were mind-boggling. I was in a whole new terrible no-good world and I would have to learn how to adapt.

When I was finally brought up to the magistrate, the charges ranged from wire fraud to mail fraud to money laundering. The case would have to be transferred to San Diego, but in the meantime, I was offered bail in the amount of $100,000, which I did not have. I was then taken to MDC – LA Metropolitan Detention Center, which is a huge concrete high-rise overlooking the 101 freeway. I spent the night in a bunk bed rack under a drug dealer in for distribution of *MDMA/Ecstacy*.

The next morning, I was transferred to the San Bernadino Sheriff's jail for holding pending bail and trial. The

Sheriff's Dept. offered the feds a contract to house their inmates. And the feds typically use 3rd party contractors to house and transport federal inmates. The transfer took place in a very off manner. I was hand shacked to two other inmates' waists as I and my new friends tried to walk together without falling over. It was not a comfortable walk or ride. When we arrived, it was quite a difference from the MDC. This was a real jail with real bars and real deputies who basically took no guff from anyone. I watched a deputy lay out a guy who was getting froggy with him. Once secure inside the jail, we were all un-cuffed, lined up on the wall and then ordered to disrobe until fully naked, turned around, bent over, squatted and ordered to cough. Then we were issued orange-colored pants and shirts and placed in a holding cell, pending an intake evaluation that would determine our housing unit.

I was placed into a general population tank with about 60 other inmates. The bunk bed racks were 3 men high, and my rack was right next to the open bathrooms and showers where men got to relieve themselves and shower without any privacy. There was a day room with a tv and a bank of phones.

I was really not doing so well. I called my mom and she to her great credit said that she would help make my bail. The next day I was transported to San Diego and had a new arraignment and then was given a bail figure of about $140,000. My mother made the arrangements to be my bail guarantor in signing over her home and jewelry and convincing my brother and father to each contribute

$10,000 apiece. However, the processing would take time; about three weeks' time.

So back in San Bernadino, I settled in until one day a fight broke out and I, having never been in jail before, did not know that alerting staff is generally disfavored by other inmates. It makes you a "rat"; and rats get killed. Of course, I alerted staff and they came and broke up the fight. But in the process, they tossed the entire dorm, doing an exhaustive search; and in finding a lot of contraband, confiscated it. When we were all returned to our dorm, I was fingered as the one who had tipped off the cops and I was surrounded by about 15 – 20 large, tattooed, and angry inmates. I thought to myself, *Wow, so this is where I am going to die.* There were, however, a number of inmates who surrounded me to defend me; and were squared off ready to fight. It was a real standoff that was not going to end well I could tell. In the end I called for staff and went into protective custody rather than risk getting my head smashed in my sleep or stabbed or worse.

I was given my own very cramped one-man cell on a tier of other protective custody inmates. Many of them were either "informants" (like me); or child molesters, none of whom would have made it 10 minutes in general population. Child molesters produce a very violent reaction from most inmates, and some suffer serious violence. It is my understanding that there are so many of these types of people that entire federal prisons are now devoted to housing them and their numbers have swelled so much that no longer are they in the minority in prisons.

We got to see the sun 3 times a week for an hour. We could walk around in a fenced area under supervision of a guard tower armed with shotguns. Along the fence line were nail clippers so you could "groom" yourself. Piles of nail clipping from years of use stood nearby. In the middle of the outdoor area were other one-man cells where inmates who were either too dangerous or too at risk for violence were placed so they could at least see the sky and walk 4 feet back and forth. But that's it.

Then there was the (kosher) food issue. They did *not* provide kosher food. So, I basically starved for three weeks. I was able to get some kosher candy from the commissary and other inmates traded me or simply gave me breakfast cereal that had a kosher certification. I was nervous and hungry with no idea when I would emerge and this saddened and stressed me.

I wrote to the head commander of the jail. The commander advised me that I would have to get the chaplain to authorize kosher fare. I wrote to the chaplain and firstly, he sent me missionizing literature about accepting Christianity; and then showed up in front of my cell door and told me that the kitchen was considered "kosher style" and that all I had to do was remove the ham from the egg and cheese muffins and that that should solve my issue. I told him *nicely* that unfortunately he was incorrect on both fronts and that I was literally starving. There was nothing else he could or would do for me.

It was a lonely, frustrating, and dark time. I came to feel like I was buried alive and would never emerge. I had flashbacks of when I was a kid in Pennsylvania. There were drainage culverts under the road and one day my friends and I tried to crawl through, but what was a large entry way began to get narrower as smaller and smaller concrete piping was inserted and then I got stuck and could not move forward. I could feel the trucks rumbling overhead and thought that I would die there. Eventually I was able to wiggle my body just enough to be able to back my way out. Being entombed alive was terrifying and here I was again, physically, mentally, emotionally entombed alive, but the worst thing was losing contact with my children.

Finally, I made bail and was released and would stay free for the next 9 months... until a federal judge had my bail revoked, and then increased to $500,000 effectively keeping me *in* jail until my release 6 years later.

Before I was able to leave federal holding, I had to have my other weapons turned into LAPD for destruction. There was the police Berretta 92FS and my backup weapon, a Smith and Wesson 6906. I was unhappy to see them go, but happier to be out of jail. Even the police detectives lamented about what a shame it was when they had to take my weapons to have them destroyed. When I returned to my home, it took a few weeks until I was able to regain my custody and visitation of my older daughter. I missed her so much! The court was initially reticent to award me 50% as before because Shannon made sure to tell the court that I had been arrested in a federal fraud case and was out on bail. I simply responded that in the US, a defendant is presumed innocent until convicted in a court of law. Since I had not been convicted of anything and planned to fight the case, my presumption was that of innocence and the Superior Court found that to be a compelling argument and custody and visits were restored.

I realized then that my Jewish wife was not coming back, but instead she was going to start her medical internship in Arizona at Maricopa Regional Hospital – She would be living in an apartment near work alone with our baby daughter. In the interim of my incarceration her parents had set her up with furniture and a place to live.

I immediately filed for divorce and full custody of our daughter. My wife was a drug abuser and I believed would place our daughter at risk.

Superior Court of Los Angeles had jurisdiction and the judge was just elevated to her position; so, she was very new to the bench. We detailed with proof the hoarding, the nodding into the soup behavior, the narcotics she was abusing, the number of doctors she was seeking and the suicide attempt and 5150 hold. The female judge was a pretty blonde. My wife was also a pretty blue-eyed tall blonde who sat up straight and batted her eyes at the judge and at the end of the day the court allowed my wife to keep our daughter and simply bring her back to Los Angeles for weekend visits twice a month.

Later, on the phone, in a moment of honestly, Miriam told me that she easily manipulated the judge by appearing very straight and that she and the judge shared a bunch of "Oprah moments" with each other. In the end, despite an overwhelming showing, the judge could not believe that the blonde haired blue-eyed beautiful medical doctor, who had been awarded a residency in Arizona, sitting in front of her was the psychological and drug addicted wreck that my attorney made her out to be. Of course, Miriam had lots of practice as a functioning addict and simply cleaned up for her trial date.

The judge later reversed herself when she found that Miriam had been arrested for parental neglect while being stoned on the street with my daughter in tow, and that my daughter was taken into Arizona CPS protective custody and later released to me. Miriam later lost her hospital residency and even later than that was re-arrested for prescription fraud. At the end of the day, I had full physical and legal custody of my younger daughter and 50% visitation and legal custody of my older daughter. That was just fine with me.

I am certain that I have attracted women in my life who somehow matched some of the dysfunctional familial affect shown to me growing up; and the reason for this seems clear enough. Given an emotionally deficient and inexplicable childhood, never being able to get to the truth or set things straight, feeling amoral and immoral, and feeling a general *"ick"* (like spiders running across my skin), I sought out women who closely matched that and then I somehow tried to fix or set them right as some sort of justification for my childhood, after the fact. Kids never stop trying to make sense of their upbringing and interactions with their parents. The dissonance between what should have been healthy and what wasn't produced a drive in me as an adult to find it and fix it, and all would be ok in the world again; a childhood fantasy lived in an adult reality.

Along with all the previous women in my life that I could not change or "set right", Miriam was so definably sick that it was obvious that I would never be able to make sense of her affect or ever fix her.

Even though I was now caring for my year-old baby full-time and for my 4-year-old 50% of the time, my custody was tenuous. The guarantor of my bail bond insisted that I meet financial obligations and other conditions for my bail to remain in force, which I was unable to meet; and because of this, I was in serious jeopardy of having bail revoked, going *back* to jail and losing my children.

A bail conference was called in front of a federal judge. On the day of the bail conference, my 1-year-old was in the care of a friend and my 4-year-old was in her preschool.

Now real reasons for exonerating bail are for issues of public safety or flight risk, and nothing short of further criminal activity or absconding should ever justify ripping someone away from their own children. My bail guarantor knowing my situation, persisted with impossible demands and then made a false allegation, with no foundation and no basis, that I would likely flee… to Israel.

Boom.

The judge was simply going to exonerate my bond and allow me to repost with someone else, no problem; but an allegation that I was somehow an international flight risk to Israel was a monstrous and catastrophic move.

And that was it. The judge was also a Jew. Here I was, a visibly Jewish defendant in a *yarmulke* in federal court and my own personal guarantor, out of nowhere, had just averred to the judge that I was a flight risk. The judge did not allow me to repost the $140,000 bond that I had available from other family members. He *increased* my bail to $500,000. I went directly to jail that day and did not see my daughters again for another 5 years.

That night, in handcuffs, I entered MCC- SD (Metropolitan Correction Center – San Diego), a high-rise maximum-security federal detention center, where I would spend the next 14 months of my life. When I think back on this painful period of losing my freedom and my children, I sometimes cry; but I don't bear any grudges. I recognize that everything is from G-d. There is a beautiful biblical story that captures this. Everyone is familiar with the narrative of Joseph being betrayed by his brothers, thrown into a pit, and then sold into slavery, ultimately finding himself falsely accused of a crime and thrown into an Egyptian dungeon. Many years later he was elevated to the most powerful position in Egypt, second only to Pharaoh. He ended up saving the world from starvation, including the lives of the brothers who betrayed him. When Joseph's father passed away the brothers again begged Joseph's forgiveness for their previous conduct; they were still concerned that he would take revenge for their awful act of betrayal so many years earlier. He did no such thing. He said to his brothers, "Fear not, for am I in the place of G-d? And as for you, you meant evil against me; but G-d meant it for the good." (Genesis 50:19-20)

"You meant evil against me, but G-d meant it for the good."

Now I am no Joseph, but I know that if my bail had not been pulled and my entire life had not blown up along with those of my daughters, I might have gone to trial and been acquitted.... *or* been convicted and served a decade more time. That act of pulling bail may have actually saved my life. I also know that if I did not go to jail and serve the exact lengthy sentence of 6 ½ actual years in prison, I would not have learned that I could donate my kidney. I would not have been in the right place or right time to have re-married. I would not now be a new father to another two children, a daughter and now a son. Those little lives would not have come into the world (G-d forbid) had bail not been revoked and had I not done every single day in prison that I did. Sometimes the greatest gifts come in the darkest packages. It just takes time to unwrap them.

Metropolitan Correction Center – San Diego (MCC-SD)

MCC-SD is a federal Bureau of Prisons (BOP) holding facility. At 23 stories, this stone and steel fortress can house up to 1,300 inmates. The upper stories are for the "high power" or more dangerous, "sophisticated" higher profile characters; though I was housed with serial murderers and drug dealers and gang members in my low-profile housing on the 7th floor. 7th floor is where most inmates are housed pre-trial, pre-conviction. It's a large, rambling and impossibly loud floor that can sleep 200 inmates at a time. There are 4 wings that sleep 50 inmates each in bunk beds called "racks" with bathrooms and phones, an upstairs and downstairs all attached to the main floor with tables and stool seats for meals; and interestingly enough, an unused pool table at the center. Apparently, some genius figured out that pool balls and cues could be used as deadly weapons and started swinging and throwing on guards and other inmates; and since no one in administration thought that might be of concern *before* introducing the pool tables to each of the housing floors, shortly after placing them, the BOP removed the cues and balls, but left the tables.

Staff on the floor consisted of one BOP guard for 199 inmates. If the number went to 200, a 2nd guard was added. The guard could be a male or a female and aside of keys, one set of handcuffs and a radio, there was no other protection afforded. With no cameras on the floor or floor mounted panic buttons, the guards' only connection to help if needed was a phone in the office and a personal panic button on the radio they carried on their person. 199 inmates to one guard is no joke, but somehow most of the time it worked. Fights were mainly between inmates; and floor guards were essentially babysitters and reporting agents. If anyone ever flew off the handle, one push of a guard's panic button or a phone call would bring a swarm of staff crashing onto the floor from other parts of the institution. If things really got bad, guards were authorized to throw flash bang grenades, and use batons followed up with shotguns. New criminal charges could be filed after any kind of melee. And everybody knew it. Staff controlled not only distribution of water and food, but also the opiate of the masses, the televisions. As silly as that sounds, nobody wanted to lose television privileges. Fighting with staff was a losing proposition, which is why only one guard was needed to supervise so many inmates.

With 200 men in a relatively small, confined and tiled space with no noise dampeners, the chatter level was unbearable. Add to that the televisions, which were usually turned up to the highest volume to compete with the ambient inmate noise, and it could drive someone insane. I had come to hell and found that in hell they also play dominos and watch Jerry Springer. After a while everything just sort of numbs out and nothing affects you any longer. The insanity of federal lock up just becomes one unfunny running joke after another.

After a few days of being at MCC-SD, I was fortunate enough to be given kosher meals and was even able to receive *Cholov Yisroel* (a higher level of kosher supervision) dairy. And my kosher diet called, "common fare", was delivered in separate containers from the regular meals and was prepared in a separate kitchen. It consisted mostly of raw vegetables, cans of sardines and mackerel and pouches of peanut butter. Hot meals came in separate double sealed and certified containers but were many times inedible. It was a hard diet to stomach, but I had little other choice. With no money coming in for commissary, I could at least eat to survive. It was a definite big step-up from San Bernadino county jail.

I was released into the general population housing unit made up mostly of Mexican nationals on drug and border violations. There were Russian nationals as well; in fact, an entire crew from a Russian naval vessel being held for transporting tons of cocaine through international waters. They were eventually sent back to Russia in some sort of diplomatic exchange to avoid embarrassing Russia. There were black Crip and Blood gang members, white drug dealers and lots of murderers. While prison population usually divided along racial lines, there was not so much of that in Administrative Holding. You got in line and ate with whoever happened to be next to you. You slept where you were assigned. Other than that, there were 6 – 8 TVs each with their own inmate boss; from Spanish Novellas to sports to *General Hospital* to *Law and Order* to cartoons to CNN and FOX News; whatever you wanted.

I would advocate that every federal judge and prosecutor be compelled to spend 24 – 72 hours in prison before they be permitted to seek or hand out any term of incarceration. If you've never experienced what it's like inside, you have no way of knowing what you are subjecting people to. I've witnessed some of the most unbelievable things, from watching inmates tattoo each other with typewriter motors, pens and ink procured from ash and melted down plastic chess pieces to actual barbaric body modifications without anesthetic or proper sterilization. The Mexican *Pisas* seemed to be the group most into the body modifications, inserting plastic beads, made from carved up dominos or chess pieces, into their male organs. A sharpened toothbrush made for the puncturing tool. And the toothbrush was sharpened on the non-slip segments of the flooring that coated each of the top steps of the stair risers; the same flooring outside the bathrooms that every inmate walks over, daily.

As much of a hellscape as general population is, a far worse fate awaits those inmates who want to fight their cases: US Marshals' transport and holding. Every inmate must be brought to court *daily* during pre-trial motions and then for the trial itself. This requires being shaken awake before dawn, usually 4 a.m., by the graveyard shift CO; then taken down to a freezing dungeon in the MCC basement dressed only in a loose-fitting prison jumpsuit. Still bleary-eyed, even as your system is producing lots of nervous adrenalin, there you are given a sack breakfast; after which you are shackled to a long chain connecting tens and tens of other inmates for a waking escort underground through a long, dark, dank tunnel that connects MCC – SD with the US Courthouse.

Beneath the courthouse building is Marshals' holding, a labyrinth of huge steel cages with nothing more than a concrete bench and a toilet. (If you are lucky there might also be toilet paper.) Inside each cage, inmates are packed in. The Mexican nationals made up most of the crowd. Most of them had never been inside the United States, or ever received proper medical, housing or nutrition… and for many, federal lockup was a step-up from their previous lives. They were already loud and fractious, making excited catcalls at 5:30 a.m. It was literal chaos. You would not be taken up to the courtroom until at least 10 a.m., and if it ended up being an afternoon hearing, you would have to sit until 1 p.m. in this concrete and steel cacophony. When you would be brought up to the court, instead of being able to sit in the courtroom, you would be placed in another cage in an adjacent room until your case was called. Sometimes your hearing would be taken off calendar without explanation and you would simply have to wait in Marshals' holding until it was time to bring *everyone* back; an entire day shackled in a dungeon with no food, but a smashed apple and meat and cheese sandwich, with no reading materials... stressed at the absolute purposeless and tormented existence you were currently inhabiting.

When you were brought back through the tunnel on a chain and reprocessed into the MCC facility and then finally up to your housing floor, it was frequently past dinner... and so an entire day had passed where you had received little to no nutrition. Sometimes you received a meal. Sometimes not. Being a kosher-requesting inmate made it even more difficult to get fed.

This routine could go for days or weeks, up at 4 a.m. and not returned until 7 p.m. In my case I was looking at being dragged back and forth for a *95-day* trial. I had no idea how I would be able to survive 3 months of this kind of torment. To say that I *dreaded* going to court via Marshals' escort would be an understatement. As incredible as it sounds, my priorities and perspectives went topsy-turvy. It was now not so much whether I even felt responsible for the charges I was held for in my pre-trial detention; it was in-fact the thought of being worn down by subjecting myself to daily Marshals' transport, which had the most deleterious visceral impact on my will to fight the case.

Yet, despite the daily horrors encountered, one still needs to survive. There is what to say about standing up for your religious rights and pushing to ensure you do all you can to be able to pray and eat and celebrate holidays in a kosher way; but without people from the outside advocating for you, it's very difficult, if not impossible to live a kosher existence in prison. To that end, Rabbi Moishe Leider visited me and made sure I had kosher matzos for Passover, and he prevailed upon the chaplain to let me keep my *tefillin* so that I could pray in them daily. Also, there is a national group run by Aleph that provided books and other holiday needs and so I owe a great debt of thanks to those individuals, Rabbi Mendy Katz and others, who visited me and assisted me.

I was able to keep and wear my *yarmulke* and my small, fringed garment called a *tallis katan*. I was also able to receive my large *tallis* (prayer shawl) and *tefillin* (phylacteries), which I was able to put on daily during weekday morning prayer. I was the only one on the floor self-identifying as a religious Jew. In fact, in my entire foray into the BOP, across numerous prisons and multiple States, over 6 years, except for one prison orderly I saw at MCC-LA who was also wearing a *yarmulke* and *tallis katan*, I never came across another self-identifying religious Jew, like me.

Sure, there were Jewish programs: Chanuka, Shabbos, Pesach, Purim, High Holidays where all the Jews incarcerated would be able to meet together; and it was during this time that many would wear the prison-issue *yarmulkes*. But as soon as services were over, off they came and oft times it would be difficult to identify many of those inmates as Jewish outside of Jewish programming.

I was literally alone. I had no group to hang out with. Nobody really knew what to do with me, because in prison, everyone needs to fall into a group. There are inmate shot-callers, loosely in charge, which prison officials unofficially endorse in order to control inmate behavior. It's informal but very important for the orderly and safe running of the prison. The groups are called, "cars". There was the Black car, the White car, the Mexican car (*Pisas* – Mexican National and/or *Sureños* – Mexican Mafia) and the Native American car (*Chiefs*).

Pisa was slang for "peasant", normally a simple guy who was a mule for drugs or illegal immigration. The *Sureños* were typically far more dangerous and violent, but not as numerous as the *Pisas*... and many times *Pisas* and *Sureños* fought amongst themselves.

Within the Black car were regular everyday guys and then you had the gangs; within the White car were also regular everyday guys and then you had the skinheads, the Nazis, the Aryan Brotherhood, etc.

When I would finally make it to Stafford, Arizona FCI, I was designated simply by my skin color as being in the White car, and therefore, by default, the head Nazi was theoretically my shot-caller; but because I was a readily identifiable Jew, nobody, not even the Nazis, ever asked me to do anything. If something G-d forbid ever jumped off and there was a race riot, the expectation was that each inmate would have to find his own race and fight alongside them. I made it clear to everyone in every institution I attended that I was in no one's "car"; and if something did jump off, I would not be participating in any riot or war and that they could find me in my cell after it was over reading a book.

None of the shot-callers really wanted anything to do with me anyway so they left me alone. I did not fit into their worldview, prison or otherwise. Though I identify with Chabad Chassidim and it's not our custom, I opted to grow out my *peyes* (sidelocks) long and let them hang down so that I would be even more recognizably Jewish. I did not want there to be any question that I was simply wearing a *yarmulke* for benefits. Many inmates tried to say they were Jewish so that they could qualify for kosher food fare. After receiving kosher meals, many would also then eat off the main non-kosher line as well. To combat this, staff was very suspicious of kosher requesting inmates and sometimes required them to go for months before they would be approved. I had to show in a physical way that I was all-in and committed to my religion. Of course, I always ate only kosher, but getting staff to sign off on that request could take weeks and more starvation. One look at me by staff and they knew I wasn't playing around, and I was approved for kosher fare at the very next meal. I was approved to keep my *tefillin* in my own locker, despite the long leather straps and danger that strangulation may have posed to myself or other inmates. Essentially, I was allowed to practice without too much difficulty. I was sincere in my practice, I observed my holidays, I prayed with *tallis* and *tefillin*, I learned, I led services and holiday programs and I never gambled, did drugs, got tattoos or participated in any inmate or staff sex. In short, I was congruent and respected for my dedication… and no one wanted any piece of me other than I continue to do my time in a quiet and sincere way. That suited me just fine.

For a few days since my arrival to the floor where I would spend the next year of my life, I had been hearing about some guy, named Derek Galanis, who was jailed on an Ecstasy conspiracy charge; and that I should meet him because I would probably get along well with him. The problem was that he wasn't currently on my housing floor. He had been taken to the *hole*, also known as the "special housing unit" or SHU, for fighting. Apparently, he was involved with a Mexican *Pisa* who was cleaning the bathroom when Derek tried to use it. The *Pisa* attacked Derek and they ended up rolling around until staff broke it up. Now Derek was no one to mess with; he was a golden gloves champion and martial arts black belt instructor and had a lot of sanctioned fights under his belt. He was also tasked as the muscle, the physical enforcer and hitman, for another criminal organization, his own family so named, the Galanis Crime Family. Though not as well-known as other crime families like the Gambino Crime Family, the Galanis Crime Family worked directly with Gambino father and son pulling off numerous financial frauds. So, when Derek returned to the floor, I half-expected some tough guy, unapproachable and mean. But to my surprise, he was actually the nicest guy you would want to meet. He was unassuming and deferential and very intelligent. We became friends and in a short period of time when his bunkmate ("bunkie") left, he invited me to take the bunk under his rack. We spent close to 12 months together as bunkies.

Derek was a great friend to me; I listened to his pain that he had from his family's betrayals and the situation he was in and he was generous with me and listened to my pain at being separated from my kids and the difficulty I had coming to terms being charged for a fraud. I was so conflicted. I gave him the entire story, omitting nothing, from the facts of the case to my perceptions of the facts at the time. Derek also had the benefit of meeting many other defendants on my case and debriefing with them as well. Derek already had an expertise in constructing money raise deals and breaking them down into their respective parts; so he was able to listen to me, validate me and give me his perspective, also coming from an admitted white collar crime dysfunctional family background.

Then years after we were released, Derek caught another fraud case, this time with his own father and brother and ended up back in federal prison. We stayed in contact and I actually visited him at the same Taft prison I was once held in. I petitioned the warden to visit Derek and I was granted permission! It was strangely anti-climactic being able to return to the Taft-FCI/Camp, arriving and leaving of my own accord. It was now simply an emotionally neutral place for me, an ancient part of a previous life.

Anyway, Derek asked me to help him bring his story to life from behind prison walls, detailing his life in the Galanis Crime Family. I did as he asked; I published his book. I also edited his book and wrote the foreward. The full title is, "Greed and Fear – The Galanis Crime Family"; and it is now available on Amazon for purchase.

In one of his chapters Derek spends considerable time detailing his time with me and his perceptions of my case, which I found to be surprisingly intuitive and accurate; and so, instead of re-writing or re-inventing my own wheel, with Derek's permission, I simply re-quoted from his book, *in italics*, "Greed and Fear, The Galanis Crime Family", Chapter 4:

If there was any open good in jail, that good in MCC-SD was from any number of other inmates. The people and their characters you meet in places like this stay with you for life. And the word "colorful" does not do it justice. The first person I got really close to was my bunkie, an Orthodox Jew, in for wire/mail fraud. He would forever change my outlook on life, and he remains a close friend to this day. But when I met him, he was a bitter man. Imprisoned on a large fraud case out of Los Angeles he was simply a salesman for one the Independent Sales Organizations or ISOs. It was an eclectic group of guys, the leaders of which had been getting away with fraudulent money raises their entire professional lives. The two bosses were both in their fifties, but one was a bit older and much savvier. The older one got the joke, or at least was willing to admit that it was all a joke early on in the indictment process and discovery phase. After raising illicit funds his entire life and making money for no one but himself, he pleaded out to a sweet six-year deal and agreed to testify against everyone else. It's called, 'rolling the top down on the bottom.' The case itself was predicated on a $50 million fraud. The younger boss either did not get the joke or was in extreme and dysfunctional denial... or worse, perhaps he was delusional.

The problem was that [the younger boss] had embraced a money raise rubric (and lavish lifestyle) that made the appearance of fraud and greed, or at least financial mismanagement, all but unavoidable, and success all but impossible. One potential endgame thrown around by these particular bosses was a reverse public merger into a shell... [T]he younger boss was extremely tough and stubborn, but I would definitely not call him clever. From the stories I gathered from the other co-defendants and from simply watching personalities it was clear that he was the other boss' whip. Defiant until the very end, ignoring pleas from his boss, other co-defendants and even his lawyer, this guy blew his trial and was handed a 24-year sentence. I recall a conversation I had with the guy during 'rec' (outside recreation time) on the detention center's roof one week. He had overheard a bunch of other inmates and me talking about our respective crimes and piqued, 'At least you guys knew you were doing something wrong!' Immediately my riposte was, 'The Government looks at all the money you lost people, whether you knew it or not, it's gone!' He responded, 'I'm very sorry about that.' But he didn't seem too upset. Perhaps it was the Seroquel they were prescribing him to sleep (cope) that made him seem toned and emotionally deaf.

The deal they were charged with was pulling out 85% in commissions off the top. Before any money make it into the deal, 85%, which was an obscene amount of a client's money, simply disappeared into operating expenses. All customers were required to physically sign the investor's agreement that they had read and agreed to this figure and understood all the potential risks. On the other hand, most likely anyone investing who had actually read the risk they were signing to could not fully comprehend the implicit bad faith of such a directive and disclosure, disclaimer or no, or certain impending loss. The 15% that did make it into the deal was either returned to the clients in earlier failures; or in later iterations, simply taken for "additional" expenses/stock options by the head organization.

By the end (after approximately 8 programs like this) the company principals had internally decided that they wanted

100% to be paid in commission. This was done by essentially hiding the money grab in plain sight by "investing" that 15% in stock shells, management companies, service providers, etc., that they controlled by their nominees. The bottom line is that no one took a fiduciary interest in the clients' best interests, and by abdicating that responsibility, even at the salesman's level, did grave harm to their customers. At the very least even the salesman, who did not know about the internal business operations, most likely should have known.

85% blew us out of the water at 50% IBTR commissions. Growing up in the Galanis Crime Family I developed an expertise at dissecting deal scaffolding. So, I was able to look at their deal structurally. It was structured as a general partnership specifically because the promoters did not want to be under those limited liability regulations. And because in legitimate investments, you have to "blue-sky" (register) the investment in each State you sell into, general partnerships are meant for a few well-heeled (what we call institutional investors) worth in excess of $1M. The SEC (Security and Exchange Commission) does not need to babysit a legitimate general partnership populated with rich investors who have money to burn and generally know (or should know) what they are doing. But the promoters in my bunkie's case stood the general partnership loophole on its head, bringing in literally 100s of investors, many with as little as $3,500 net worth at a time. I have no doubt that structure was meant to push back the investors once things went bad and to avoid State Blue Sky laws. The worst thing the operation faced from any State was a Cease and Desist order. [My father] would have been proud. In fact, during our proxy fight over FAM we tacitly threatened the limited partners saying their vote may make them general partners and thus create for them significant liability. The *commission breakdown in my bunkie's deal was 50% to the ISO and 35% to corporate. Only 15%, and later zero, went into the deal. It was an organization built totally around greed; again, [my father] would have been proud. Looking for the first time at a deal outside myself, I reflected on a few things. The head guy who was willing to own his crime got off very lightly. The number two guy who refused to acknowledge even a mistake got slaughtered. And they had been getting away with things like this their whole life. I could not understand how stupid my father was and how stupid [my brother] would prove to be, until I met my Bunkie, that is.*

From the moment I met him, he too had refused to accept any responsibility for his actions. He was 'just a salesman believing that the deals could have worked, and everything sold with best efforts was with the express approval of his boss. If a falsehood in good faith was uttered how was that then committing an intentional fraud?' That was his mantra. And technically he was correct. How could he be held accountable for a fraud that he never knew about? But he had one problem. He was not just any salesman; he was the best salesman in the entire organization. Other co-defendants would call him brutal, in that he would take every nickel from his clients that they had available for investment.... And sometimes funds they did not have.

What was plainly apparent to me was a full-on display of how intransigence, even in very smart people, can destroy them. My bunkie was previously involved with similar-type investments to the one he was being held for. When juxtaposing previous conduct against the current deal under indictment it was hard, in my opinion, for him to claim innocence. But by paring away at it, he did just that. And he did so in a very clever fashion. He was motivated to put off his guilt to a large extent, as it pained him that he was perceived as the fulcrum of so much of his clients' losses. [My brother] and [my father] used their own logic in an even more diabolical fashion. They absolutely didn't care.

It's hard to depersonalize what is very personal. But the bottom line is sooner or later, both my bunkie and my father and brother had to plead out. In the federal system, the earlier the better. My bunkie waited until the end and got a much harsher sentence than his boss. In his case, my bunkie's intransigence was based on a dissonance of moral perception. His likely amoral actions of the past conflicted with his moral present. As such, he was unresolved to admit guilt, attempting to deconstruct his previous conduct as somehow less than criminal and therefore less than immoral.

He would confirm for me things [my father] had told me my whole life, but that I had never seen in person. As I would tell him later, he was a living breathing chimera, a whimsical fantasy I thought only existed in [my father]'s mythological story-world. Incidentally, his interaction with me and his wordsmith acumen would be the beginning of a massive expansion of my vocabulary in prison. That's the thing about prison; you can use it to improve yourself if you are willing. But it's all self-help. No one will do it for you.

As I got closer to my bunkie he opened up about his life, his previous marriages, his children and his return to Judaism after he ended his relationship with investment fundraising.

And eventually, because the actions he previously committed were deeply at odds with his new ethical outlook, he was able to come to terms with his actions in the conspiracy and ultimately the guilt associated. He still maintains to this day, though, that if he had known for a fact that what he was selling was actual fraud, even then, he would have walked away.

But he also acknowledged that there was enough bad behavior he witnessed from those above him, including the two bosses, that when taken as a whole, delineated, that he should have known better; which in federal law is considered negligent, and therefore unlawful. And therein lay the problem with high pressure sales like these: Greed. The desire to make the sales and huge commissions will absolutely color one's judgment. My bunkie did not want to believe it was fraud until it came down on his head in a criminal indictment. When you are so close, individual details can be justified or brushed away under the color of high commissions. It's why my father loved to cultivate greed in his salesmen. My bunkie had been involved in several deals to this point in his life and by his own admission did not understand the underling liability or risk to himself. I recall one he told me about was a lottery for cell phone coverage areas. He was negotiating a higher percentage of the deal with the promoter, and the promoter agreed to pay him more if he could take his name off it and replace it with my bunkie's name. My bunkie agreed, not understanding the liability. PPMs like this have a 9 in 10 failure rating. The waters were replete with disingenuous salesmen fleecing investors, and it was why my father had always steered us away from the market when he was incarcerated. In the particular deal for instance the lottery never took place but that did not mean the investors got all of their money back. My bunkie explained to me the concept of force majeure, an unforeseen, catastrophic event. He also explained how the money earned was justified, 'Fees, Derek'; always with the caveat that the customer signed, had read, understood, and agreed to the risks and fees before they were allowed to invest.

187 // Making Music With What Remains

It was the line that removed my bunkie from full responsibility as a fiduciary for his clients' best interests and moved him into the role of salesman of a high-risk investment, simply placing risk in plain sight, veiling it with his honed verbal skills, thought processes and radio announcer voice. His whole persona fit an image that the customer wanted to embrace. He painted a picture of what could be, but the customer never internalized the words "could be" or "if this works out" even though he constantly used those qualifiers. They were just felled by the ether of potential financial success and the power of his pervasive persuasion.

But jail has a way of taking away all of the distractions and for some people forces a serious self-reflection and honest appraisal. My bunkie took that path, though it took him almost a year inside to come to terms with an honest reckoning.

And I truly believe that the Government likes to remand people pretrial not only for the legal reasons they have, danger to community and flight risk; rather they do so because they need people to reflect on their acts, fraud guys in particular. These people spend so much time "thinking on their feet" as [my father] puts it, that they land up creating excuses for any eventuality, which is my father's definition of intelligence. People with a conscience, however, are able to learn from their mistakes. It doesn't happen overnight; it's a gradual process that oft times comes quicker in jail.

I recall vividly when my bunkie came to me at the beginning of his mea culpa. He was trying to come to terms with participating in a fraud and then having to plead guilty, thereby avoiding trial and risking 14 or more years in jail by losing in front of a jury. He told me that his whole life he was able to extricate himself from any uncomfortable situation, but for the first time he was not able to make his way out or walk away from something discomforting.

It was a watershed moment for him, and it prevented him from going all the way to trial. He did have a co-defendant (another salesman who had worked directly with my bunkie) on the case, who did go all the way to trial, and he won. However, he was not that good as a salesman. It was specifically my bunkie's success in the salesroom that would have been his Achilles heel and most likely his downfall at trial. But that co-defendant's win at trial showed how tenuous the case was against my bunkie, and the stretch my bunkie had to make to come to terms with accepting that he should have known better. He could have just as easily come to the opposite conclusion. In the end he took a guilty plea instead of risking losing 14+ more years of his life.

Some of the prison staff may have felt that my bunkie's embrace of rabbinic Judaism was simply for show, but today my bunkie is an ordained Orthodox rabbi. He is proof positive that you can turn your life around, and I respect him immensely for it.

The path, however, was far from easy and sometimes even dangerous. One of the less intelligent guards at MCC-SD by the name of Fred Tolentino took an active (and some would say anti-Semitic) dislike to him and tried to get some young black gang members to beat him up. He created fake stories about him and also made anti-Semitic remarks; suggesting how the beds could be disassembled to reveal steel bars with which to beat him. But the young black gang kids liked us; they even gave us nicknames. My bunkie they named 'Sizzle' and I was 'D Nasty'. It's true that we used to fight full contact to the body to relieve stress, but that was not the source of my nickname. The origin had to do with my lack of understanding and how to protect myself in such a filthy environment....

189 // Making Music With What Remains

And the guard, Tolentino, who was trying to start a proxy war with my bunkie....? Well, things went far worse for him for attempting to hurt my bunkie. It was not long before he was suspended and not allowed above the third floor at MCC-SD, which effectively barred him from interacting with any other inmates. In fact, I was on the floor when my bunkie actually had Tolentino served by US Marshals with a civil rights complaint under color of authority, suing the guard in federal court. My bunkie ultimately settled with the guard pre-trial for thousands of dollars for his harassment, but not before serving him with copious interrogatories, requests for admission and multiple legal motions he himself prepared/filed from behind a wall. Tolentino actually had to write a check to my bunkie and sign his name to it to get him to dismiss the case.

It's fair to say that I think he won the war and his point. No one in the BOP ever bothered him again when it came to his religion. An inmate's file follows him everywhere he goes in the BOP. I'm sure in my bunkie's file, next to his order of confinement was a copy of the federal complaint he filed against Tolentino with a warning in bold print stamped, 'Do Not Fuck with This Inmate.'

As Derek's book editor, and his former bunkie, I can attest to everything in Derek's account. And the source of my honorary Gang name, "Sizzle"? Let's just say that I knew how to dance, and those black gang kids could appreciate it. They almost named me, "Hustle".

All told I pleaded guilty to 7 counts of a 66-count indictment, 3 counts of mail fraud, 3 counts of wire fraud and 1 count of money laundering. The mail and wire fraud counts carried a maximum of 5 years in prison, to be run concurrently. It was the money laundering, with a 20-year maximum; that allowed the judge to lengthen my sentence by 2 ½ years over the 5-year max. That money laundering count was added by the prosecutor as a *go to hell* parting "gift". There was never any talk of a money laundering count in my original dealings with prosecutors. Money laundering is normally reserved for RICO and actual criminal enterprises. I was only a salesman. And all I did was deposit my paycheck into the bank. But because the funds came from an alleged criminal enterprise, those proceeds were deemed criminal and therefore by my conducting commercial business (by making a bank deposit) subjected me to that charge. Money laundering in my case was a *major* stretch and may not have survived a trial by jury, but I did not want to challenge it and then be charged with ten or twenty more counts.

That's the thing with federal prosecutions. They make you accept their theory and the crimes associated and if you refuse, they throw the entire kitchen sink at you. In my case, I had declined so many previous offers from prosecutors to settle along with their relatively light sentencing recommendations, that even if I could come to terms with being dragged to court daily, the odds, (the reader will recall that 98% of all federal cases end in conviction), were not in favor that I was going to beat this… *and* there was still a way I could conterminously end my suffering by pleading out; I had taken my case all the way to *in limine* motions days before trial was supposed to start. I realized that if I lost at trial my world would be over.

So, I asked for and took the deal prosecutors were then willing to offer me, in order to avoid being forced to trial. In all fairness, prosecutors did have to prepare for trial and went through great pains to structure their case with me as their "star" defendant. When I pleaded out, the Government did not have their main punching bag and it is for this reason (among others) that I believe my co-defendant, Steve, who admitted to me that he believed he was selling a fraud, was able to win an acquittal. After all the Government evidence was presented, I was told that the jury kept asking, "But where's David Diamand?"

By my forcing the Government to prepare for a case so heavily reliant on my presence, and then me being a no-show, perhaps truncated their case's effectiveness when it came to some of the other defendants. I was to be used as the Government's truncheon and fulcrum to spin and flip everyone else; at least that was their strategy, and it fell very much flat.

It was still no less stunning that my co-defendant, who worked *directly* with me on the same customers, was acquitted. It took a considerable amount of time for me to let his acquittal sink in. He endured that 95-day trial (though he was not subjected to incarceration or Marshals' transport and housing before or during the trial) and was found "not-guilty". Maybe I had made a mistake in pushing myself to come to terms with, and accept, the Government's theory of guilt for something so flimsy, so tenuous; something that 12 federal jurors unanimously agreed was *not* fraud. In the end, I could not retract; I had entered a guilty plea before trial as the "safer" known option and there were no "do-overs".

The Government always gets its "pound of flesh", even from those who ultimately win at trial. From the pre-indictment target letters to arrest and pre-trial detainment, attorney's expenses, transfers from prison to court daily to a trial and possible conviction risking years of your life and the *horrendous* stress this creates in your family and friends; no matter what damage I may have done to the Government's overall case, they hurt everyone associated in powerful and profound ways. There will always be for me a sort of PTSD, and though I take it in stride, I will always remember waking up daily in my prison cubicle looking at the steel racks and painted over cinderblock walls and wondering incredulously how the hell did I find myself there. It was absolutely beyond belief and yet there I was confined behind prison walls.

In the end, I had taken prosecutors all the way to the day before trial and pleaded guilty; and my direct co-defendant went to trial and won an acquittal. Neither fact was lost on the judge. My sentencing took place after that three-month trial and I naively figured that after hearing all the evidence and then seeing my co-defendant be found not guilty by a jury of 12; that he would sentence me to a relatively light term of incarceration. After all, my boss, Tim got three years and the leader of the investment who was ordered to pay back $49 million, received six years. And I was only a salesman. No such luck. The judge gave me Steve's time as well as my time for a total of 88 months. It was a devastating blow. 88 months. Longer than even the top boss. I called my father that evening because he was present in court and I needed to talk to someone. I asked him what he thought. He said that when he told his friend what had happened to me, receiving the longest sentence of anyone who pleaded out while having the lowest position in the organization... and knowing that I wear a *yarmulke*, my father's friend said that the judge must have been an anti-Semite. My father told his friend that the judge was Jewish. My father's friend's riposte was, "Then the judge is definitely an anti-Semite!"

None of the above is meant to rehabilitate (or redeem) my reputation, nor diminishes my responsibility in bringing people into the investments. No matter where my ultimate culpability lay on the spectrum, it was my voice and my advice that caused many to invest. Beyond the patent and very-clear high-risk investor prospectus that each person had to agree to before investing was the Government's assertion (and now conviction) of fraud hanging over my sales like a constant, low, dark raincloud. My customers had invested because of my counsel. And therefore, I do bear that responsibility and I have accepted as much. I decided long ago that it should be a matter of honor to make amends; and that it is my duty, even if it takes me the rest of my life, that I repay my customers/clients who invested and lost through my recommendations.

This also comports with an important concept in Judaism called "teshuva"; (Hebrew for "return", but also meaning "repentance", "atonement for sin"). To fully atone for any wrongdoing means, in addition to admitting to a misdeed, being accountable to repairing (if possible) what you have damaged. Ultimately, 10 years after being released from prison, having worked toward meaningful repair, I was able to submit formal application for a full pardon to the President of the United States via the US Pardon Attorney.

Despite that, at the time of incarceration, having to endure such a harsh sentence was not made any easier not ever seeing my children. In my entire 14 months in that high-rise building Shannon never once brought my 4-year-old daughter to visit me. When I would get visits from other family, I always noticed kids in the visiting room. The feds allow contact visits and so other inmates had their children climbing all over them, but Shannon would not allow my daughter in for fear that seeing her father in prison would damage her. This would be the beginning of an insidious exercise of denying my daughter her father and diminishing/negating my importance as a parent in her life. It was cold-hearted parental alienation of affection. And she did it in a very devious way, under color of "protecting" my daughter from a hard reality of life. I think that having had my daughter *in my life* would have been much more beneficial to her than any perceived "damage" such knowledge would have done to her. We did see each other briefly years later at another institution, when she was already much older, and then twice when I was released, but the alienation was done. And today my daughter is 21 and refuses to speak to me or communicate with me in any way. She has been brainwashed into thinking that I did not care for her; she certainly has not been supported in maintaining a relationship with me. She is carrying her mother's anger and distorted view of me, relying on false rumors and manufacturing "reasons" not to see me in some sort of feting allegiance to her mother - an obsequious casualty of parental alienation of affection.

Still, I love and miss my child. It's part of the buried alive feeling I will carry with me for the rest of my life. It's like a death. I lost a child. And that is my fault; because while the feds are expert at destroying families, the responsibility of my being subject to the feds' incarceration in the first-place rests on me alone. And while Shannon could have chosen to do the right thing by me and our daughter, she was given (and took) a path of walking away with my daughter... and eventualities like losing a young child are part of the price of going to prison.

After I accepted responsibility and took a conviction, I was sent from the 7th floor to the 8th floor at MCC-SD, which is the post-conviction floor. I met up with Derek again for a brief time before I would be transferred to a real prison destination. I made a half-hearted attempt at appealing my conviction on grounds that the court improperly applied a couple of upward departure points and unfairly enhanced my sentence, but that appeal failed and so around November of 2002, I was designated to Federal Correctional Institute – Taft, CA. Designation in the feds is based on a number of factors, type of crime conviction, previous criminal history, violence and flight risk. I was on the low end of security points and this enabled me to be sent to a prison camp, with no walls and no fences. The only threat to being returned behind a wall was if I were to break prison rules.

The day of the transfer came and instead of the BOP placing me on a chain gang on a prison bus and then transported through San Bernadino for who knows how long of a period of starvation, the US Marshals, upon receiving a letter from me about my kosher food transport issues, did something very solid for me. Most inmates must suffer weeks in transit until they arrive at their final destination. But I was to be given a direct transport, unheard of unless you happen to be *El Chapo*. Perhaps the Marshals got wind of my previous lawsuit against Tolentino or perhaps they had compassion. Maybe it was both. Anyway, I was brought to the original intake floor and allowed to change back into my suit and civilian shoes. Then I was shacked belly to wrist and ankle to ankle and brought down to the prison basement where I was given a readymade kosher lunch and handed off to two US Marshals who would be escorting me directly to camp.

"Do not pass Go! Do not collect $200! Go directly to jail!" Usually a pejorative phrase in Monopoly; in my case, going directly to jail suited me just fine. I was so happy to be relieved of the transport nightmare that most other inmates in the system have to endure.

We set off from San Diego for the 3 – 4-hour direct drive to Taft. I was in the back seat. It was a bit surreal driving through and seeing my hometown and freeway off ramp, being so close to my old life, yet still worlds away. When we finally made it down the 5 FWY *Grapevine* and turned onto the road that led to the prison, a CHP officer pulled us over for speeding. It was a female officer. As she approached our unmarked vehicle, both Marshals flashed their badges at her and advised that they were transporting a prisoner (me) to prison. The officer looked

197 // Making Music With What Remains

at their badges then glanced at me cuffed in the back. She paused a bit longer as she gazed at me. And then it hit me how I knew this CHP officer and how she recognized me.

Exactly six years before, a group of Porsche owners had organized a Porsche event at Willow Springs International Raceway, a private track where you could take your car to speed and also practice cornering, shifting and braking in as aggressive a way as you wanted without fear of a reckless driving or exhibition of speed moving violation. The course was about 80 miles north of Los Angeles and the route to get there would take us through a speed trap near Taft; the same speed trap that this CHP officer had just used to pull over my US Marshal escorts.

Shannon had been with me that day in the passenger seat, convertible top down. As we descended past the 5 FWY Grapevine northbound, I noticed a CHP cruiser up ahead. Instinctively I checked my speed and made sure I was at or under the speed limit. My brand-new Porsche analogue speedometer read exactly 65 mph. I maintained that speed throughout the duration of my driving encounter with the CHP. I began to gain on the cruiser and the officer switched to the number 2 lane allowing me to pass. I passed the cruiser at *exactly* 65 mph. The officer, a blonde female noticed me and the blonde female passenger in my car.

A few moments later the CHP cruiser reentered my lane and lit me up, pulling me over. Hands on the steering wheel, I waited for her to approach my vehicle. I was wondering if she might have recognized me from a previous Sheriff operation or maybe she thought the car might be stolen. She approached the passenger side and asked for my driver's license and registration and proof of insurance, all of which I handed to her.

Anyway, after about 5 minutes and all of the other cars in our Porsche convoy passing us with quizzical looks, the officer came back, handed me all of my documents and said with a bit of a cheeky smirk, "I clocked you at 67 mph. I pulled you over to make sure that you know that the speed limit is 65 mph. I'm going to let you go with a warning."

I arrived at Willow Springs now late for my pre-race briefing. When I shared the story of why I was pulled over; because a CHP officer wanted to make sure that I knew that she knew that I knew that the speed limit was 65 mph, which they saw unfolding as they drove by on the 5 FWY, they all laughed. Six years later my US Marshal drivers had been pulled over by the same female CHP officer; only this time I was wearing handcuffs, a belly chain and was being chauffeured to prison. And no one was laughing.

Taft Correction Institution (TCI - Camp)

A short while later we pulled into Taft Correctional Institution, a federal prison built by the feds but staffed and managed by a private 3rd party contractor called *The GEO Group*. Aside of one BOP liaison at the facility, the entire operation was run by civilians who had the power to detain and write incident reports (called "shots") and have good conduct time taken away from you. In short there was no real difference (as far as inmates were concerned) between the private guards and the federal ones; except that the private guards seemed to have more to prove and were oft times harsher, though not as well-trained as their federal counterparts.

I was escorted still shackled in my black suit into the main FCI, which at that time was a medium-security facility housing flight-risk-inmates, violent inmates, child molesters and inmates with immigration violations and higher security ratings with significant time still left to do. In the feds there are Administrative Detention centers, which are maximum security pre-trial holding sites, USPs (United States Penitentiaries), FCIs (High, Medium and Low) and Camps. There is also an ADX which is a kind of administrative super max USP that houses the worst of the worst, inmates who are considered too dangerous to be housed in general population, with security management risks or are simply too high profile to be out and about.

The Federal USPs have gun towers, 40-foot walls, 4 fences including one stop fence, one electrified fence and two 18' high chain link fences perhaps 20 feet apart both topped with razor concertina wire and then rolls and rolls of concertina wire piled up between those two chain link fences. Concertina is essentially razor wire and is hideous to encounter. If an inmate could get over the wall and the electrified fence and was able to scale the first chain link fence without being shot by the guard in the gun tower, he'd find that if he tried to climb over or crawl through the razor wire that it's actually engineered to pull you in, then collapse on you and cut you horrendously in the process. Once you are caught in that sea of razor wire there is no mortal escape, without first bleeding to death, and then specially trained staff have to physically cut you out.

Outside most federal facilities is a road that encircles the fence perimeter. 24 hours a day, two BOP rovers circle the perimeter, one driving clockwise, the other driving counterclockwise. Both vehicles are equipped with shotguns and M16 rifles and the drivers are also armed with handguns to repel escape attempts from the inside and unauthorized entry from the outside. In the extremely unlikely event that an inmate would find himself on the wrong side of the fence, he can be shot dead on sight. Escape, aside of being unlikely, is also ill-advised.

FCIs (Federal Correctional Institutions) don't have the walls or electrified fencing or gun towers. But they do have the chain link fencing and razor wire and two armed rovers circling outside. And camps have no escape prevention security at all, no fence, no locked units, no cells. A walk off from a camp is still considered an escape and brings with it serious consequences like lots of time in the hole, 5 more years added onto your sentence and a big red warning in your jacket that you can never be sent back to a camp. You may also be sent on diesel therapy, which is a tactic the feds like to employ on inmates who don't behave. You are shackled belly to wrists and ankle to ankle for up to 12 hours a day and forced to ride a bus from BOP destination to BOP destination, eating sack meals and sleeping in county jails at night. The journey can be weeks or months and it's grueling and debilitating and extremely uncomfortable. You feel absolute purposelessness, robbed of all dignity. When that is over, you will do the rest of your time behind a fence or a wall. The only thing you don't have to fear if you decide to walk off from a camp is necessarily being shot. You *may* get shot, but it's not a foregone conclusion. All prison campers are considered more or less non-violent by the time they reach camp. Anyone with more than 10 years left on their sentence, or someone with violence, or who is a child molester can never reach a camp level rating.

The US Marshals escorting me inside the main building ditched their duty weapons in the front gun lockers and then took me inside the secure portion of the building. I was handed off to my contract civilian captors and led into a holding cell. I was instructed to strip out of my suit and was issued a t-shirt, khaki scrubs–type pants and a khaki medical scrub - type pullover. (Author's Note: I will *never* put on another pair of khaki pants, even "dress" khaki pants, again. Having spent over a year in them incarcerated was enough for me.)

As before, they allowed me to keep on my *tallis katan* and *yarmulke*. The intake manager came over to me and told me that she had not yet received my file from the BOP, and was unsure of my security rating; therefore, I would have to be admitted to the FCI until my camp management variable could be confirmed. It had already been a long morning, traumatic in so many ways and now it was real. I had just seen the outside world for the first time in 14 months, passed my home on the way, and now here I was in actual prison (not a camp) and I still had *years and years* to go before I could ever see my children again. Once I was left alone in my holding cell, while they were preparing to admit me into the FCI, I started to cry, to weep actually. For the first time I felt truly adrift, lost and alone. It was a bitter-few-minutes of reckoning until I came to terms with, and was able to embrace, my situation.

Thirty minutes later a case manager arrived back at my holding cell and told me that my paperwork had arrived, and I was now cleared to go to camp. I was released from the holding cell without handcuffs and escorted to the front of the building that I had just entered a half an hour earlier under armed US Marshal's escort in handcuffs; and now I was told to wait outside *by myself* for another inmate to arrive in a golf cart. Sure enough, an inmate from the camp arrived and I jumped into the cart and away we went to the other side of the prison grounds where the camp was located.

When I got to the camp I met with my case and unit managers and was assigned a bunk in a three-man cube amongst a 200-man warehouse of two and three-man cubes. There was a total of four 200-man warehouses in this camp, a dining hall, law library, television room, commissary, medical clinic, multi-purpose rooms and a large running track, handball courts, basketball courts, tennis courts and a well-manicured grassy soccer field. It reminded me of a public middle school campus. I actually got my work assignment that very day. I had arrived early at camp and my job started at 11 a.m., so I walked over through administration, across the parking lot to a development of buildings where I found my new boss, an 80-year-old farmer with the camp landscaping crew. He was nice enough, actually very nice. He drove a bunch of us over to the FCI fence line, the fence that I was behind an hour before and handed me a flamethrower. My job was to burn out all the weeds that had started growing between and around the two chain link fences with the razor wire attached. The razor wire prevented anyone from grabbing those weeds by hand; hence Inmate Diamand was now manning a *freaking* flamethrower.

To appreciate the irony and insanity of the above is to be a federal inmate who was taken down by the FBI at gunpoint, incarcerated with murderers, considered so much of a flight risk that I was refused reasonable bail and had to be housed in a maximum security high rise, had not seen the actual civilized world's light of day for 14 months until just then, having arrived just 2 hours prior in belly chain and handcuffs and who was locked in an FCI behind the very fence I was now on the other side of. Suddenly all of that overkill security hysteria no longer applied?! One second, I'm considered a dangerous felon, and the next second there I was with a flamethrower, shooting flame at fence weeds. In the BOP there are many ironic and insane cognitive dissonance situations an inmate will find himself in on a daily basis. The idea is to keep your wits, your sanity and your sense of humor, and *embrace the suck*.

I settled into my new life, inherited a pair of running shoes and a radio and started running the track again. Cooped up in a building for 14 months with one *rec* day a week on a building roof with helicopter wire above you and 100s of other inmates crowding for the same free space was not conducive for running. I recall I was able to convince a really nice BOP guard, Baronowski (everyone called him

"Ski"), to let me out into the main dining area on our housing unit when he locked everyone else down 30 minutes before meal delivery. For those 30 minutes he let me run around the entire perimeter of the dining hall as my workout. No other inmates; just me. It was a novel idea I'm sure no one ever thought of before and soon other inmates grew jealous. Tolentino found out about it during his period of intensive harassment of me, and he shut down my running escapades in what he termed, *running of the bulls*. That was alright with me, because Tolentino's harassment of me would be permanently shut down by the US Marshals serving a civil rights violation lawsuit under color of authority on him.

Now well into my routine at Taft, I had time to focus on one huge priority in my life and that was my youngest daughter, who was now living with her non-Jewish grandparents in Louisiana. When I was arrested, my youngest daughter was taken into CPS foster. She was alone for weeks waiting for someone from my family to take her home so that when I got out of prison, I could reunite with her.

Though the dependency court found that I made a proper plan for the care of my daughter, the only choice available was to turn my daughter over to the care of her non-Jewish grandparents in Louisiana in the hope that the mother would rehabilitate and regain custody. The court placed my daughter into a guardianship in the State of Louisiana, but subject to the laws of California.

But the grandparents also alienated my daughter from me. They were bitter that Miriam returned to them a basket case and blamed her pervasive drug use and bombing of her medical residency on me. The only problem with that is that I don't do drugs and never did drugs and have no intimacy with addiction. It turns out that the grandmother was a narcotic and methadone addict, who used to work as a nurse. According to her daughter, after a vial of narcotic was drawn into a syringe and administered to a patient the remainder was supposed to be trashed. But the grandmother would secrete theses remnants out and eventually had enough to fill her own syringe which she and my wife would inject in each other. Years later during another custody fight, when my daughter once came to visit, out of one of her bags rolled one of the grandmother's 10 mg Methadone pills that could have killed my daughter had she ingested it.

So, my daughter was being cared for by two addicts and a grandfather who was in active denial about how sick his wife and daughter were. The grandparents had bad intensions; they took advantage of my incarceration by trying to have my parental rights severed so that they could adopt my daughter. They never intended that I should ever have the chance to reunite with or parent or enjoy providing care for my daughter. But the courts were very clear on the matter, "Just because you go to jail, does not mean you lose your parental rights."

I'm not sure the reader can appreciate the despair and hopelessness I faced. I literally felt like a drowning man. I had no resources, save a ribbon-based electric typewriter (with no spell check or cut and paste functionality and no access to the internet); I had no counsel, and I was behind a wall with no access to my child, while I was fighting millionaire non-Jewish grandparents for the life, care, companionship and soul of my baby. But my despair gave way to granite resolve, and I poured my *everything* into legally fighting for my baby.

I wrote and filed all my briefs from inside the Taft legal library. After many months of filing brief after brief on my own with only facile assistance from an appointed attorney, I won the case and kept my parental rights to my daughter. The grandparents appealed that, and I won again. At least I could look forward to the love and joy of raising one of my daughters when I got out, I thought.

I tried to stay in contact with my older daughter too and would initiate multiple calls per week to hear her voice and assure her that her daddy loved her even though I was away. She never understood why I never came to see her, but her mother told me that I should not tell her where I was, and I respected her wishes for the time being. One day when I called, Shannon answered and told me that she was getting married to someone named John. She broke down in tears as she told me. She seemed sad about what was once a happy life with me being over and perhaps she felt a little guilty for moving on; she seemed to be conflicted in her continuing feelings for me and her desire to begin a new life. I wished her well and that she should not feel badly for her decision to move on. It turned out that my older daughter would begin to call this man, "Dad"; and as part of the heartbreak of prison would have it, I ultimately lost the heart and soul and love of my eldest daughter. I had been replaced; and even to this day, I still feel the bite of that sharp knife, which forever remains... the loss of my child.

I found out shortly after that call that my grandmother, Hannah Diamand, had passed away. I would not be able to attend her funeral and it would not be until many years later when I could visit her (and my grandfather's) cemetery plot in New York, stand by the gravesite and cry.

Grief in prison takes on a different kind of cold isolation; you eventually just become sort of numb to all of the crushing psychological and emotional pain. But then Taft wasn't without its funny moments. In the BOP, there is a mandatory standing count once a day. Every inmate must stand and be counted. The BOP count is sacrosanct. Every inmate in its custody and care must be accounted for and that number *must* match the confinement register. According to official BOP statistics in 2003 there were 172,499 federal inmates and that included inmates housed in county jails, in US Marshal housing and transit and in administrative lock up. The sheer volume of transfers by the Marshals and their ability to coordinate these transfers, including the housing and transport logistics thereto; in addition to being able to provide an accurate inmate count each and every day, was all quite impressive.

If any inmate interfered with the count, there were severe consequences; and until the number of all the inmates was tallied by each of the facilities, the count could not be cleared. An inmate interfering with a count carries a charge approximating that of rioting and mayhem. And, if the count was not cleared, then count was not over, and you were required to remain standing. This could stretch on for hours, especially if someone was missing.

The inmate is required to stand. It used to be that the counts were done with inmates being allowed to lie on their bunks, but soon it was discovered that BOP staff was counting dead bodies for days until they began to smell. To ensure that all their inmates were alive, the BOP implemented the *standing* 4 p.m. count. The count was also designed to mitigate escapes and it keeps the BOP accountable to the one job they really have, which is to maintain their exact prison population, per Legislature's order. The BOP is really big on rules, but it doesn't really have a contingency or institution rule for an inmate once he escapes, so they try to mitigate them as best they can.

At Taft, we all simply returned to our bunks by 4 p.m. daily to comply with the count; until one day when we were all forced to return to our bunks at 10:30 a.m. for another standing count. Apparently, an inmate from the FCI had escaped. Inmate Orosco who was working in the FCI food service behind the fence apparently found a way out of prison. On a trash pickup day, he placed himself inside one of the huge waste containers behind food services by the loading docks after breakfast. The entire area is double fenced, but those fences open when the trash trucks come through. One such truck lifted the massive trash container and dumped all of its contents, including inmate Orosco, into the trash repository of the truck and then simply drove back out the gate on the way to the dump. Standard count would not be until 4 p.m., so Orosco had a 6 to 8-hour head start.

Orosco's plan sounded creative, but it was not without peril. Those trash trucks have crushers designed to *crush* the trash into compact bundles. Orosco almost got crushed to death as he was inside the metal jaws of that truck. Then the trash truck broke down on its way to the dump. Orosco had set it up with friends on the outside to meet him at the dump with a car, so that when he emerged from the truck, he could make his getaway. Because of the delay, his friends got spooked and took off, so that when Orosco's truck finally arrived and he tumbled out of the dump truck, he was on his own. The driver noticed a small, thin Mexican man in prison khakis rolling end over end out of the truck, wild eyed, looking around and then running in the opposite direction. The driver called the prison and soon enough Orosco was back in Taft, in the hole this time, facing an additional 5 years for escape.

From that day forward, the Orosco Standing Count was instituted at 10:30 a.m. daily.

There were issues at Taft that would ultimately get me thrown out of camp. One of their rules was that no food served in the dining hall could be removed from the dining hall. This was a very difficult if not impossible rule for me to observe. The tables were very small and there were 4 inmates to a table. Each tray had lots of non-kosher food on it and cross contamination was certain. Think "squirting hotdog syndrome." There was no way I felt I could open up my meal and not get non-kosher food flying into it, so time and again, I would simply stick my saran wrap meal under the arm of my jacket and secrete it out of the dining hall and up to my bunk where I could open it and enjoy it in peace.

But time and again, I would get caught violating this rule by the unit manager who was not very sympathetic to my concerns. She would invariably issue me a verbal warning and then started writing me formal incident reports. I tried to be creative about it and change up my eating times, but after about the 4th time of her finding me in my cube eating my prison issued meal, she had me sent to the hole on a "stealing" violation. She actually charged me with stealing my own food! And that charge was unbelievably upheld by the Hearing Officer. Well, that sent my security points and management variable up so that I could no longer be housed at a camp. I spent 90 days in the hole and then was transferred to a higher security prison out of State simply because I was eating my own lunch (in my cube).

In the BOP, a charge of stealing is treated very seriously. It's up there with murder, rioting, mayhem, hostage taking, sexual assault, or assault with any deadly weapon like stabbing someone.

The camp administrator called my name to the front lobby. Guards from the FCI came over and handcuffed me and drove me back to the FCI. Meanwhile camp guards rolled up my rack and boxed all my personal items. I was brought back into the FCI and taken to the special housing unit and given a tiny cell with a toilet, open shower, bunk bed and small desk with a steel seat attached. Once a day I was given *rec;* handcuffed while being escorted to the small outdoor cage that I walked around for an hour, then re-handcuffed and back to my small cell. I did get my kosher meals delivered to me through a slot in the door and happily got to eat them on my bunk with no one telling me that I had stolen them.

I spent 90 days like that. I did a lot of pushups and writing and reading… and sleeping. Surprisingly, the hours and days moved. There was a routine, and it was not as terrible as it might sound. I was even invited to bunk with another Jewish inmate named Mike, who had been with me in the camp. Mike was in prison for Medicare fraud and never stopped moaning/grumbling/complaining about his 10-month sentence. He was aghast that my original sentence was 88 months. Anyway, he wanted to petition the warden for some sort of camp privilege, so he wrote a letter. But instead of mailing it through proper channels, he took it with him and asked the inmate with the golf cart to shuttle him up to the main lobby where he could deliver the letter personally. When Mike got inside, he was challenged, and it was determined that he was way out of bounds and they hooked him up right there and took him to the hole. Mike thought he was being funny; that was just the type of guy he was.

Actually, on his first day of prison, he was permitted by his sentencing judge to self-report to the institution. He showed up to the camp parking lot in a nice suit having just been dropped off by his wife. In the parking lot were a number of portable grills and the prison staff was enjoying an employee party of some kind. Instead of going inside the camp admin building, Mike sauntered over to the gathering of staff and began to schmooze with them. Mike knew who they were, but they had no idea that they were talking to a self-surrendering prisoner. He shook hands with everyone gathered there.

Mike, being dressed in his nice expensive suit, caused everyone to think he was actually a BOP liaison; and the staff wanting to impress him, chatted him up and offered him BBQ food. Mike, of course, being Mike played along by passively assuming the mistaken identity. Mike actually started eating one of the hot dogs offered to him until some of the prison staff asked from which BOP office he had come.

Mike told them, "Oh, no. I'm a camper. The judge told me that I'm supposed to self-surrender today. So here I am. And by the way, really nice party."

The entire group went slack jawed. Two prison staff grabbed Mike under the armpits with his hot dog still in his mouth and dragged him to a waiting van and over to the main facility for processing. I laugh whenever I think of the kind of *shtick* he used to pull wherever he went. It was indeed fortuitous that I got to spend about 30 days with Mike. I put *tefillin* on him every weekday and we spent a lot of time listening to each other's pain. He actually left from prison from the hole on his way to halfway house, and then home. I saw him leaving the facility in civilian clothes from my special housing unit bullet proofed glass window. We stay in contact to this very day.

One day about half-way into my administrative punishment, I met with the Discipline Officer to discuss the charges against me. He advised me of three things.

Number One: I would not be going back to camp. I would be going to an FCI, and that final designation was still pending. Number Two: I would be losing 6 months of commissary privileges. Number Three: I would be losing 27 days of "good conduct time"; which meant that I would have to spend approximately another month in prison *more* than calculated from my original sentence. To me numbers one and two were a pity, but number three was unacceptable.

In prison there are different types of inmates, some like my friend Derek Galanis, who would never even write a *cop-out* (informal request), much less file a federal lawsuit. I was certainly not one of those laissez-faire inmates.

I immediately got busy appealing the punishment through the so-called, "administrative remedy process." First appeal went to Hearing Officer. Rejected. Second appeal went to the warden. Rejected. Third appeal went to BOP Regional Office. Rejected. Fourth appeal went to BOP Washington Main Office. Rejected. Since I had exhausted my administrative relief options, my only and final avenue for injunctive relief was to appeal directly to a federal magistrate judge, whose name was Judge Coffin.

In the BOP, in general, each response could take 60 days or longer if an extension was requested; and so, by the time my 27-day loss of good time complaint got to federal court, over a year and a half had passed and I was already in Oregon by then.

I filed a four-page legal brief on the court describing the incident and my arguments as to why the stealing charge and resultant good time sanctions were improper. My main argument attacked the flawed reasoning of the original civilian Disciplinary Officer who likened my taking a meal designated for me only as "theft". He compared the kosher meal prepared exclusively for my personal consumption to the general milk available for all the inmates. He wrote that if I were to take a bladder of milk out of the dining hall it would be considered the same thing as me taking my kosher meal out of the dining hall; that either type of food removal would be considered stealing from the institution. But that comparison was his argument's downfall.

As a kosher food recipient, I wrote, I had a good faith expectation of receiving a specific kosher meal that no one else had an expectation of receiving; and that that kosher meal was wrapped and designated to one and only one inmate, namely me. I was not depriving anyone of my meal, nor did anyone have a legitimate expectation to that specific kosher meal other than me. (Now, if you want to know the level of pettiness involved at TCI specifically and in the BOP generally, the meal in question contained 4 pieces of sliced bread, 2 tomatoes, a hardboiled egg and some chopped salad.) In the case of the milk, I argued that had I removed milk from the dining hall, then that would have been theft because all the other inmates had a legitimate and good faith expectation of being able to drink that milk and the institution would have had a legitimate expectation for the milk's return. In the case of my kosher meal, no one, not the inmates and not the institution had any good faith expectation of use of or return of my meal. Therefore, the removal of my meal did not meet the legal or operational definition of theft (or stealing) in any BOP rules manual or under any federal law.

I then advised the court that if anything, removing *my* designated food from the dining hall amounted to only a minor rule violation of possibly being "in possession of minor contraband", whose penalty is simply to have the meal confiscated; a non-serious charge that would never have contemplated any loss of good conduct time. And since the charge of stealing was improperly applied; so too the penalty of 27 days loss of good conduct time was improperly applied. I asked that the charge be dismissed and that my 27 days good conduct time be restored.

My brief was well-reasoned and well-received. The court completely gutted the BOP's punishment and sanctions, writing in its ruling that my arguments were "persuasive". The court reversed the Disciplinary Officer's charge of stealing and ordered that the BOP restore my 27 days of good conduct time. For the 2nd time in my BOP tenure, I felt completely vindicated in federal court. But there was still one hurdle to go. I had to meet with a new Disciplinary Officer to deal with the charge of being out of bounds with my meal.

My lawsuit, (argument and ruling), was originally published online, but that was taken down. The Government does not want federal inmates filing lawsuits thinking that they can win. That's why Congress made the process of getting any kind of meaningful relief while incarcerated onerous and full of time delay. Only once you exhaust your administrative remedy options, then can you file on the court. It's rare that an inmate will make it all the way to court and even rarer for an inmate to win his case. In my case I won, but the last thing the Government wants is the kind of publicity that suggests other inmates should file lawsuits as well, so my case is no longer public.

I kept a copy of my federal lawsuit against the BOP, entitled, "CV-06-37-TC" (Civil case, year filed, case number, judge's initials); so here is the ruling and judgment on my case:

*"**Findings** – Petitioner argues that his conduct did not constitute 'stealing'. I [Judge Coffin] agree. It is undisputed that petitioner was issued the food for his personal consumption. Petitioner's argument that these circumstances are distinguishable from the 'milk' example cited by the Hearing Officer is persuasive. Petitioner acknowledges that he may have violated institution rules or program statements against 'possession of contraband' by removing food from the dining hall. However, as noted by petitioner, such a violation would not carry the sanction of loss of earned good conduct time. Respondent has not identified any institution rule that defines or could reasonably be construed as defining petitioner's conduct as 'stealing'. Under these circumstances, I find that the 'some evidence' to support disciplinary decision requirement was not met.*

*"**Judgment** – Petitioner's petition is granted to the extent that the Bureau of Prisons is ordered to restore the 27 days good conduct forfeited by petitioner as a result of the incident giving rise to his claims herein. /S/ United States District Judge"*

The BOP, generally, is very much loathe to be told what to do by the courts. Being established by the Legislature, for most things they take court rulings as advisory only, and in this case the new BOP Hearing Officer did not want to implement the court's ruling. He told me that even though I had been punished with 90 days in the hole, 6 months loss of commissary and a disciplinary transfer for a malapropos charge that was now dismissed; that I would still have to lose my 27 days good time for being in possession of contraband, that being my own meal, and that would be his ruling on the matter.

I balked. A federal district judge had just ordered restoration of my good conduct time; and essentially, I was now being intimidated into accepting the continued loss of good time. I told the Disciplinary Officer that the federal judge had specifically restored my good time and that what the officer was trying to do was illegal and unethical. Of course, I told him those things *nicely*. Then I told him that his recommendation amounted to BOP retaliation for winning my case and that if he did not immediately restore my good conduct time per court order that I would file *another* (turnaround) lawsuit asking for a contempt of court charge and sanctions on this officer. By then he knew I was serious. He dismissed the theft charge and restored my good conduct time. Case closed.

And so, with almost two years to wait before I would actually win my case in federal court, I would now be subject to an illegitimate and baseless punishment. I was informed about 10 days before my disciplinary transfer that I was re-designated out of State to an Arizona FCI, considered a "Low" in the BOP, called FCI Safford. It had a fence around it and all of my movement would be controlled and henceforth subjected to monitoring. When your security rating goes up, your coterminous residence security also goes up.

Being in the hole, you are not afforded many things and one of them is a hardcover book. Only paperbacks are allowed. Staff was concerned that the hardcover could be removed to fashion a weapon, yet they provide every inmate with razors, whose blades can easily be removed; and for me they allowed me my *tefillin*; long "dangerous" leather straps and all. This hardcover book prohibition took on significance for me because as the High Holidays (Rosh Hashana and Yom Kippur) were approaching, the only prayer books available were hardbound. I wrote to the chaplain, a non-Jew, who was purported to have a fascination with Nazi propaganda and war memorabilia in his office and someone who had never been a strong advocate for the Jewish community in prison. I explained my situation. He refused to allow me the book.

As fortune would have it, the rabbi to our camp was a man named Shmuli Schlanger. He's currently the head rabbi of Chabad of Bakersfield. He visited our group in camp and when he heard that I was in the hole, he made a special visit to see me. I was taken in handcuffs out of my cell to meet with him. It was the day before Yom Kippur. While I was shackled, he sang a very moving Kol Nidre for me and I wept openly. I thought that I would keep that melody in my heart and head and that would see me through the fast day. I'll never forget Shmuli pouring his heart out to me in song. The next day, two hours before the fast came in, I received the Yom Kippur prayer book through my meal slot. There was no hardcover attached, though. Shmuli, upon beseeching the chaplain to allow me to have this prayer book, but getting nowhere with the guy, took the book and tore off the hardcover and told him to deliver the prayer book to me immediately. G-d bless Rabbi Shmuli Schlanger.

Finally, at the end of my stint in the Taft hole, I was shackled up and taken to a waiting bus for my disciplinary transfer to Arizona. This would be my first experience with BOP intra-institution transit. The BOP maintains a fleet of transit busses, costing upwards of $500,000 apiece, complete with caged interior, satellite tracking and other fun items known only to the BOP. There are three armed escorts on the bus and there is only one open splashing toilet at the back… but considering how you are shackled it's more of a joke than a place to relieve yourself. There's no way for you to be able to lower your pants to be able to effectively use the facilities for voiding; and forget about evacuation.

Some inmates are black boxed, a device that was developed by an inmate. It's a metal box that locks over the handcuff chain making it impossible to move your hands at all. This control device is placed on inmates with a history of violence. Your only food is a sack lunch with a smashed meat and cheese sandwich and an apple usually also smashed. Of course, for inmates like me, I normally just starved.

I recall sitting next to a particularly interesting Mexican fellow who had numerous tattoos all over his arms and his face. One particular tattoo that he had inked into his forehead read, "*FUCK THE FEDS*".

I realized then and there that I was indeed a long way from home, shackled belly to wrists and ankle to ankle on a BOP prison bus riding next to some guy named Paco with a face tattoo telling his BOP captors exactly what they could do to themselves.

I started to laugh. Then one of the BOP transport guards also noticed Paco's forehead and challenged him, getting right in his face, bullying him. Of course, I'm physically chained and seated in between all of this.

The guard admonished him, "You think that's cool, inmate? You think you're a tough guy with a *tat* like that?"

It went on for a bit like that, the guard bullying and posturing and there's really nothing for the inmate to do; he's defenseless, so he puts up with it. BOP guards also really don't take kindly to being called "guards"; (they prefer to be called, "CO", as in, "Correctional Officer"), and they definitely don't take kindly to tattoos like the one my seatmate Paco was sporting on his face.

The drive was uneventful, and we stopped at, you guessed it, San Bernadino, where in about 3 weeks another BOP bus would be along to take me to Arizona. Since I had been a previous guest of the facility, they returned me to one-man special housing in case anyone might still be there from before and recognize me. In San Bernadino; once you are designated a "protective custody inmate", you are always placed in special housing.

I immediately got to petitioning the captain and chaplain to provide me with kosher meals. And then I began to threaten legal action. As a federal inmate I had a right to eat kosher. My rights did not just disappear because I was being housed in a contract facility. After about a week of this, they bumped another inmate off the Arizona transport and gave me his spot. I was on my way, two weeks early.

We left San Bernadino the next morning before light and were on the bus for close to 10 hours. We had a stopover for about 3 days in an FCI – Medium in Phoenix. We were housed in transport holding, which is like special housing, just more crowded. We were as a group marched over to the dining hall to eat our meals and I was afforded kosher fare. It was noticeable that most of the servers were of the white race, sporting tattoos with Nazi symbols and propaganda all over their arms, heads and necks. I've never seen so much Nazi ink so close up. There were blazing pictures of Hitler and swastikas and iron crosses inked into skulls and cheeks and chins and necks. Of course, then there was me, "sporting" *yarmulke* and *tzitzis*, getting my kosher meals and washing for bread. The stares I caught were epic. There was a palpable feeling of *incredulousness* that here these guys were in their own little prison Hitler world and this Jew had just popped their bubble, and they were reeling in discontent. It was serious and I could imagine that none of the skinhead, white supremacist food service Nazis were happy to see me; but the institution staff was very vigilant and stood close guard, so I ate in relative peace.

The one thing I learned along the way. Be respectful. Go out of your way to be respectful. But never, ever, back down from your principles and values. Those kinds of guys were what prison staff would call predators. I would call them jackals, looking for weak people to dominate and tear apart. Of course, any one inmate can be overpowered by a group, but depending on how you held yourself determined whether or not you would become a target.

Three days later we boarded a bus for our final leg to FCI - Safford.

Federal Correctional Institution – Safford

We arrived at a wasteland called Safford, Arizona, population: 9,500; a one-horse town northeast of Tucson not that far from the Mexican border. The BOP likes to build its prisons in remote areas, and this was no different.

We all hobbled off the bus under shotgun watch of the BOP rover vehicles that had stopped to lend escort assistance to the offloading guards. We were mustered up in a line-by-line formation and it was made very-clear to us that escapes would not be tolerated; in point-of-fact the guard gestured at us with his shotgun... you would be shot dead. *Welcome to Fantasy Island.*

Inside, the place looked like a high school campus; there was a main intake building which tumbled out onto a campus surrounded by housing units and in the center of the quad was a concrete and grassy area where televisions were mounted. No TVs in the housing units. A good start. At the end of the complex was the dining hall and commissary. To the left of that was the Lieutenant's office and further in was medical. To the right of the housing area were laundry facilities, a chapel and the weight pile and law library. I immediately got a job on the weight pile, picking up after inmates. It was a great job because I was able to bulk up and do my cardio exercises quite often. I ran miles daily, lifted weights and had a Pilates core and bar workout routine, ongoing. I was in the best health of my life.

My food was all kosher and I sincerely never had any food related issues while at Safford.

Being that I was now in a "Low" (fenced low security prison) provided for an interesting set of characters available in my new orbit. I was on my way up in security points because of being falsely charged with stealing; but many of the inmates I met were on their way down in security points because of good behavior and less time left to do. Many inmates had been in USPs and FCIs – High/Medium because of the severity of their crimes and the sheer amount of time still left on their sentences. Lots of these inmates were on their way ultimately to camps and so mostly all of them were well-behaved.

There were a few notable differences in the inmate make up. While there had always been lots of white guys where I had been, here the makeup was more hardcore supremacists, though mostly non-violent by this time. They ended up hanging around one another sporting their Nazi-influenced ink. The white supremacists' head art was memorable. One guy had what looked like a gigantic scrambled egg inked into his forehead and bald scalp. I asked others about it and was told that he had been trying for a large tarantula tattoo. So, either the "artist" had been on meth when he set the ink; or the guy had it done in prison by an amateur... or perhaps both. Another Nazi guy had the word "HATE" in 72-point lettering on the side of his head. Others had swastikas inked on their chests. (One black guy was advertising a non-existent verse from a Jewish psalm, inked into his neck, Psalm 25: [verse] 75.)

Also, I noticed that for all their "toughness" that the white supremacist crew was very insecure and most, if not all, were into homosexual behaviors. There were a number of effeminate inmates who would advertise for attention and invariably it was always a white supremacist who was giving it to such an inmate.

I also noticed in this new environment an explosion of child molesters. They had their own large group; and as their security points dropped, they started gathering more and more in these types of FCI Low prisons, because they could never get a management variable to go to an unsecured camp location. So, their numbers ballooned. They were regarded with disgust and revulsion by most of the other inmates, me included. But they were mostly safe from inmate reprisal because no one wanted to go up in security by striking one of them.

Lastly, I noticed significant numbers of Native Americans, mainly Navajo. They were of few words but mostly very respectful. I learned words like "hello" and "friend" and "what's up?" so I could address them; and one day off-hand I asked one how to say, "I'm sorry, forgive me."

I was told by the guy that their language had no such expression. I looked at him quizzically. I said, "What if I bumped into you accidentally and I wanted to tell you that, 'I'm sorry?'"

He shrugged his shoulders and said, "If I thought you did it by accident and didn't mean anything by it, I wouldn't beat the shit out of you. No need to apologize."

In prison, especially in the higher security facilities, the strangest paradoxes existed. Take for instance a Jewish inmate named Gutheim, whose mother actually taught me in Hebrew school at a Conservative Temple called Ramat Zion in Northridge, CA. He was best buddies with a Nazi sporting a swastika on his chest and this Nazi would frequently sit shirtless on Gutheims's bed with the swastika right in his face. Neither seemed to mind. It may have been the case that the guy with the offensive tattoo had reformed and no longer held by those beliefs, but who knows?

Then there was the head Nazi, who was enormous. Double muscled, prison savvy and very violent, he was no one to mess with. But he respected me. And he did me a solid favor near the end of my stay in Safford.

Once every 30 days or so, we received a visit from a Chabad Rabbi, Dan Hayman, who would come from 3 hours away to the 15 or so inmates who identified as "Jewish". Most of them were not actually Jewish; there was one Israeli and maybe one or two others who were halachically (according to Torah law) Jewish.

Even though I did not yet have rabbinical ordination, aside of the monthly two-hour rabbinical visit, I was the closest thing to a rabbi on the prison campus. I led Shabbos services and made sure that Pesach meals and prep conformed to kosher standards. I also counseled Jewish and non-Jewish inmates and staff on all things Jewish.

There was of course a huge population of Christian inmates and my presence certainly sparked lots of talk. Many of them had grown up steeped in their Christian New Testament churches and had never seen a religious Jew up close and some were genuinely curious. Some even approached me to ask how my *yarmulke* stayed on my head. I said with a deadpan coyness, "My horns...."

A group of Christian inmates asked for a meeting; they could not understand, based on their upbringing and understanding, how a Jew could reject the Christian messiah. I agreed to take the meeting.

Three inmates and I met in the chapel and I explained very clearly the misunderstandings and mistranslations and actual fraud that the New Testament writers tried to foist on their unwitting Gentile audience. I explained context and translation, even how Matthew took passages out of context and then mistranslated, including in Isaiah 7 the words for, "*the* young woman", who was Isaiah's wife. Matthew made up a novel and illegitimate NT prophesy simply by changing the specific biblical Hebrew words, "הָעַלְמָה" (*ha*-almah – *the* young woman), who (in context) was known to be Isaiah's wife *and* was *already pregnant*... into the NT words, "*a* virgin", and nobody would be the wiser. Had Isaiah wished to speak about a virgin, he would have used the word, "בְּתוּלָה" (besulah), *not* almah.

Matthew's audience, at first, was supposed to be the Jewish people; however, they rejected his heresy outright, because they could read the original Hebrew text. It ended up being that Matthew's forgeries were picked up by a bunch of pagan Gentiles who were used to "virgin births" and "god-men" and who were unable to read the original Hebrew text. I let my new friends know that the so-called "virgin" birth, like most of the New Testament was a fraud, a fallacy; and that is why the Jewish people rejected it... and for no other reason.

I gave more and more examples, including the biblical requirements for the messiah, but only one of the inmates sitting there seemed to be engaged. The others' eyes glossed over, and they seemed unwilling to grasp what I was saying. I realized that they were likely not there to learn from me; they were in fact totally unprepared to hear from a Jew that there was no basis to their faith.

So, I simply finished my talk by saying, "It is (biblically) forbidden for a Jew to participate in this (Christianity)."

I wished them well and started to leave, but then the third inmate, whose name was Sean, wanted to know what my operational definition was for the word, "Jew". I told him simply if you have a Jewish mother (and Jewish grandmother on your mother's side) or a proper conversion, then you are Jewish.

He said, "My mom is Jewish."

I told him in front of his friends: "If so, then you have no business worshipping Christianity and you need to return to the faith of your fathers. Now that you know you are a Jew you need to act like one."

Sean and I would spend many hours together learning about Judaism after that. He never went back to church and he changed his religious preference (to the chagrin of the chaplain and other Christians) to "Jewish". He began to keep Shabbos, put on *tefillin* and eat kosher meals.

Sean's path was not an easy one. Sean admitted to me in a moment of pain, having never told anyone before, that he was a serial killer. He had killed over 19 people in his short life as a drug dealer and had maimed scores of others. I never lost sight of the fact that the man I was sitting next to was (hopefully reformed as) a killer. He grew up in an abusive home with a non-Jewish father who beat and raped him repeatedly. He had never been charged in any of the murders he had committed and instead was in prison for a short time on a drug charge. But his life up until that point had been one of violence and drugs and since he was white, he had unwittingly joined the skinheads and Nazi prison gangs; and was the right-hand man of the head Nazi.

So, here's Sean realizing he's Jewish with tattoos and a shaved head and lots of white guys who look up to him, now sitting with me, wearing a *yarmulke* and eating kosher. The head Nazi took it in stride; he respected me, and he respected Sean.

I've come to realize that most white guys who join the Nazis in prison only do so because they need to belong to something. They have no real idea what the Nazis actually stood for, their socialist agenda, other than they were "tough whites" who wanted to be perceived as hating everyone, which is all a scared, lost and alone inmate wants to have in his life when he goes to jail. He wants to belong to a tough group and have friends.

When you go to prison, you leave a lot of loose ends. One of the many torments of prison is the ongoing knowledge that you have left so many things undone. My debts and defunct marriage both began to weigh on me. Having been in prison for so long and not having the means to pay off my credit cards and other obligations was untenable. At some point I knew I would be releasing and having to come back to mountains of unpaid debt accruing interest and having a terrible credit rating was not something I wanted over my head. So, by October 2005, I filed in Arizona federal court for bankruptcy protection and had all of my civil debts discharged under federal law. The year I filed was also the last year that credit card obligations could be discharged in bankruptcy court. Congress changed the law as of January 2006. So, when I emerged from prison and applied for credit again, I had no obligations on my record and my FICO score was already into the mid-700s.

I also was able to finalize my civil divorce from Miriam. I had already given her a *gett*, (a religious divorce) while I was in MCC-SD and then I obtained a dissolution of marriage order from the Superior Court of California, also while behind a fence in Arizona; because I was able to convince the clerk of the court to have me "appear" in front of the judge, telephonically.

My grandparents on my mother's side came to visit. My grandfather, Paul, was already in failing health. He was suffering from prostate cancer. That visit behind a razor wire fence would be the last time I would ever see him in this world, and I think we both knew it. I know my grandfather loved me; he made a very arduous trip to see me in order to say goodbye.

I had been in Safford for about 9 months when my security points went down, and I was rated for camp again. While Safford began the process of getting me transferred back to camp, I was moved to a special dorm called Echo Unit. Unlike the other dorms on campus that were locked by staff, Echo Unit was open, and our movements were not controlled. So, we were afforded camp-like status while still being in a Low. It also required that we work outside the fence being on menial and excruciatingly boring work details like picking weeds and moving dirt piles, digging holes to nowhere, and essentially wandering around the perimeter of the prison in 102-degree heat for 8 hours a day. It was actually one of the *worst* experiences I've had in prison. I felt like a zombie trudging around trying (and failing) to look busy with mind numbingly meaningless "work".

In my unit was a white guy, perhaps 55 who was in on a weapons charge. He had previously been convicted of a felony on a drug charge and was ineligible to possess firearms. But he had a .22 rifle, minding his own business on his property and was doing target practice. His neighbor heard the gunfire and called the FBI. He was re-arrested for being a felon in possession of a gun and given an additional 36 months.

In the feds, the felonious possession of a firearm can get you up to 15 years in prison. Each bullet you possess can give you up to 5 years, apiece. If you have one handgun and 20 bullets, run consecutively, you are looking at a life sentence. So that guy was fortunate that all he got was a relatively short prison sentence.

Fortunate or not, he was a bitter, ignorant racist and not apologetic about it. My presence in the Echo dorm was difficult for him. He began to challenge me and harass me. He made me feel that it was only a matter of time before I would be in a fist fight with him. In my entire tenure in the BOP, around murderers, bank robbers, rapists, drug kingpins, Nazis, etc., etc., I've never felt so certain that I would be forced to come to blows with this angry white guy in on a gun charge.

One fateful day our outside crew was in front of the prison, and we were tasked with raking leaves. This guy came right up to me and told me that he'd had enough of me and he was ready to let his fists do the talking. He actually raised his fists to me threatening to hit me. I have no recollection of what stupid thing set him off, but it was likely nothing except an excuse for him to try and brutalize me. He had no idea what was about to fly off on him, though.

I threw down my rake. As I did so, I switched my left leg back, leaving my right hand and right leg forward, knees slightly bent, ready to kick low/high and strike... my fists immediately coming up in a tight, trained boxer's pose. It was actually a southpaw kickboxing stance. I squared off with him, measuring my distance and then waited for his attack. Never, before that moment aside of sparing with my bunkie Derek, had I done anything remotely like what I was contemplating I was about to do. Never, before, had I raised my fists to anyone in prison.

But, just from how I came up into a fighting stance it was clear to that guy, right then, that I was a trained fighter, and I knew that the guy knew. I felt a rage begin to surge in me; a quiet sort of fury, controlled, but also ready to unleash a great force of intensity. I had some choice words for him, and I was seething, now ready to beat the hell out of him. I would go to the hole. I would lose my camp transfer. But I was not going to let this guy threaten me any longer. His eyes grew big... and then he dropped his hands and walked away.

I walked around for the rest of the day with all this adrenaline and the awful feeling that I would never be able to go to sleep again for fear of this angry white guy, who was clearly "off", snapping and attacking me while I slept. I had embarrassed him in front of the entire inmate crew, and I knew that he would want revenge.

Later that evening I told my new Jewish friend Sean what had happened; and since they were in the same white guy prison "car", I asked what he suggested I do. Sean told me that he would take care of it.

That night my tormentor got a visit from the head Nazi. He came into our Echo dorm unit, which for him could have gotten him thrown into the hole because it was out of bounds for any inmate not so designated; and they had a heart-to-heart conversation. I was listening from my rack, as this enormous head Nazi woke him up and told him to stay away from me.

He said, "You let Diamand do his time. You stay away from him or you and I are going to have a big problem. Do you understand? *You stay the fuck away from Diamand.*"

My tormentor could not believe what he was hearing. The head Nazi was running interference for me! He was incredulous, bleating, "He's a Jew. How could you?"

The head Nazi said, "You just let him do his time. Don't make me come back here again."

And that was it. That angry white guy never looked at me or spoke to me again.

As the date for my transfer got near, I realized that my transfer was being scheduled very close to the Jewish High Holidays, Rosh Hashana and Yom Kippur. I went to my counselor and unit team to try to explain that I could not leave until after the holidays, so as not to risk traveling *on* those days.

Normally inmates transferring *to* camps are allowed to self-report; that is, the BOP releases the inmate on his own recognizance, gives him a bus pass and allows him a certain amount of time to report to the new facility. My problem would have been that if they released me without enough time before the holiday, due to Jewish law restrictions, I would be stuck not being able to travel and therefore be technically AWOL and in a lot of trouble. To mitigate this, I suggested other dates for my transfer. My counselor and unit team responded by simply having me shackled and forcibly transferred to Oregon on a BOP bus 1 day before Rosh Hashana. Apparently, they did not appreciate the significance of the Jewish holidays or simply did not care.

After 12 hours shackled on that bus on our way to Sheridan, Oregon we stopped at a USP holding facility to await the next BOP bus to our next destination. I'll never get over coming into a USP, with the gun towers and death fence; high voltage electrified fencing and huge solid walls, *in addition to* the two chain link fences and razor wire. We were off loaded and housed in a special housing unit. The next two days were Rosh Hashana and I celebrated them as best I could with another Jewish inmate who was housed with me. After a week our next transport arrived, and we were re-shackled and boarded the next bus. It was the day before the holiest day of the Jewish year, Yom Kippur.

After *another* 12 hours on that BOP bus with nothing to prepare for the fast the next day except for a minimal kosher sack lunch, we arrived at the BOP regional headquarters in Dublin, California and offloaded into the FCI-Low. There was no time to order kosher food and no time left to eat. The fast had already begun. I arrived to my holding cell just at sunset and began Kol Nidre (the beginning of the Yom Kippur prayer) in tears. I said the holiday evening prayer and fell asleep.

The next morning, I was awoken before dawn and brought a non-kosher breakfast, which, even if it was kosher, I couldn't have eaten anyway; and then I was led to another holding cell for transfer to my final destination. Expecting that I would be left alone for this holiday, I was actually surprised when they came for me. At that point, I simply gave up trying to explain the situation to the early morning CO, who clearly wasn't taking religious requests. I was forcibly shackled and reloaded onto the next bus.

So, on Yom Kippur, October 13, 2005, I was put onto a prison bus, hands cuffed and locked to a belly chain with ankles shackled. Though I knew I would not be eating or drinking that entire day, I also had no idea when my next meal would come, if ever; and the thought of ending my fast without anything to eat was just a tiny bit discomforting. In preparation for this fast, I had only had that small lunch the day before.

I hobbled up to the CO riding literal *shotgun* in the front of the bus, asking if there would be any kosher food available. He advised me that there was nothing available. I told him then I would just fast. I don't think he realized I was also voluntarily fasting. But he seemed concerned because there was no kosher food available and advised me that he would radio ahead to our destination to make sure that there would be something kosher waiting for me when we all de-bussed.

About midway into our journey, the CO driving the bus thought it would be funny to pipe in Christian music to the inmate section of the bus. I'm not sure if the reader can appreciate the physical and spiritual hell in which I found myself; metal chaffing my wrists and crushing my ankles, leaning back against a metal chain around my waist, unable to use the restroom, fatigued, thirsty, starving, with a fractious headache, being jostled and bounced around on a 12 hour bus ride on the holiest day of the Jewish year; and now the *coup de grace*, being forced to listen to some Christian music group singing, "You got a friend in Jesus."

Knowing, even then, that I would be laughing about this in 10 years, didn't quite quell the animus I was feeling right then, though. It was a definite low point for me. However, I also understood that being in that specific position at that specific moment was deliberate and Divinely Providential. It was all from G-d. And since I believe that G-d is good, then being placed there was for the good, and only for the good, there could be no anger. There could only be an appreciation of the need for an *aliyah* (ascent/elevation) from this *yeridah* (descent). In life the descent is usually obvious; but perceiving the ultimate ascent? What possible good existed on this prison bus?

As one of the greatest Chassidic masters, the Alter Rebbe, wrote in his Torah Ohr on Bereshis p. 30a.: "*Yeridah* (decent) is for the sole purpose of a subsequent *aliyah* (ascent)."

The whole point of descending is in order to be able to reach/elevate even higher. A person can regard the descent critically, blame G-d, blame the system and beat his head against a wall; become angry or worried or frightened. Alternatively, he can view this low place devoid of any apparent holiness or purpose, and recognize that the *lower* you go, the *higher* you can reach; that the loftiest revelations can be discovered in the lowest places.

The Rebbe has a famous letter where he replies to somebody that an alien from another planet entering an operating theater would not imagine that the surgeon and his team, cutting the patient open, were doing something intended for the ultimate good of the patient. But, in fact, what was happening in that operating theater was that, leaving aside personal gratification, that medical team was dedicated to doing something positive for that person.

So, I took everything in theoretical stride, shackled as it were. As the sun began to set, I recognized it was the time for Neilah, the holiest part of the day of Yom Kippur, and though I did not have a siddur (prayer book) with me, I offered up my confessions and prayers to G-d.

As dusk descended, our bus arrived at the main administrative detention center in Sheridan, Oregon. I hobbled off the bus and into a maximum-security holding facility for the final time in my stay with the BOP.

Federal Correction Institute - Sheridan

Inside the holding cells in the main detention center, shackles finally off, the horrendous day of travel was over… and I noticed by that time that Yom Kippur had just ended. I felt as though my suffering of late had to be an atonement of sorts for so many blunders and missteps in my life until then, and I felt that G-d had accepted my prayers and I was surprisingly grateful for my lot. Just then the steel door opened, and staff delivered to me a beautifully saran-wrapped kosher meal with lots of raw vegetables, bread and the biggest muffin I had ever seen all with proper kosher certifications stamped thereon. It was a perfect ending to one of the most messed up days I have ever had.

We were all marched into the bowels of the maximum-security building for what was supposed to be three weeks of evaluation. Every inmate who arrives must wait in transport holding while evaluations are conducted as to camp suitability and to ensure there is room at the camp. Three weeks of being boxed up lay ahead!

The next morning, I alerted the babysitting CO that I needed to be let out to pray. The staff had confiscated my *tefillin* and large *tallis* and I asked for them back. After a lot of back and forth and significant push back, a lieutenant was called in and he let me out of my small cement and steel cube, gave me my bag and led me to the law library where I was left alone to pray. When I was done, I returned to my unit and went back to my locked cube. I was so happy! Having just succeeded in meeting my morning religious obligations under the most onerous of circumstances, I was quite incredulous at my good fortune.

Then, 30 minutes later, I was summoned to the lieutenant's office, given my religious bag and sent over to the camp. Apparently, administrative staff did not want to have to deal with my continuing religious requests. The whole concept of being subject to high-power lock down security became a non-sequitur in my case because every time I had to be let out of my cell to pray turned their vaunted high security protocol on its head. My camp transfer was approved in record time and I was pushed to the front of the line. I left other camp-designated inmates who came in with me in that holding facility that I would not see again for weeks, while my transfer was approved in minutes.

I walked myself over to Sheridan camp to begin what would become the last 2 years of my prison sentence. Sheridan camp, like most other camps in the BOP system, was a satellite facility attached to the larger FCI situated on the other side of the sprawling prison grounds. It had 4 main dorms, two wings each attached to two buildings. The grounds looked more like a posh golf course complete with two lakes in the close distance. But looks can be deceiving. The lakes were literally human waste receiving treatment ponds with a steady flow of raw FCI and camp sewage flowing into those lakes. At the end of the greens, right before the pond, was a gigantic fecal collector that caught all the solid waste before it entered the pond and then compacted it and spit it out the other end in dried waste pies. Welcome to Sheridan camp!

Sheridan was the first prison that afforded me four full seasons; but each season was very mild. I actually enjoyed the weather. It was never too cold, even when it snowed.

I was able to get an evening shift, making 17 cents per hour weekdays at the Powerhouse. This was the facility that provided all the electricity and heat to the FCI and the camp, and my job was to monitor and record the gauge readings to ensure that there were no spikes or drops in pressure. The COs were mostly good guys, more into the engineering component of their jobs than the security and punishment component usually relished by most BOP guards. I even got my prison driver's license so that I could drive the staff truck on the reservation.

I got kosher food, was able to build a kosher Sukkah and make kosher Pesach. I began to run long distances, like 13 miles at a time and worked out on the weight pile.

The warden at the time was all about his forward movement in the BOP and tried to come up with innovative programs to impress his superiors, so he had his lush grounds plowed and seeded with hearty string bean and strawberry plants and when they sprouted, forced all the camp inmates onto those fields to harvest.

Now it's a long way from chain gangs and forced labor camps, but right there in Sheridan, Oregon, the warden did not seem to care. It was an all hands on-deck operation. If you did not want to be rolled up and sent to the hole, you had better be out in the field harvesting beans or picking strawberries. A number of inmates were sent to the hole for malingering, and I was almost one of them. I had a night shift job ensuring that the camp got heat and hot water and electricity and did not blow up… and what the warden was asking of me was to work a 2nd job for no pay in order to impress his superiors. Inmates clean every spot in prison including the warden's office. And those inmates came back with reports of the warden's bean folly from reading correspondence left on his desk.

It turns out that the cost of the seeding and watering the fields was far and away more expensive than simply purchasing the beans from a local vendor. The warden had accrued so much wasteful irrigation expense, and to cover for it, he made the inmates shoulder the work burden of harvesting and eating those beans, all the while concealing the actual cost of his fool's errand from the BOP main office. When the BOP main office found out about it, we all figured he would be discharged. But like all great governmental bureaucracies, cronyism rules the roost. Instead of firing the warden, they gave him a promotion. He got a cushy oversight job in Washington at BOP HQ to "reward" him for spending the BOP's money on an irrigation road to nowhere.

I was non-too interested in participating in the warden's incompetent scheme to exploit his inmates, having mismanaged the prison's budget under his watch. The boondoggle was meant only to benefit his appearance. So, I went to medical and got a clearance not to have to go into the fields and pick the warden's beans. While inmate after inmate hemmed and hawed and ultimately got rolled up and sent to the hole, I simply pulled out my pink medical release and was left alone. Of course, when the other inmates came back from a day in the field after having worked a full day doing their other assigned duties, I caught a lot of hard stares and some unseemly comments; but I wasn't going into that field if I could help it. Some things I just would not bend on. And on the bean fields, I found a way not to have to bend.

I ended up being at that camp for just over two years. I kept my job at the Powerhouse throughout. There was one "senior" inmate at the Powerhouse, but he was assigned to the day shift. Still, he set rules and protocols that he expected all the other inmates (and COs) on the other shifts should follow. Also named David, he was a bit of a prima-donna; but no one would fire him or tell him to "cool it" because he knew more than the COs about how operations ran. He kept records and files; and losing him would have created a huge amount of additional (if not impossible) work for the COs. Most COs were ex-military, having done their time in the Armed Forces; they were just looking for a way to collect their pensions, while expiring out their government contracts without having to work too hard.

Anyway, this David was very particular about his office, which was situated in a bird's nest location in the Powerhouse, up some stairs and overlooking the main floor. He had a special chair that was his alone. Of course, no inmate has their own office, but David felt that that area was his and sacrosanct. However, on evening shift, when all the other inmates were seated at the desk space allotted on the main floor, there was nowhere else to sit. So, as the senior inmate on duty, I took the bird's nest desk. In between gauge readings once an hour, there was literally nothing else to do, so I would bring Torah to learn, Hebrew and Yiddish and write letters to my family and friends.

Invariably I would forget to push his high-backed faux leather chair into the exact position I found it in when I arrived for my shift, and the next night I would find a note addressed to the evening shift that read, "No one is to sit in my (David's) chair or at my desk."

I had had enough of this. I asked another inmate to join me in the bird's nest and assist me in lifting "David's chair" down the stairs and then with the help of a third inmate, (and under the amused supervision of the night watch CO), into the actual boiler room. There we crammed that chair into a corner, wedging it in so that it was fairly well-hidden. In place of the chair in his bird's nest I placed a plumber's bucket upside down. On top of that bucket, I left his note.

The next morning Mr. Murrell, the senior day-watch CO at the Powerhouse, called over the camp loudspeaker, "Inmate Diamand. Inmate Diamand. Report to the Powerhouse. NOW!"

Murrell clearly sounded upset. I knew exactly what it was about, and I wondered if I would be fired or worse; sent to the hole. With a bit of trepidation, I walked over to the Powerhouse. When I opened the door, I found a number of staff commiserating with that senior inmate, trying to assuage his sensibilities about finding a bucket (and his note) where his chair used to be.

Murrell turned his attention from listening to the inmate pule to me, ordering me into his office. Once we were both inside, Murrell shut the door.

"Diamand, do you see that inmate over there bellyaching?" Murrell asked.

"Yes, sir," I said.

"Do you understand that we need that inmate to ensure our operations run smoothly?" Murrell continued.

"Yes, sir," I said.

"Diamand, I am only going to ask you this one time. Did you take that inmate's chair and replace it with a bucket?"

"Yes, sir," I said.

I waited for him to fire me or order me to turn around and cuff up, thinking I was on my way to the hole. To my surprise, Murrell started to laugh. He turned slightly away from the window so that the very upset senior inmate could not see him cracking up.

"A bucket!" He guffawed, "A bucket. You should've seen the look on his face when he saw that bucket under his desk with the note you left on it…. and his chair in the boiler room! Diamand, you crack me up. I appreciate your honesty, owning up to this. Now, in all seriousness (as he began to chuckle), don't do it again."

Other duties of the evening Powerhouse crew were to clean the BOP transport busses; the same type of bus that I had arrived in handcuffed and shackled. It was a bit surreal walking freely onto this $500,000 jail on wheels, walking past the seats I used to sit in, picking up the uneaten sack lunches strewn on the floors, thinking about the mass of humanity that sat in that very bus, not an hour before, chained, in pain, scared, lost, cold, tired and alone. True they were all there to pay for a crime, but their humanity is what grabbed at me. My crew and I mopped and disinfected the bus. The CO's tactical bags were left on the front seats; attached were their batons with a steel ball at the end of them. It was odd to me that a BOP weapon, a deadly weapon, was so casually left by the COs for any inmate to happen across. On one of those night cleanings, as I was finishing the bus, a large black CO came back on board and recognized me by my *yarmulke*. Then he addressed me:

"Weren't you the one who said you needed kosher food that day on this bus... and we didn't have anything for you? Did they give you something kosher to eat at the jail when we let you off the bus?" He asked in a genuine concern.

I replied, "Yes, I was finally able to eat when I got to the jail. They had kosher food for me. Thank you so much for radioing ahead on my behalf. I was literally starving. I hadn't eaten since lunch mid-day before."

He nodded and said, "That's a long time to go without food."

Smiling, I said, "It was only 26 hours I had to go without food. It's not like the end of the world...."

He was shocked and looked at me like I had a plant growing out of my head.

He said, "Inmate, you are as cool *as fuck*. I never met anyone who didn't complain about mealtimes. Most inmates throw a shit fit if you are late serving them *one meal*. You went without food for a whole day and, 'it's not the end of the world…?!'"

He maintained a look of incredulousness, perhaps even a wrinkle of admiration. I smiled, thanked him again and exited the bus.

Shortly thereafter, I received a call from the chaplain. He had my grandmother on the phone. He said that my grandfather was in serious decline and that I should call as soon as possible. When I called, my grandmother told me that my grandfather had literally days if not hours to live and was there any way I could get a furlough to say goodbye in person. The BOP would not give me a furlough. I asked to speak to my grandfather.

"David?" I heard my grandfather weakly say into the phone. It was a voice I could hardly recognize. I immediately began to tear up and then cried openly.

"Papa…. Tell me something good," I wept into the phone.

"I love you David," came his definitive response and they were the last words he ever spoke to me.

My last words were, "I love you, too. Goodbye, Papa."

He passed away that night. Two of my grandparents had already left this Earth and I had not been able to be present with them. I felt like I had been kicked in the gut and I walked around for a week after, grieving. Eventually, the cloud lifted a bit, and I could function again.

Every 30 days we received a rabbinical visit from the local Chabad Rabbi, Chayim Mishulovin. I bring him up because as I was getting ready to release from prison, I realized that I had nothing to go home to and one of my biggest concerns was that I did not have any proper clothes to celebrate the Shabbos in; everything had been thrown away or destroyed when I went to prison. He offered the black fedora off his head and his long black silk Shabbos jacket (called a kapote) to me. I ended up walking out of federal prison wearing his silk kapote the day I left, and I have never forgotten his selfless act of clothing a fellow Jew with something so special and dear to him.

I had a few friends on the outside and as I was getting nearer to my release date, I wrote a letter to one such friend, Leonard, my accountant, about my concerns. He wrote me back saying, "Don't you worry. I will have clothes, a car, a job... and a wife for you. Don't you worry." True to his word, he gave me his car and clothes, found me a job... and introduced me to my future wife.

There were many Shabbos days in prison that I would read a Jewish newspaper called *The Jewish Press*. One Shabbos afternoon I turned a page and there I saw an article about a rabbi who had donated his kidney to save someone else's life. Everything for me came into clarity. I knew exactly what I wanted to do when I had the chance and seeing that I could alleviate someone's suffering was a huge uplift for me. I wrote to my surviving grandmother that I wanted to donate my kidney when I got out. She did not seem pleased with the idea, so I let it sit in the back of my head. It took me over a decade since reading that article to come to terms with the fact that I would have to part with one of my organs, but on March 13, 2018, a full 11 years later, I had the merit of donating my left kidney, and saving someone (and his family) from a life of pain and misery.

January 2008 had arrived. I was allowed to complete my last 6 months of prison in a halfway house. I was told to report to the main jail to get my plane ticket and change back into my civilian clothes, suit and tie, and long black coat courtesy of Chayim Mishulovin, for my ride home.

I had to then go to the main administration building to pick up some traveling money, but I stopped over at the Powerhouse first to say goodbye. I opened the door for the first time dressed in a suit instead of grounds' keeper inmate clothes and the effect was immediate and dramatic. No longer did the staff have CO authority over me; neither was I subject to the world that all the other inmates were in. My release date and change of clothes made me a "person" again; the staff addressed me respectfully and the inmates were giddy, if not a little wary of me now. I was no longer one of "them". I felt like a butterfly just emerging from the cocoon with new wings and I was about to fly. It only lasted a moment, before I realized that the door to that CO/inmate world was closing forever and it was time to leave. When I got to administration, the same thing happened. Staff that used to address me as "Inmate" no longer had that authority or desire. I shook hands with some of them. They saw before them a man, now, just like them and wished me well.

I arrived at the airport and took my ticket to the counter for my boarding pass. While I was waiting in line at the TSA to pass security, I realized that I did not have any real identification with which to prove that the ticket belonged to me. All I had was my bright red prison issued ID, which had my name, a mugshot, my intake number; and the words, "Federal Bureau of Prisons INMATE" stamped on it. Oh well, I thought, this will be embarrassing.

As I got closer, I saw a little old lady in a wheelchair in front of me. She provided her ID and then she got called aside and searched like no one I've ever seen searched before. This lady was so feeble she needed two TSA agents to stand her up while a third agent ransacked her bag and her wheelchair before they set her back down to continue through security check. I thought, if that is what they do to a geriatric in a wheelchair, what are they going to do to me, a felon just released from prison showing inmate ID?

I showed my prison ID and held my breath. The agent, at first seeing what looked like a rabbi standing in front of him caught a clear look at my prison ID. He raised his eyebrows thoughtfully, pursed his lips together, then nodded as if he understood… and waved me through the rest of the TSA screening process. I walked through the metal detector and didn't even have to remove my shoes. I boarded the plane and was now on my way back to Los Angeles.

Finally, after 6 ½ years I was coming home.

Chapter 6

What Remains

"I never saw a wild thing sorry for itself. A small bird will drop frozen dead from a bough without ever having felt sorry for itself."
- D. H. Lawrence

Upon landing at LAX I immediately went to Jerusalem Kosher Pizza, the first pizza I had had in almost 7 years. I then made my way to the Gateways Federal Halfway House in Echo Park, which is a private contract facility meant to provide the inmate with a means to slowly re-integrate into society, while still maintaining BOP custodial supervision. In reality, I was still an "inmate"; property of the BOP, however the BOP was allowing me 6 months to shake off the 6 plus years of institutionalization and slowly come up to speed within the free community.

I was allowed to leave the facility for work every day and I was given additional passes up to 4 hours on top of that to leave the halfway house for any legal reason. I had to sleep at the halfway house and give them a percentage of my paycheck as "rent". And they provided me with all my kosher meals.

I came to the halfway house with little more than the clothes on my back and a few t-shirts and briefs I had purchased from the prison commissary. When the Jewish community learned that I was out of prison, a fundraiser took place and they raised enough to be able to clothe me properly. I was so grateful for that kindness.

My grandfather, Israel, took a fall in his New York apartment, which landed him in the hospital and then his condition worsened until he was literally on his deathbed. He never left the hospital. My father called me from the hospital and told me that end of life preparations were underway and that if I wanted to say goodbye, I would need to come quickly.

I had not seen my grandfather since 1994 and by this time it was 2008. When he was told in 1996 that I had embraced a non-Jewish wife and her religion, he forbade all contact; he refused to see me or even speak to me. I can recall phoning him up to say hello; upon hearing my voice, he would simply hang up the phone. That hurt me a lot. When I finally came to terms with, and ended, my folly; throwing all that off and returning to Judaism, I tried him again. He was resolute in his eternal upset with me and would never forgive me for what I had aligned myself with (even though I had acted in ignorance). Even when I attended an Orthodox *yeshiva* in Morristown, New Jersey and was only a short distance away from him, he would not take my call. I could not really blame him. In his mind Christians were responsible for the murder of our entire family; the feeling of betrayal must have been felt by him on so many levels.

Until one day, when I was already in Taft prison camp and my grandmother Hannah died. While I remained imprisoned, my father and brother went to New York to be with my grandfather while he buried his wife. The entire religious side of his family was also there from Williamsburg. My grandfather shared his angst with one of his elder cousins about my leaving, but then returning to Judaism via Chabad. This cousin told my grandfather that if I had returned to Orthodox Judaism, then he must forgive me. He said, "You have to forgive him, Israel."

And my grandfather listened to him.

I began to learn conversational Yiddish in prison, which was my grandfather's first language. I would write letters to him now in Yiddish and he would respond in very open and dear ways. I could tell he felt a pride in me that I had returned sincerely, fully embracing Judaism; it's just that I could not see him. My father, not wanting to send my grandfather into another upsetting tailspin decided not to tell him I had gone to prison. I could not call him on prison phones because every few minutes a recording would play that the call was coming from a federal prison, so we had to set up phone calls via the chaplain's office, which was not monitored. My father just told my grandfather that I was working and traveling and not able to visit. That went on for 4 years.

Now that I was in halfway house, I was certain I could get a pass to say goodbye or go to his funeral. Neither request was granted. My grandfather died and was buried without my attendance. Another tragedy; still, at least my grandfather died knowing that his grandson loved him and had come home.

True to his word, my accountant, Leonard found me a job, transportation and a romantic introduction. He gave me his mother-in-law's Chevy Cutlass and a job at his accounting firm. I had transportation and income. Then he introduced me to the woman who would later become my wife. She, being a recent divorcee, was looking to re-marry; having just moved from Crown Heights, New York to the Jewish community in Northridge where she was studying at CSUN for her teaching credential. Leonard told her that he had "this great guy" for her; then when she showed some interest, he told her that I had just gotten out of prison. She wasn't expecting that, but I think she was intrigued because she agreed to meet me.

So, one Sunday, about three months into my halfway house she came by the accounting office I was working at to meet me. There was an instant attraction and I felt certain that we would marry. We spent a lot of time together, both of us older and having had previous committed relationships that had failed. We had a lot in common. Her previous husband, an Orthodox rabbi, revealed to her that he had health related issues that would prevent the continuation of their marriage. We were both Jewish from birth, both raised in secular households, both returnees to Orthodox Judaism and both committed to living a religious life. We both had two children each and we both wanted more.

One week to the day that I met her, I asked her to marry me. She accepted. Three months later, exactly one week after I left the halfway house for the last time a truly free man, we married in the *same* Chabad synagogue I had visited for the first time (and become observant in) so many years before as a returnee to Judaism... and then I moved in with her in her student housing apartment.

I was working by that time at an advertising agency in the city and we began trying to have our own biological children and to restore the one who had been taken from me 7 years earlier. Being that my wife was a bit older than me, we had a few years' trouble trying to get pregnant, and we began to consult fertility doctors.

I also began to file legal motions in Louisiana in an attempt to restore my daughter to my custody and care. Acting as my own attorney, I was able to force the grandparents to allow me visitation and sued them in court for the return of my child to my State and custody. Thus, would begin one of the most enduringly painful sagas of my life over the next 3 years.

Because I was now on three years of probation, I had to go back to federal court to ask my sentencing judge to allow me to travel to Louisiana to prosecute my case against the grandparents who were now refusing to return my child. When the federal sentencing judge originally imposed his onerous sentence on me, he told me that I would still be young enough when I got out of prison to have a life and begin again; that it was not hopeless for me. I never lost sight of his words of encouragement even as he sentenced me to a lengthy prison term.

The Government, as usual, opposed my motion. But the judge, I believed, remembered his words to me and overruled the Government. He said that my term of incarceration and probation were meant to be rehabilitation and that he was not going to punish me by denying me the ability to reunite with my daughter. He said that it would be part of my rehabilitation if I could reunite with my child and so he ordered that I be allowed to travel to Louisiana as often as I liked.

Before I left the courtroom, the court had some last words for me. The federal district court judge who had originally sentenced me to 88 months in prison stated on the record:

"When I think about you, [Mr. Diamand] I think about – didn't you save some people's lives? Right, you were like an EMT or something like that. I think about all the good things about you. What happened in the past happened in the past, and I am really hoping that you take all the brilliance that you have and use it for the good."

Wow. When I left that courtroom, I was on top of the world. It would only be a short time before I would get to see my beautiful daughter again, cruelly kept from my love and care for almost 7 years. But the cruelest cut was yet to come. What was meant to be a beautiful reunion and homecoming turned into a bitter child custody battle between the grandparents and me. The venue would be Benton Parish, a southern French-law Christian court that enabled the grandparents' continuing parental alienation of affection and helped to turn my precious daughter against me, making her into a shell of a child in my presence.

With the help and moral support of my wife, we journeyed to Louisiana for the first time seeing my daughter since she was 14 months old. It was a wonderful first visit. We melted into a corner and just caught up with everything since I had been taken away. We spent about 2 hours our first visit. The next day in court, the judge affirming the grandparents' guardianship was valid, gave them temporary custody, but would have a subsequent trial to determine who should ultimately have permanent custody of my daughter. I was offered one Sunday per month visit in Louisiana until the trial.

Having very little money and realizing I would need help prosecuting my case, I tried to find a Jewish community I could reach out to. All I found was a Reform congregation, so I reached out to their congregational leader, who agreed to meet with me. She advised me there was a lawyer in the community who might be interested in taking my case. His name was Joel Pearce, and when he heard about what happened to me, he agreed to take my case *pro bono*.

Joel ended up becoming a close friend. He offered out his home to us for visits and allowed me to use his car when I came monthly to visit my daughter. In exchange for providing me with free legal representation, I taught him all things Jewish. In Shreveport/Bossier, there is no longer an Orthodox Jewish presence and Joel had only been exposed to Reform Judaism and Christianity. He had a voracious appetite to learn about authentic Judaism and its proper practice.

At the next court hearing, Joel met with the judge, a man by the name of Jeff Cox, privately in his chambers. When Joel emerged, he was visibly shaken and upset.

He said, "I told the judge that your daughter is a Jewish child and needs to be raised by her Jewish father. The judge said, 'I am not letting a Jewish child leave the State of Louisiana until and unless she becomes a Christian. She needs to accept Jesus as her savior before she leaves this State....'"

Joel said that Judge Cox's comments were off the record and could not be used to impeach him. Welcome to Louisiana "justice".

Joel was able to get the judge to order a child custody evaluation to determine which home my daughter should live in. The judge advised all parties *on the record* that he would implement the recommendations of the child custody evaluators, *whatever* they recommended. At that point I believed that for once I had a better than good shot at being awarded full custody. I knew I was the better parent for my daughter and the evaluation on Louisiana home turf would prove it in a big way. But the judge apparently only meant that he would implement the recommendations *if* the results were favorable to the grandparents. They were not.

Almost three years after I initially found a beautiful and sweet daughter that I imagined I might someday be able to care for full-time again; an *exhaustive* child custody evaluation was entered into evidence. The court appointed evaluators came to the stunning conclusion that my daughter living with her father in California would be in her best interests, that she should immediately come to live with me full-time, and that I should have full physical and legal custody of her. The evaluators acknowledged that there might be a period of adjustment but that they were confident that my daughter would do just fine living with her father.

The recommendations were categorical and unambiguous in support of *full reunification* with me, my daughter's father; so, we went back to court confident that at the very least, the judge would do as he said and implement the recommendations.

In the end the judge advised us that though he initially promised to implement the recommendations of the evaluators; he now declined to do so. Instead, he divided the baby in half. For his "legal" standing, he cited *one* obvious, but innocuous assessment that the evaluators included in support of the custody change; that it *might* be a challenge initially for my daughter to adjust to California. (The evaluators also stated in the very next line of their report that my daughter would also easily overcome the challenges of adjustment.) The judge seized on the first part, saying that a "potential challenge of adjustment" showed a *likelihood* of potential harm, which outweighed her best interests coming to California. He found that to be an imminent threat, which overrode best interests! The judge gave me, (with the grandparents), joint custody of my daughter and all visits would take place in California. When confronted with being stripped of all their custody by the evaluation, but actually retaining half legal custody and full physical custody, it was a clear win for the grandparents. They lost the case on evidence and expert recommendations but won on decision.

We appealed the case and the Appellate Court found that Judge Cox had indeed erred. But they still affirmed his ruling under a different legal theory. Citing the fact that when Judge Cox made the temporary custody order in favor of the grandparents for the purposes of determining who would ultimately win full custody via trial and the child custody evaluation; the only way to undo the grandparents' *temporary* custody order would be to prove to a court that leaving my daughter in the custody of the grandparents would be an *imminent danger* to her welfare. Once an order for custody had been ordered, the standard changed from *best interests* to *imminent danger*.

According to the Appellate Court, Louisiana law did not recognize *best interests* of the child once a temporary order for custody had been entered, *if evidence had been accepted*. At the original hearing I made oral arguments, which were treated as "evidence". Baring a showing of *imminent danger* to my child, a finding of *best interests* could not trump the original custody order, even though it was only meant to be a temporary order. This new interpretative theory was previously unheard of in the State of Louisiana and clearly meant to miscarry justice towards a preconceived end. In an effort to deny me my Jewish child, my case had turned the entire Louisiana Child and Family Law Circuit on its head. In interpreting law in a manner that it was never meant to be interpreted, there could no longer be a temporary custody order for the purposes of gathering information for a proper ruling, if either party ever wanted that order to be changed, absent a showing of *imminent threat* to the child's life. Everyone in Louisiana Family Law now knows my case. And they hate me for it.

And even though there was evidence that the grandmother was a methadone addict and had made methadone available to my daughter; and that both grandparents had alienated my daughter from her father, none of that raised the bar in the court's mind to be an imminent threat of harm. Outside the gates of the Catholic Church after the Holocaust, if ever there was a more concerted effort to steal a Jewish child from a Jewish father this was it.

For 2 years I had visited my daughter every month, taking the redeye to Bossier, only to find a recalcitrant and angry little girl who was told that I was a bad man and that I was trying to take her away from her grandparents. Our visits were awful, and still I persisted. I tried to find any way into her heart. She went out of her way not to let me in, as if letting her father into her life would somehow kill her grandparents. The alienation of affection was so severe that I almost did not want to get on the airplane. She met me with hostility bordering on contempt each and every time. There were times, though, that she forgot to hate me, and she would laugh and be free and playful; but as soon as she realized she was having fun with me or smiling or laughing, she would scowl her face and withdraw back into her grandparents' imposed shell. The only way I would have been able to save my child from a life of hatred would have been a full custody change. And now that would never happen.

For a year after I "won" joint legal custody, my daughter came to California for visits and even those were miserable between us. She acted unkind and was withdrawn and alienated from me, as if she believed that showing me love would somehow be an affront to her grandparents. They had spent so much time telling my daughter how bad I was, that to love me would have been an admission that they were wrong or lying to her and my daughter was unwilling to admit that to herself. I also believe that the grandmother would have beaten her down so badly psychologically that not loving me was literally saving her psychological life. I found letters that the grandmother wrote to my daughter that bashed me. It was all in a desperate psychopathic effort to immorally manipulate my child's affections against me. And it worked.

When my daughter was 12, she simply refused to get on the plane. Of course, that was likely a set up and plan by the grandmother. She recorded my daughter having the fit and refusing to get on the plane and since you can't force a 12-year-old onto an airplane unescorted, my daughter never came to California again to visit me, never wrote me a letter, never spoke to me on the phone. I had lost my 2nd child.

Severely dejected from the loss of my child, I took about 18 months off from work to enter Kollel Tiferes Menachem, a rabbinical *shiur* at *Yeshiva* Ohr Elchonon Chabad (YOEC), which is a Los Angeles based Jewish seminary. While enrolled, I successfully completed the program. In May 2013, I earned *smichah* (rabbinical ordination), becoming an Orthodox rabbi. It seemed that after all those years of being secular, then wandering in various and different paths, finally finding my way back home and then achieving one of the loftiest credentials available to a

Jewish man, made my journey more worthwhile. I don't think I would have had the impetus to seek a rabbinical degree otherwise.

Immediately after ordination I was tapped by a local *sofer* (scribe) to completely re-write and edit two of his authoritative Halachic compilations; one on Mezuzah and one on Sefer Torah. The author graciously gave me the following approbation in his Acknowledgements: *"I would like to thank the English Editor, Rabbi Dovid Diamond, for his keen insight in fixing the grammar of this sefer into a fresh, easy reading English and at the same time keeping all the Halachic concepts of this sefer intact."*

My wife and I were still devastated from the loss of both of my children, but we never gave up hope for our own children. We changed our fertility doctor to one who had good success and decided to try to have children via IVF (*in vitro fertilization*); this was an expensive proposition and if not for a generous loan from a rabbi friend of hers, rabbinical approval and Orthodox supervision through *Puah*, we would never have been able to go through with the procedures. About a year after we started with the IVF, we had a baby. The doctor, unsure of how well my wife would fare, even tried to dissuade our first attempt because according to the ultrasound some of her uterine epithelial cells were not perfectly arrayed. Out of money to try another round, I insisted we do the implantation against his medical opinion/recommendation. Thankfully, his opinion was incorrect and 9 months later we welcomed our first child into the world, a baby girl.

After our daughter turned two, we decided to have another child. Our embryos were in storage, frozen, so we began the medications and shots and got ready. The embryos were thawed under supervision and the best one under microscope was chosen for implantation. The doctor was so impressed from my wife's first pregnancy and delivery that he offered to implant 2 embryos. We chose to stay with one. It took, and 9 months later we welcomed our second baby, a son, and my first boy.

My son's embryo had remained frozen for over 2 years. Fertilized at the same time as his sister, I like to think that my kids are fraternal twins, three years apart. And it could be that my son is technically older than his sister, even though she was born first. He may have been conceived *before* her.

It's unbelievable, the miracle upon miracle that these two children represented and if not for medical expertise and advances and the circuitous swooping route my life took; if not for every single day in jail; if not for all of it… those two miracles would never have come into the world, G-d forbid. Today they are 5 and 2 respectively. I feel with each of their births and being their daddy on a daily basis, as though I have been re-born.

Friday nights and Saturdays (Shabbos) were very special, and I treasured those days because much of the time was family oriented. One such Friday night my wife and I and the kids went to shul for a Shabbos meal. The table was open to whoever happened to be in the neighborhood. Some people I knew; others were people who just needed a meal.

An elderly man wandered in and sat down. I later came to learn that he had Alzheimer's and had wandered away from his family's Shabbos table. He had somehow found our shul.

He was invited to our table and began to eat with us; however, he did not speak, and no one knew his history. About 20 minutes into the meal, a few of us noticed that he had placed his head on the table (perhaps to rest?); but his eyes were wide open, his face turning gray. There was food in his mouth… and he was not breathing. He looked like he had died.

I somehow intuited immediately that he was chocking. Food was lodged in his mouth and presumably down his throat. The strain that his face and neck muscles showed made it clear to me that he was having a choking emergency.

At that point, I did not think of anything else other than clearing his airway. I was able to reach him while he was still in the seated position. He remained unresponsive to my touch, but I still felt tension in his body. I placed my hand and fist into the abdominal thrust position from the rear, also known as the Heimlich Maneuver and began delivering thrusts. After the second thrust I felt a lower rib pop. On the third thrust, another of this man's ribs popped. I thought, *Great. Not only does this poor man have to suffer the trauma and pain of choking to death, but here's two broken ribs for him as a parting gift….*

Anyway, I was unable to completely dislodge the obstruction from the rear and the man was now 100%

unresponsive and all tension had left him. He no longer supported any of his own weight. I lifted him between his midriff and axillary up out of his chair (full adrenaline now) and placed him on his back on the floor to begin to do abdominal thrusts and to start chest compressions. My goal at that point was twofold, to clear the airway and ensure that his heart kept beating.

The shul's rabbi's wife called *Hatzalah* (an organization of volunteer EMTs), whose response time was usually much quicker than the Fire Department and LAPD; and then 911.

Shortly after I placed him on his back to begin compression, I rolled him to his side to do a mouth sweep. A friend of mine I had gone to rabbinical school with, Yisroel, performed a deep sweep and cleared the patient's mouth of food. That act had a pronounced effect on the airway obstruction; and soon the man was breathing again on his own, thank G-d. Between the thrusts, compressions and mouth sweep, I am fairly certain we saved this man's life. EMS showed up shortly thereafter and took this man to the hospital. I later found out that his family was searching for him and was very happy when he was returned to them. He disappeared for two hours and then he came back with two broken ribs. *But he came back alive.*

As I approached my 50th birthday the commitment I made while in prison to someday save a life by donating my kidney to someone in need resurfaced. *Someday* was here. I began to feel an urgency to save a life and end someone's misery, and I believe saving the man with Alzheimer's made it real again. I contacted my rabbi (even rabbis have rabbis) to ask him to confirm for me if it was permitted to donate an organ to save a life. He advised me firstly that I did not have to do it since I would be risking my own life; but that it was permitted under Jewish law. Saving a life is a paramount mitzvah (Divine commandment/good deed) in Judaism. I contacted an organization that makes living kidney donation matches, *Renewal.org*, and told them what I wanted to do. After I answered a few of their questions, I was told that there was a potential match in my own city who was being treated at Cedars-Sinai. It turned out that the potential recipient was a friend in my own Jewish community; and his father was also a friend. I knew the family and could only imagine the suffering they were enduring as my friend's kidneys shut down and he began dialysis. When I went to visit my friend, he literally looked like he was on death's doorstep.

I contacted Cedars-Sinai Comprehensive Organ Donation Coordinator and told them who I wanted to donate to, and they set me up with an intensive battery of testing, both physical and psychological. I passed the tests and was cleared to donate. A date was chosen a few months out. In the meantime, I continued my physical training and conditioning to stay very fit.

Most Sundays my wife gave me a few hours to ride my mountain bike while she spent time with the kids. One such ride took me from my home in the Pico-Robertson neighborhood in Los Angeles to a local mountain range in the Santa Monica Conservancy called Franklin Park. I had a great ride to the top of the park, near Mulholland Hwy and then back down city streets on my way home. As I was cycling southbound through Beverly Hills, I heard and then noticed an Infinity Q60 pull up alongside of me and begin to pace me. Then a passenger side window rolled down, and something flew from the car and struck me. It was a full Starbucks iced coffee drink. It exploded upon impact and soaked me and my crash pads. The car revved its very-powerful engine, chirped its wheels, and sped off.

Had I lost control, and crashed, it would have been a nasty fall. At that speed, I could have ended up in the hospital or worse. As soon as I had composed myself and realized what had happened, I gave pursuit of that Q60… on my mountain bike. I clearly had no real expectation that I could catch the car, but I was going to try, nonetheless. I was certain that I was not the first person to be a victim of their dangerous game. I could imagine that innocent people on bus stops probably also got sprayed or had items thrown at them by the occupants of that car; and here were these spoiled entitled elites, having no regard for the lives or the dignity of others. They never considered that at the speed I was rolling I could have crashed and been put into hospitalized spinal traction. They did not consider that I might have small children at home who depended on me or even cared if I was injured.

The car turned the next corner, blowing the stop sign and I pedaled faster. I felt a familiar rage begin to flow in me; the same feeling I had when I was forced to confront that racist inmate who had raised his fists to me, quiet and controlled, but now giving way to resolve. That driver and his passenger(s) had just picked the wrong guy. If I caught them (in my pipedream), I intended to be the last person they ever threw something at again, because we were going to have words... and maybe even more than words.

When I turned the corner, I expected to see only a small fragment of the Q60 in the distance; however, the car was very-close now, stopped in traffic, and I was gaining on it! The driver swerved, jumped into a right turn lane, made another turn... and I gave chase. As I rounded the corner, he was again stuck in traffic and by now he knew I was in pursuit. He floored it. If he had just continued straight on a main thoroughfare, he could have easily lost me; but he insisted on making quick turns down residential streets as if he wanted to stay in the neighborhood. That was fine by me because this allowed me to stay in the race. Every single street he turned onto was impacted with traffic.

I could feel that the driver was getting nervous. He did not want a confrontation with me under any circumstances; and his driving took on an erratic and ultimately destructive bent. He turned sharply right and then tried to navigate another right into an alley. If he had succeeded in entering that alley, I would have lost him, but he overshot it and wrecked between the Cardiff Drill Tower Building, an architecturally designed oil derrick, and a telephone pole. His entire front end had crumpled; both sides of the car were completely smashed.

I now had two choices. I could keep on riding by the wrecked car or engage with my attackers.

I chose to engage.

I dropped my bike right behind the car and ran up to the driver's side as the driver was getting out. I was intent on subduing the guy in order to hold him for the police. Normally well in control of my affect, I allowed myself to enter the fray quite aggressively, feeding off adrenalin and my resolve to restrain the driver. He was much taller than me and as I grabbed him, he was trying to push me away. I pummeled him. He swung on me. I parried his punches away, and then I hit him again. Three passengers jumped out of the car and swarmed me; one of them pushed me off the driver and then as I turned to engage the others, two of them ran away altogether.

The driver was no longer a threat, stunned and reeling from having gotten the worst end of our initial exchange; and I turned my attention to the passenger who was still blustering aggressively, but clearly in shock at how things were unmercifully unfolding for him and his friends. Since he had also put his hands on me, I advised him (not nicely) that I was about to "wreck" him too.

As I advanced toward him, now ready to lay hands on him, he began to panic. He backed away from me and spread his arms out, palms open, in a sort of universal sign of surrender; and then he dropped an unexpected bomb.

He entreated, "Don't hit me, we're minors."

I immediately stopped my advance. The driver was so tall that he looked like an adult to me. I told him that I would be placing them all under citizen's arrest and that I would be holding the driver for police. I then called 911 and reported the situation.

By this time, I had removed my helmet. I wear a *yarmulke* at all times, except when bathing (or rolling in Jiu Jitsu) and I stood there watching the driver so that he did not flee. I also decided to hold the car keys so that he could not run. When I entered the driver's cabin, there were no keys; it was keyless, but as I was rooting around looking for them, I accidentally nudged the gear shift into reverse and the car began to back up. The driver's door was already opened in front of the telephone pole and as the car moved backwards the door began to shear off its hinges. I heard the driver crying that his car door was ripping off. It wasn't intentional, but I also wasn't sorry about it, either.

Then something interesting happened. As their parents and the police would soon be pulling up, all four 17-year-old "minors" pulled out their *yarmulkes* from their back pockets and put them on. Up until then, nobody but me was wearing a *yarmulke*. Then it all made sense. These kids attended a religious school in my religious neighborhood driving daddy's car and had decided that they wanted to do mischief but did not want to be identified as religious Jews while they did it. They were either ashamed of their hypocritical actions or looking to influence law enforcement and their parents by appearing religious, when their actions suggested otherwise.

Just then the driver's father came on scene with the driver's brother. His brother was much bigger than me and seeing his little brother holding his swollen face and being comforted by his father began to glare at me.

I turned squarely at him and challenged him, "What are you looking at?!"

He quickly looked, and walked, away. I was still very much dialed up from being targeted by his brother and by my subsequent hot pursuit.

Just then, LAPD rolled up. The officer who came over gave one look at this beautiful car in a heap of wreckage and then looked at the kid who was driving and just sighed, "What a shame!"

I stood my ground and waited for him to come over to me so I could give my statement. There was a lot of pointing at me; the kid who I came to blows with was still holding his swollen face; and I wasn't quite sure how this would play out. Then the officer approached me.

I told him roughly what I have already described above. The officer asked me if I was hurt. Aside of the divot in my calf from the secondary impact of the laden cup, which I showed him, and the fact that I smelled like a mocha latte, I told him I was unharmed. But I told him that the driver and his friends were guilty of hit and run, reckless exhibition of speed and evasion and that I was sure that I was not the first person to be their victim. I also told the officer that I could have been severely injured had I crashed. The officer said that the driver and his occupants claimed that I had punched them. I told the officer that I did place my hands on the driver but only in my effort to hold him. I said that because he committed a hit and run, that I was in fear that he would try to run again or continue to physically assault me; and I had a right hold him for arrest by the police... and of course he *had* resisted me.

The evidence of the kid's reckless driving was clear. When coupled with the fact that it was illegal for the kid to be transporting underage kids with him, the officer told me that my story was credible. He said that I could have also just as easily left the scene and since I stayed, he was satisfied with my account. He said the kids were anyway in a lot of trouble and then asked me if I would like to press charges. I declined. They had enough problems and I figured they had learned their lesson. The officer was surprised, and then shook my hand and wished me well. He never asked me for ID.

As I was pedaling away, I heard the driver's father pleading with the LAPD officer, "You're letting him (referring to me) leave…?"

I allowed myself a smile. Indeed, he was.

I found out later who those kids were. The Jewish community is small; and I had a heart-to-heart talk with their school's principal. I was almost satisfied, but not quite. I found the name of the parents of the driver and sent them a letter. I was appalled that neither he nor his son had reached out to apologize and that if I did not get an apology, I would contemplate pressing formal criminal and civil charges. I was concerned that unless there was serious remorse, that the behaviors would continue, and more people would be hurt. I was concerned that a rich daddy was going to let this incident slide like I am sure he had let so many other incidents slide.

I met with the fathers at a local café and after a nice talk and heartfelt apologies; I gave the father of the driver a hug and invited him and his son to my home. A week after I donated my kidney, all but one of the occupants of that car, including the driver and the kid who had thrown the drink at me, showed up at my home. We spent 30 minutes discussing it until I felt satisfied that they were indeed remorseful. I hugged each one of them and wished them well.

The day of my surgery was fast approaching, and I was very excited, palpably. I felt as though my whole life had come to this one beautiful moment. But I was met with some pushback. I wanted to share this joy of what I was about to do with those closest to me. But everyone I spoke to had two things in common. They were all medical professionals, and they were all a little less than thrilled, which translated in every case to literally, "Are you crazy?"

My Big Brother, an ER doctor, advised against it. My mother, now a nurse practitioner and not a fan, mordantly quipped, "When are they *harvesting* your organ?"

And my uncle, who happens to be the head of medicine at Harvard Medical School and arguably the top nephrologist/kidney doctor in the world told me not to proceed with donating the kidney.

So much for 1st opinions... which is why I believe G-d created 2nd opinions. The Comprehensive Organ Donation staff of doctors and nurses at Cedars educated me to understand that there was little to fear, that the risks were minimal, versus actually saving a life. And it was not just the recipient's life; it was his entire family who would have to deal with his dialysis, sitting with him in despair.

The day of surgery arrived, and I met Josh, the recipient, and his family at the hospital at 5 a.m. I was prepped for surgery first and was told that once the transplant team on my case had my kidney out, it would get a short ice bath and then Josh's right abdominal wall would be opened and my kidney would be transplanted and connected to his aorta, inferior vena cava and finally the ureter, which would hopefully start the flow of urine to his bladder. It was no less amazing how my kidney was removed. Three laparoscopic incisions were made in my abdomen for the camera, scope/cutter and stapler. Once the facia was cut away and cauterized, the aorta, inferior vena cava and ureter were located. Each was stapled on two sides and then severed until the kidney was free of any mooring. Then a 4-inch incision was made near my pubis; today it looks like a smaller version of a C-section scar. My abdominal cavity was inflated with CO_2, so that the surgeon had room to maneuver, and she reached her hand inside and simply pulled my kidney out. Of course, I was unconscious through the entire thing. I was wheeled into surgery and the next thing I knew I was in recovery.

When I woke up Josh was still in surgery, but my kidney had been re-attached and was already producing urine, which was flowing into his bladder. I was told that my kidney (now Josh's kidney) started working the second it was re-attached! I started to weep openly. I was so happy. Josh's mother was there with me. To see her expression of relief and love was one of the best moments of my life.

The surgeon came into recovery and told me that she had never seen a more beautiful kidney. She had taken a picture of it in its ice bath and sent it to me. Then she unexpectedly leaned over and kissed me. As she stood, she said, "I can't believe I just kissed you."

Clearly outside official protocol, I wasn't exactly complaining. I suppose we were all caught up in the miraculous magnificence and gratitude of that moment. I've never forgotten it. When they finally brought me to my room, I stood up from the gurney and walked myself over to my hospital bed and lay down. The nurses were amazed that I was already so mobile, unassisted.

I want to be clear that aside of holding each of my 4 babies for the first time when they were born; giving that kidney was the highlight of my life. I came out of surgery elevated. When the kidney came out, something changed - I started seeing people on levels I never imagined. I began to feel love and appreciation for people almost immediately. Apparently, giving away your life opens you to the beauty in everyone and everything around you. So, for me, while people told me how grateful they were for the gift I gave, this experience was a gift to me beyond all gifts.

I believe that G-d provides the cure for every illness. I realized that I had the merit, from the moment of my birth, to be my recipient's cure 50 years later. What is amazing is that I had been holding his cure my entire life. The entire process has shown me that when you make a healthy self-sacrifice; when you give your life for another, the most amazing things happen.

I've never felt more whole.

Chapter 7

Delusion of Consciousness

"A human being is part of the whole, called by us 'Universe,' a part limited in time and space. He experiences himself, his thoughts, and feelings as something separate from the rest; a kind of optical delusion of his consciousness. The striving to free oneself from this delusion is the one issue of true religion. Not to nourish the delusion but to try to overcome it is the way to reach the attainable measure of peace of mind."
- Albert Einstein

It has been generations in my immediate family since anyone was remotely religious, practicing Orthodox Judaism. Looking at my parents' largely secular, reformed upbringing; and also seeing that *after* my parents divorced each other they both remarried non-Jews, I had previously married a non-Jew and my younger brother remarried a non-Jew and he now also has a non-Jewish child, which for all practical purposes is the beginning of assimilation and the end of the Jewish people.... How is it that I had the impetus to intentionally re-embrace and marry *back* into the Jewish faith, have Jewish children, and live my faith as my great-great-grandparents surely lived it in Orthodox fashion? In short, why me?

I read an interesting theory in a book by Rabbi Benjamin Blech called, *Hope, Not Fear* (Rowman and Littlefield). In it he posits that G-d likes to give "second chances" in this life by giving us the opportunity to clean up our acts and change direction; or by bringing us back in a reincarnation. Reincarnation is a very Jewish concept written about in Kabbalah, which is the ancient Jewish Tradition of mystical or esoteric interpretation of the Torah. G-d gives us "encore" performances: Even if you didn't do it right the first time you are encouraged to come out again until you do get it right, in this life or another.

When Hitler killed six million Jews by gassing, shooting and burning them alive, over a million were children. Many Jews, born into religious families, never got to live out their allotted time as religious Jews. So, G-d gave them their religious lives back, as it were, by sending down those souls again into newly born Jewish babies. But by then, with much of Judaism decimated there were not enough religious families to send those souls back to. So, G-d placed them in secular Jewish families. Today, we see a resurgence of a return to Orthodox Judaism like we have never seen before from families who for generations were irreligious.

In my case, against the flow of my family's irreligious progression, I felt impelled to return and I can't explain it. Perhaps my soul was one of those million children, returning to complete my mission, which will become my encore.

As a colleague/friend of mine reminded me, there is a Mishna (a compellation of Oral Law) – Mikva'os 7:7 read each time before the final mourner's prayer, "Regarding a(n impure) needle on the steps of a cave (of a body of water suitable for purification), if one was moving the waters back and forth, once a wave passes over it (the needle), it is pure."

The Lubavitcher Rebbe explains that on a mystical level this legalistic teaching is describing the mission of the soul. In Kabbalah the soul is referred to by many names, including "needle". In the same way that a needle sews separate garments together, the soul joins the spiritual world with the physical. To accomplish this joining, the needle requires a hole and thread. A needle can pierce through a garment. However, to sew garments together, a needle needs a hole at one end to receive a thread. The hole represents humility to accept a thread. The 'thread' alludes to the entire Torah and commandments, which are the means by which we connect the world with G-d.

To accomplish this, a person must be in exile – represented by the cave – and encounter the challenges of life. The "waves" of water passing over the needle allude to these challenges, which the Torah refers to as "raging waters." (Psalm 124:5)

The Rebbe concludes that by surmounting the challenges of life in exile, such a needle becomes pure, i.e., it becomes connected with G-d, the Source of all purity as alluded to in the verse, "The mikvah (gathering of waters) of Israel is G-d." (Jeremiah 17:13)

So, in addition to elevating the physical world, exile (darkness, challenges) can elevate and purify the soul.

There is also a concept of "sparks" or those elements within the challenges of creation that wait to be reunited with their Source, and this needs to be explained. In Jewish esoteric thought, originally when G-d created our existence, He began with a world called *Tohu*, which means "chaos", "confusion". The light in that world was very powerful; much too powerful for the vessels that were tasked to contain it and those vessels shattered, creating the world that we live in called *Tikkun*, which means "repair", "restoration". This world requires fixing. Within the materialistic shell of everything we encounter are "sparks" from the world of *Tohu*. Those sparks are elevated or redeemed when we indeed interact with the material world, specifically in the ways G-d intended. By elevating those sparks, we redeem the world and our own souls in the process. And since G-d placed those sparks in His creation, He also leads every person to his or her personal sparks that need to be elevated. Life is not a purposeless journey. Every moment is rich with opportunity and the realization that G-d is the One Who calls on each of us to participate in the elevation of the world should cause intense joy and satisfaction even in seemingly mundane activities.

I have come to realize that through every horrendous event I have endured, something unbelievably beautiful came out of it. And while I would have a hard time having open *hakares hatov*, (Hebrew for "recognizing the good/having gratitude"), for the imposition of familial dysfunction and trauma during my formative years… in a big way, I owe G-d a debt of gratitude because two essential things necessary for my specific mission in life occurred:

Though I have chosen not to give explicit details, it is important for the reader to know that my upbringing was so emotionally traumatic/dysfunctional, that while I was not always successful at slaying the dragons, I still learned not only how to survive, but how to literally, and without fear, unwind falsity from the truth; to *persist* in finding and embracing the true narrative. I learned, even though at times I acted out in despair and frustration; that after a while I realized that I was still "whole" and did not have to act the way I had been treated. I didn't have to rebel against the "unjust" environment; though painful, I could still have a positive effect on the world around me. And, in point of fact, my life's accomplishments depended precisely on the harsh environments in which I found myself.

I also found that at times I was drawn toward things and people that were destructive; people and places that matched in some way the dysfunction of my upbringing... perhaps as a way to try to work out those formative parental issues in another venue, since I could no longer currently work them out with my parents. But that was also a gift, because if there was a way to liberate such a "spark" trapped in that darkness, then *someone* had to engage with it. And it might as well have been me.

None of this is to say there was no grieving; even to this day I feel deeply about what I lost, but I had to forgive those who hurt me, and I had to forgive myself... or risk staying shackled to a perpetual prison of anger. As Dr. Edith Egar writes so movingly in her book, *The Choice*, page 212, "... [T]o forgive is to grieve—for what happened, for what didn't happen—and to give up the need for a different past. To accept life as it was and as it is." (Simon and Schuster)

But acceptance is only half the equation – You also have to attach meaning. As Tzvi Freeman writes in his book, *Wisdom to Heal the Earth*, "The events of the past have not changed and neither has their sequence... all remains as all was. But their meaning is now vastly different. And that is what really matters. Because nothing is real in this world, all is transient, here only for now, vanished in a time later, all except for meaning. The meaning of each event, that is forever. And according to where you take those events, so will be their meaning." (Ezra press)

So, I chose to believe that I was given a gift, which became a strength. Specifically, because of the toxicity I endured, I learned to be able to persist and prevail through more damage than most others. I do have limits, but I am able to function in challenging circumstance because I am so used to them. Since, on some level, I believe I participated in choosing the challenging events of my life, in large part because of the influence my parents had on me; I have had to be in flux and endure complexities that might have completely shattered someone else less suited.

Today I acknowledge that my early childhood prepared me for life's battles by toughening me. Clearly, if I had another childhood, I might have had an easier life. But I would not have engaged with the kinds of darkness whose sparks are concealed by the veils of this world, and succeeded in unwinding what I dove into, thereby elevating the sparks assigned to me by G-d.

But it wasn't without casualty - I certainly wouldn't have lost the love and companionship of my first 2 daughters. Yet, even looking at the 6 ½ years I had to sit in prison because I could not come to terms with taking an 18-month plea deal; it's specifically *because* I did not accept that deal and then suffered from horrendous turmoil that today I am the father of two new little children for whom my life revolves again. I got a 2nd chance in this life, a rebirth.

An encore.

If I had changed one day, one minute, let alone changed years, not gotten involved with investments, not engaged with the darkness then I wouldn't have lived my life; the life that G-d wanted for me. I would be a different person and would have missed the opportunity to be a father again at 50. I can't image life without the joy of my son and daughter in it. Therefore, I have to thank G-d for *every single day* I sat in prison; for every block wall I stared at and for every link of fence and razor wire. I thank G-d for the sparks that were assigned to me that only I could elevate by diving into deep dark pools no one else wanted to; and since G-d directs the paths of every man to his intended destination, I attach great meaning to the path that I took and for the influences that pushed me in directions I needed to go.

So then, on the highest levels, there is no such thing as being a "victim" of life's circumstances. Just the opposite. We all volunteered and therefore, nothing is wasted. Everything has purpose and what looks like a "fall" is really a preparation for the next elevation.

Making Music With What Remains

There is a Midrash (a rabbinical explanation or commentary) on Genesis 27:1, "When Isaac grew old, his eyes became dim, so that he could not see..."; that the challenge of contracting difficulties as well as finding the faith to overcome them will make one a better person.

This can include any suffering one endures; from being incarcerated, to losing one's children, G-d forbid, to the utter obliteration of one's entire life. As Viktor Frankl demonstrated by living through the Holocaust, he was able to find meaning in his suffering: "Everything can be taken from a man but one thing; the last of the human freedoms – to choose one's attitude in any given set of circumstances, to choose one's own way...."

The challenge is that we all operate, as Einstein put it, in our own "delusions of consciousness", perceiving ourselves as separate from our Source and from each other. "True religion" is finding our Source and our connection to it, which will give us the deeper meaning that we are all connected to one another. The delusion is that there is a separateness. Take, for an extreme example, the death of a loved one, G-d forbid; something none of us should ever know, but far too many of us already do. How can one make sense of the separation, the loss?

In our perception of eternity, we join with a loved one for a short period of time and then they are gone; yet we continue on through time, seemingly without them. But this (mis)understanding is the delusion, the gap in our consciousness. The reality is that we never lost contact with our loved one. Even the pain we feel in our "loss" is actual proof of our (continuing) attachment. Only what is living, what is attached, can produce pain. Our pain signals we are still attached, still connected. And this realization can bring comfort and healing.

The only thing is that materiality and time place veils over our physical eyes. But our souls can see beyond; that we are all part of an eternal continuum. Eternity does not countenance "time". Loved ones never separate from their bond with eternity nor to the connection with those still subject to time. As Mitch Albom writes in his book, *The Five People You Meet in Heaven*, "Lost love is still love. Life ends. Love doesn't." (Hyperion)

Picture a Ferris wheel. This is eternity. We all ride this wheel. Because you can't see the person behind you or on the other side of the wheel does not mean they are not there; we simply go through life deluding ourselves that we are alone, when it's not possible to be alone. Everyone who ever lived or will live is riding the same eternal wheel. What happens when someone dear to you seemingly exits your passenger's cabin on the Ferris wheel? They die and are no longer physically with you as you continue your journey. You may have traveled 50 years without your loved one thinking that they are only a distant memory. But that gap in time is the delusion. The reality is that your loved one is still on the same eternal wheel, moving through eternity *with you*, just veiled from view by the coarseness of the time-based "reality" we who are living are still subject to. Your loved one's soul *is still on the same eternal wheel* that you are. Time is the construct. The soul is eternal; not left behind, but transcending time and space *with you* for eternity.

I believe that a measure of comfort can be taken in knowing that nothing can separate you from your loved ones, in this life and in the next life, and that you can close those delusional gaps of "separation" by acknowledging the simple truth that we are all part of the Whole. In the recognition of reality, you can reunite with those loved ones who have physically departed; and also create new loved ones to journey with you through eternity.

I suppose that is what the world of Moshiach (Redemption, World Peace and an End to the Darkness of Exile) will look like; when the sting of death will no longer prevail and we will all literally see our loved ones again, because we will have recognized the truth and acted accordingly - This happens when you realize that your loved ones are not really "gone" or separated from us; and even more so, one-time strangers can become friends *and even loved ones* as we endeavor to end our separateness simply by acting like a friend to whomever we meet. Based on Jewish Proverbs (adapted from Mishlei 27:19), "Words that come from the heart enter the heart."

Any kind word can turn a stranger into a friend, giving way to transcending the entire concept of the word, *stranger*. A stranger is just someone who has not yet registered in another's heart.

And though the world has not yet been perfected or refined to that level, even as we anticipate it every day (Rambam's 12th Principle of Faith, based on Sanhedrin 10:1); I can still live *with* (the ideal of) it right now, by creating a reality and a world that would welcome its arrival.

When you open your eyes and are able to see the dignity and nobility and G-dliness in every person you meet, then this is a vital portion of the redemptive world that we will inhabit… and indeed, it's the world that G-d has tasked us to create.

As the Lubavitcher Rebbe spoke so forcefully to his adherents in a series of well-known sichos (talks), "I have done all I can. Now it is up to you. It's not necessary to change the world. Change yourselves."

The knowledge that we are all part of eternity is powerful and uplifting. It ennobles and dignifies every single encounter we have with another human being and it gives new meaning and comfort to all of us who have endured suffering and/or the physical loss of those who have gone before us, creating a purposeful shift in consciousness.

In the end, (which is also the beginning), we are all able to create symphonic works out of the challenges of our lives, arranging notes to our own musical scores that are more beautiful, more compelling and more meaningful than anything ever heard before. We are indeed able to make music with what remains of our lives.

In the words of the Lubavitcher Rebbe, "All you need to do is open your eyes and see."

Appendices

Cedars Comprehensive Transplant Center – Where it all began.

aha! MOMENTS

Rabbi Yoel Gold, rabbi of Congregation Bais Naftoli in Los Angeles, California, and a ninth-grade rebbe at Mesivta Birkas Yitzchok, has inspired hundreds of thousands of people with his stories. To watch some of his videos or to share your story with him, please visit InspireClips.com

BY RABBI YOEL GOLD

RENEWED OPPORTUNITY

Working at Renewal, an organization that matches kidney donors with patients in need, Menachem Friedman gets to see the best of *klal Yisrael* every day. The donors' generosity never ceases to amaze him. Each time the office phone rings, he marvels at the way people are willing to give up a part of their bodies to save a stranger.

He received one such phone call five months ago, from a father of two named Rabbi Dovid Diamand. A young mother in his Los Angeles community needed a kidney, and he wanted to know if he could donate his. Menachem added him to Renewal's registry. As part of the initial screening, Rabbi Diamand had to submit his blood type to ensure that he and the patient were compatible.

To his disappointment, he was not a match. The woman was type O, and he was type A.

"Would you consider becoming a donor for someone else?" Menachem asked.

"Of course," Rabbi Diamand said. "But I'd like it to be someone in the Los Angeles community. Can you arrange that?"

"No problem," Menachem said confidently. But when he checked Renewal's database, he saw that there was no one in the Los Angeles area who needed a type A kidney donation.

A few days later, he checked again. The

Recipient Josh Zipp (left) and his donor, Rabbi Dovid Diamand, on the morning of the transplant.

database had been updated, and there was now a new patient, 28-year-old Josh Zipp of Los Angeles—blood type A. A new patient was never something to celebrate, but Menachem felt heartened.

When he visited Los Angeles for Renewal's annual fundraiser, he called Steve and arranged to drop by. With his son on the waiting list, Steve wasn't allowed to make a donation, but they could sit and talk. "Don't get excited," Menachem told him, "but we may have a potential donor lined up."

There were still months of testing ahead, but at last Rabbi Diamand was approved to donate. The surgery could not be scheduled for another five months; it would take place a month before Pesach, at Cedars-Sinai Medical Center in Los Angeles.

In the interim, Rabbi Diamand became curious about the recipient. Menachem told him he would have to find out if the recipient was willing to share his identity.

When he called back, Rabbi Diamand asked, "So who is my kidney going to?"

"Josh Zipp," Menachem said, adding, "His father's name is Steve."

"Steve Zipp?" Rabbi Diamand was flabbergasted. "I know him very well!"

It wasn't just because they both lived in the same city. Five years earlier, Rabbi Diamand had been learning alongside *bachurim* who were preparing for *smichah* in a local *yeshivah*, Ohr Elchanan Chabad. He was making great strides in his learning, but the realities of life caught up with him—he was expected to pay a certain amount to the *yeshivah* in order to be part of the program and receive *smichah* together with the *bachurim*, but he couldn't afford it.

And then, suddenly, the *yeshivah* told him that the fee was paid for and he had nothing to worry about. He was welcome to earn his *smichah* together with the rest of the program.

His fee had been covered by a member of the community—Steve Zipp. ●

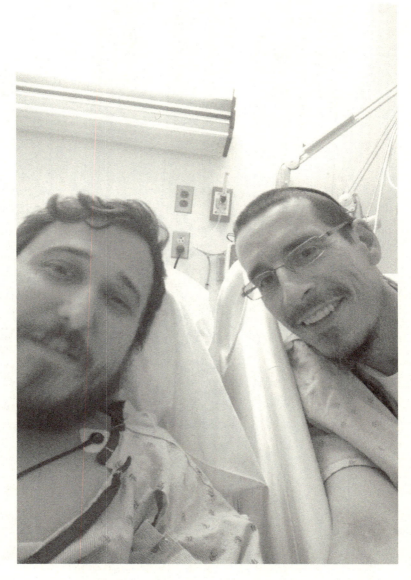

1-day post-kidney transplant; recipient and author feeling good!

291 // Making Music With What Remains

34 days post-kidney transplant, preparing for a mountain bike ride – now ensconced in full body crash pads.

292 // Making Music With What Remains

Nine months post-kidney transplant, staging for a climb at base of mountain trail head.

293 // Making Music With What Remains

2 years post-kidney transplant; top of Santa Monica Mountains.

294 // Making Music With What Remains

2 years post-transplant, now riding a *Triumph* -- Mulholland Hwy.

295 // Making Music With What Remains

Author having just received Orthodox rabbinical ordination.

Rabbi Dovid Feld, (architect and illustrator), Rabbi Dovid Bressman (author), Rabbi Dovid Diamond (English editor).

297 // Making Music With What Remains

LASD Rescue Team- Author is tallest standing under the pilot.

Air 5 rappel training out of Barley Flats.

299 // Making Music With What Remains

Author with his Big Brother and flight training helicopter.

Author's eldest daughter with her father, age 4.

301 // Making Music With What Remains

Author's eldest daughter with her father, now at age 12.

Author's middle daughter with her father, age 7.

303 // Making Music With What Remains

Author's middle daughter pictured on her 12th birthday.

Author's youngest daughter with her father, age 5.

305 // Making Music With What Remains

Author's son with his father, age 2.

Acharon acharon chaviv.
(The last is most precious.)

Afterward

My life is like a movie and I do my own stunts.
- Dwayne Michael Carter, Jr.

Fade In:

Present Day - The sun is almost directly over my head. My feet sink into the beach sand as my two children run ahead toward the Pacific Ocean, dirty blonde hair getting lighter by the moment in the late summer sun. Seagulls float effortlessly above in the onshore breeze. Helicopters and planes carrying banners buzz the coastline. The lifeguard station has not yet opened, and the beach is relatively quiet. Sand, sunscreen, and ocean smells permeate the air. I can hear, and then I see, the waves crashing onshore. I stake claim to a little patch of beach about 15 feet back from the waterline, lay down towels, chairs, sand toys and then turn my attention to my children.

My kids are excited, if not a little tentative, from the power of the surf crashing onto shore.

"Tattie (Daddy), can we go in the ocean?" my son asks.

"Tattie, will you hold our hands?" my daughter asks.

"Yes. Come. Let's go in. Stay close to me. I love you," I respond.

Grasping one child's hand in my left and one in my right we walk to the shoreline and wait for the inevitable waves to roll onto us. The ocean does not disappoint. It soaks us and pushes us and pulls us. My kids are delirious in the excited reality and power of this force of nature. I remain extremely vigilant, and I also see other parents with their kids in our proximity inhabiting the same emotional space: excitement, in the moment happiness and vigilance. I know that they are also watching out for my kids as I am watching out for theirs.

Suddenly my daughter lets go of my hand and steps into the foam and return swell. She holds her own. She runs in and out to match the wave height that is most comfortable for her. She is seemingly able to do this for hours. Wasn't it just yesterday that I was carrying her in my arms into the ocean and she would not allow me to put her down? And now she's totally independent. I'm amazed.

My son still wants me to stay with him and I do. Gladly. The waves, even onshore, are still too powerful for him; so, for now I get to hold my son, at least by the hand… until he too will be able to join his sister as an independent.

My kids are drenched, smiling, hair stringy from the salty water; now my son is shivering so I carry him to the blanket, wrap him warmly in a large towel and hold him. He falls asleep in my arms as I watch my daughter run in and out of the surf like a shorebird.

Fade Out.